He has been called "one of his generation's most original and exhilarating writers" by *The New York Times*, and "Shteyni-dawg," "Mr. Shygart," and "Poochie" by his former girlfriends. Now, in *Little Failure,* Gary Shteyngart tells his most heartfelt and unlikely story yet: his own.

AUTHOR OF

SUPER

SAD

TRUE

LOVE

STORY

Praise for *Little Failure*

"Of the many enormously gifted authors now writing about the immigrant experience . . . Gary Shteyngart is undoubtedly the funniest. . . . *Little Failure* is as entertaining as it's moving."
—MICHIKO KAKUTANI, *The New York Times*

"What makes this memoir a rich, gratifying piece of writing is that in addition to the self-loathing . . . there's also pride, confidence and exuberance. And brilliance, which makes small, glittering appearances along the way. . . . This is a mature book in all the important ways."
—MEG WOLITZER, NPR

"Russia gave birth to that master of English-language prose named Vladimir Nabokov. Half a century later, another writer who grew up with Cyrillic characters is gleefully writing American English as vivid, original and funny as any that contemporary U.S. literature has to offer. . . . [Shteyngart] isn't capable of being anything but engaging, and his erudite, witty and self-mocking voice carries the day."
—*Los Angeles Times*

"Funny, heartbreaking and soul-baring . . . [Shteyngart is] one of his generation's most original and exhilarating writers."
—*The Seattle Times*

"What a beautiful mess! . . . [Shteyngart has] all the loose ends and unresolved contradictions out of which great literature is made."
—CHARLES SIMIC, *The New York Review of Books*

"Brilliant . . . funny, unflinching, and, title notwithstanding, a giant success." —*Entertainment Weekly*

"Hilarious and moving . . . The army of readers who love Gary Shteyngart is about to get bigger." —*The New York Times Book Review*

"So you've read Shteyngart's three antic, comic, unfailingly energetic and vaguely autobiographical novels. Do you really need to read the memoir? Actually, yes, you do, because *Little Failure* is terrific—the author's funniest, saddest and most honest work to date."
—*The Guardian* (UK)

"Remarkable . . . [Shteyngart] has dismantled the armor of his humor to give readers his most tender and affecting gift yet: himself."
—*The Boston Globe*

"[*Little Failure*] might just be the funniest, most unflinching memoir ever about coming to America."   —*W Magazine*

"The tragic story of what makes a great comic writer."
                                        —LEV GROSSMAN, *Time*

"Frenetically funny, even overwhelmingly enjoyable."
                                        —*Financial Times*

"Surely some enterprising scholar is already gnawing at the question of why two of the brilliant outliers of American writing were Russian immigrants. One, of course, was the great Vladimir Nabokov. The other is the youngish Shteyngart. They both have the qualities of sly humor, secret griefs."   —*San Francisco Chronicle*

"Enormously entertaining."   —*The Wall Street Journal*

"Shteyngart's achingly honest, bittersweet comic memoir . . . is a winner."   —*Vanity Fair*

"[Shteyngart is] a successor to no less than Saul Bellow and Philip Roth."   —*The Christian Science Monitor*

"Shteyngart is a great writer—there's no arguing his literary merit—but he's also very, very funny, which is a rare quality in literature these days."   —*GQ*

"Literary gold . . . [a] bruisingly funny memoir."   —*Vogue*

"A near-perfect account of the churning state of one man's inner life."
                                        —*The Sunday Times* (UK)

"Shteyngart possesses a rare trait for a serious novelist: he is funny—and not just knowing-nod, wry-smile funny, but laugh-aloud, drink-no-liquids-while-reading funny."   —*The Economist*

"Hilarious . . . an affectionate take on growing up in gray Leningrad and Technicolor Queens."   —*People*

"[*Little Failure*] should become a classic of the immigrant narrative genre. . . . [Shteyngart's three novels] encourage us to laugh at darkness, even when it emanates from within ourselves. *Little Failure* reveals how he learned that lesson."   —*The Miami Herald*

"This Shteyngart, sad and longing and desperate for connection (with his parents, with his readers), seems the most fully human person this author has ever created."   —*The Jewish Daily Forward*

"The best memoirs are ones that are perfectly individuated, particular—and yet somehow speak to every reader's life, every reader's family. This is one of those rare books."   —*New Statesman*

"By turns poignant and hilarious, *Little Failure* contains echoes of Franz Kafka, the Marx Brothers, and Philip Roth."
                                          —*Santa Barbara Independent*

"Entrancing and unsparing . . . Few writers have written about the soul-scorching experiences of their lives with such wit and ferocity as Shteyngart does in *Little Failure*."   —*BookPage*

"An immigrant's memoir like few others . . . [A book] this compelling and entertaining—one that frequently collapses the distinction between comedy and tragedy—should expand his readership beyond those who have loved his novels."   —*Kirkus Reviews* (starred review)

"Poignant, vitriolic, wistful, always moving and painfully honest, this memoir is . . . a self-examination that is entertaining and devastating in equal measures. Highly recommended."
                                          —*Library Journal* (starred review)

"[*Little Failure* is] told with honest and generous helpings of off-kilter wit . . . fully satisfying."   —*Shelf Awareness*

"Gary Shteyngart has written a memoir for the ages. I spat laughter on the first page and closed the last with wet eyes. Unputdownable in the day and a half I spent reading it, *Little Failure* is a window into immigrant agony and ambition, Jewish angst, and anybody's desperate need for a tribe. Readers who've fallen for Shteyngart's antics on the page will relish the trademark humor. But here it's laden and leavened with a deep, consequential psychological journey. Brave and unflinching, *Little Failure* is his best book to date."
                    —MARY KARR, *New York Times* bestselling author of
                                          Lit and *The Liars' Club*

"Many, many people in this world have received blurbs from Gary Shteyngart, but I happen not to be one of them. So you can trust me when I say: *Little Failure* is a delight. You ask me if it's funny? Naturally it's funny—he's always funny. But this book is also a super sad true love story: between Gary and Lenin, Gary and his parents, Gary and women, Gary and food, Gary and America, Gary and Russia, Gary and the English language itself. And alongside the jokes and the (frankly unbelievable) photos, you'll find deep feeling on display here, and shimmering sentences, and a marvel of a story. How did an asthmatic seven-year-old Jewish-Russian immigrant in a sailor suit become one of the most beloved of contemporary American writers? Not without struggle, both historical and personal, and with a great deal of humor and grit. But mostly through paying close attention: to the way people speak, move, love, and hurt each other. It's what gives his novels their joyful energy and what makes this memoir, in the opinion of this reader, his finest book yet."

—ZADIE SMITH, *New York Times* bestselling author of
NW and *White Teeth*

"I'm always wary when a young writer offers up a memoir, but Gary Shteyngart delivers big-time with *Little Failure*. His family's story is quite remarkable, and it's told with fearlessness, wisdom, and the wit that you'd expect from one of America's funniest novelists."

—CARL HIAASEN, *New York Times* bestselling author of
Bad Monkey

"I fully expected Gary Shteyngart's memoir of his search for love and sex in a Russian-Jewish-Queens-Oberlin upbringing to be as hilarious and indecorous and exact as it turns out to be; what I wasn't entirely prepared for was a book so soulful and pained in its recounting of the feints and false starts and, well, little failures of family love. Portnoy meets Chekhov meets Shteyngart! What could be better?"

—ADAM GOPNIK, *New York Times* bestselling author of
The Table Comes First and *Paris to the Moon*

"If you, like me, have often wondered, 'How did Gary Shteyngart get like that?,' *Little Failure* is the heartfelt, moving, and truly engaging memoir that explains it all. Dr. Freud would be proud."

—NATHAN ENGLANDER, author of *What We Talk
About When We Talk About Anne Frank*

BY GARY SHTEYNGART

Little Failure

Super Sad True Love Story

Absurdistan

The Russian Debutante's Handbook

LITTLE FAILURE

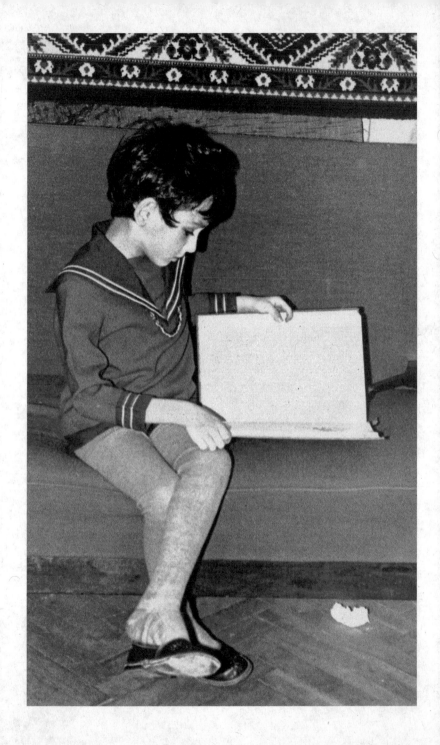

LITTLE
GARY
SHTEYNGART
FAILURE

...

A MEMOIR

Random House Trade Paperbacks

New York

2014 Random House Trade Paperback Edition

Published in the United States by Random House Trade Paperbacks, an imprint of Random House, a division of Random House LLC, a Penguin Random House Company, New York.

RANDOM HOUSE and the HOUSE colophon are registered trademarks of Random House LLC.

Originally published in hardcover in the United States by Random House, an imprint and division of Random House LLC, in 2014.

Grateful acknowledgment is made to Moldy Fig Music for permission to reprint four lines from "And She Was" by David Byrne. Reprinted courtesy of Moldy Fig Music.

Photograph on page 258 courtesy of J.Z. All other photographs from the author's personal collection.

LIBRARY OF CONGRESS CATALOGING-IN-PUBLICATION DATA
Shteyngart, Gary.
Little failure : a memoir / Gary Shteyngart.
pages cm
ISBN 978-0-8129-8249-7
eBook ISBN 978-0-8129-9533-6
1. Shteyngart, Gary. 2. Authors, American—21st century—Biography. I. Title.
PS3619.H79Z46 2014
813'.6—dc23
[B]
2013013217

Printed in the United States of America on acid-free paper

www.atrandom.com

2 4 6 8 9 7 5 3 1

Book design by Simon M. Sullivan

To my parents—the journey never ends.
To Richard C. Lacy, M.D., Ph.D.

LITTLE FAILURE

1.

THE CHURCH AND THE HELICOPTER

During a lonely period in his life, 1995–2001, the author tries to put his arms around a woman.

A YEAR AFTER GRADUATING COLLEGE, I worked downtown in the immense shadows of the World Trade Center, and as part of my freewheeling, four-hour daily lunch break I would eat and drink my way past these two giants, up Broadway, down Fulton Street, and over to the Strand Book Annex. In 1996, people still read books and the city could support an extra branch of the legendary Strand in the Financial District, which is to say that stockbrokers, secretaries, government functionaries—*everybody* back then was expected to have some kind of inner life.

In the previous year I had tried being a paralegal for a civil rights law firm, but that did not work out well. The paralegaling involved a lot of detail, way more detail than a nervous young man with a ponytail, a small substance-abuse problem, and a hemp pin on his cardboard tie could handle. This was as close as I would ever come to fulfilling my parents' dreams of my becoming a lawyer. Like most Soviet Jews, like most immigrants from Communist nations, my parents were deeply conservative, and they never thought much of the four years I had spent at my liberal alma mater, Oberlin College, studying Marxist politics and book-writing. On his first visit to Oberlin my father stood on a giant vagina painted in the middle of the quad by the campus lesbian, gay, and bisexual organization, oblivious to the rising tide of hissing and camp around him, as he enumerated to me the differences between laser-jet and ink-jet printers, specifically the price points of the cartridges. If I'm not mistaken, he thought he was standing on a peach.

I graduated summa cum laude and this improved my profile with Mama and Papa, but when I spoke to them it was understood that I was still a disappointment. Because I was often sick and runny nosed as a child (and as an adult) my father called me *Soplyak,* or Snotty. My mother was developing an interesting fusion of English and Russian and, all by herself, had worked out the term *Failurchka,* or Little Failure. That term made it from her lips into the overblown manuscript of a novel I was typing up in my spare time, one whose opening chapter was about to be rejected by the important writing program at the University of Iowa, letting me know that my parents weren't the only ones to think that I was nothing.

Realizing that I was never going to amount to much, my mother, working her connections as only a Soviet Jewish mama can, got me a job as a "staff writer" at an immigrant resettlement agency downtown, which involved maybe thirty minutes of work per year, mostly proofing brochures teaching newly arrived Russians the wonders of deodorant, the dangers of AIDS, and the subtle satisfaction of *not* getting totally drunk at some American party.

In the meantime, the Russian members of our office team and I got totally drunk at some American party. Eventually we were all laid off, but before that happened I wrote and rewrote great chunks of my first novel and learned the Irish pleasures of matching gin martinis with steamed corned beef and slaw at the neighborhood dive, the name of which is, if I recall correctly, the Blarney Stone. I'd lie there on top of my office desk at 2:00 P.M., letting out proud Hibernian cabbage farts, my mind dazed with high romantic feeling. The mailbox of my parents' sturdy colonial in Little Neck, Queens, continued to bulge with the remnants of their American dream for me, the pretty brochures from graduate school dropping in quality from Harvard Law School to Fordham Law School to the John F. Kennedy School of Government (sort of like law school, but not really) to the Cornell Department of City and Regional Planning, and finally to the most frightening prospect for any immigrant family, the master of fine arts program in creative writing at the University of Iowa.

"But what kind of profession is this, writer?" my mother would ask. "You want to be *this*?"

I want to be this.

• • •

At the Strand Book Annex I stuffed my tote with specimens from the 50-percent-discounted trade paperbacks aisle, sifting through the discarded review copies, looking for someone just like me on the back cover: a young goateed boulevardier, a desperately urban person, obsessed with the Orwells and Dos Passoses, ready for another Spanish Civil War if only those temperamental Spanishers would get around to having one. And if I found such a doppelganger I would pray that his writing wasn't good. Because the publication pie was only so big. Surely these blue-blooded American publishers, those most Random of Houses, would see right through my overeager immigrant prose and give the ring to some jerk from Brown, his junior year at Oxford or Salamanca giving him all the pale color needed for a marketable bildungsroman.

After handing over six dollars to the Strand, I would run back to my office to swallow all 240 pages of the novel in one go, while my Russian coworkers hooted it up next door with their vodka-fueled poetry. I was desperately looking for the sloppy turn of phrase or the MFA cliché that would mark the novel in question inferior to the one gestating in my office computer (idiotic working title: *The Pyramids of Prague*).

One day after courting gastric disaster by eating two portions of Wall Street vindaloo I exploded into the Strand's Art and Architecture section, my then $29,000-a-year salary no match for the handsome price tag on a Rizzoli volume of nudes by Egon Schiele. But it wasn't a melancholic Austrian who would begin to chip away at the alcoholic and doped-up urban gorilla I was steadily becoming. It wouldn't be those handsome Teutonic nudes that would lead me on the path back to the uncomfortable place.

The book was called *St. Petersburg: Architecture of the Tsars,* the baroque blue hues of the Smolny Convent Cathedral practically jumping off the cover. With its six pounds of thick, glossy weight, it was, and still is, a coffee-table book. This was in itself a problem.

The woman I was in love with at the time, another Oberlin graduate ("love who you know," my provincial theory), had already criticized my bookshelves for containing material either too lightweight or too masculine. Whenever she came by my new Brooklyn studio apartment, her pale midwestern eyes scanning the assembled soldiers of my literary army for a Tess Gallagher or a Jeanette Winterson, I found myself yearning for her taste and, as a corollary, the press of her razor-sharp collarbone against mine. Hopelessly, I arranged my Oberlin texts such as Tabitha Konogo's *Squatters & the Roots of Mau Mau* next to newly found woman-ethnic gems such as Lois-Ann Yamanaka's *Wild Meat and the Bully Burgers,* which I always imagined to be the quintessential Hawaiian coming-of-age story. (Someday I should read it.) If I bought *Architecture of the Tsars* I would have to hide it from this girl-woman in one of my cupboards behind a scrim of roach motels and bottles of cheap GEORGI vodka.

Other than failing my parents and being unable to finish *The Pyramids of Prague,* my main sorrow consisted of my loneliness. My first girlfriend ever, a fellow Oberlin student, an attractive, curly-haired white girl from North Carolina, had gone down south to live with a handsome drummer in his van. I would spend four years after graduating college without so much as kissing a girl. Breasts and backsides and caresses and the words "I love you, Gary" lived on only in abstract memory. Unless I'm telling you otherwise, I am completely in love with everyone around me for the rest of this book.

And then there was the price tag of *Architecture of the Tsars*—ninety-five dollars, marked down to sixty dollars—this would buy me just under forty-three chicken cutlets over at my parents' house. My mother always practiced tough love with me when it came to matters fiscal. When her failure showed up for dinner one night, she gave me a packet of chicken cutlets, *Kiev style,* meaning stuffed with butter. Gratefully, I accepted the chicken, but Mama told me each cutlet was worth "approximately one dollar forty." I tried to buy fourteen cutlets for seventeen dollars, but she charged me a full twenty, inclusive of a roll of Saran Wrap in which to store the poultry. A decade later, when I had stopped drinking so much, the knowledge that my parents would not stand by me and that I had to go at life furiously and alone drove me to perform terrifying amounts of work.

I twirled through the pages of the monumental *Architecture of the Tsars,* examining all those familiar childhood landmarks, feeling the vulgar nostalgia, the *poshlost'* Nabokov so despised. Here was the General Staff Arch with its twisted perspectives giving out onto the creamery of Palace Square, the creamery of the Winter Palace as seen from the glorious golden spike of the Admiralty, the glorious spike of the Admiralty as seen from the creamery of the Winter Palace, the Winter Palace *and* the Admiralty as seen from atop a beer truck, and so on in an endless tourist whirlwind.

I was looking at page 90.

"Ginger ale in my skull" is how Tony Soprano describes the first signs of a panic attack to his psychiatrist. There's dryness and wetness all at once, but in all the wrong places, as if the armpits and the mouth have embarked upon a cultural exchange. There's the substitution of a slightly different film from the one you've been watching, so that the mind is constantly recalculating for the unfamiliar colors, the strange, threatening snatches of conversation. *Why are we suddenly in Bangladesh?* the mind says. *When have we joined the mission to Mars? Why are we floating on a cloud of black pepper toward an NBC rainbow?* Add to that the supposition that your nervous, twitching body will never find rest, or maybe that it will find eternal rest all too soon, that is to say *pass out and die,* and you have the makings of a hyperventilating break-down. That's what I was experiencing.

And here's what I was looking at as my brain rolled around its stony cavity: a church. The Chesme Church on Lensovet (Leningrad So-viet) Street in the Moskovsky District of the city formerly known as Leningrad. Eight years later I would describe it thusly for a *Travel + Leisure* article:

> The raspberry and white candy box of the Chesme Church is an outrageous example of the neo-Gothic in Russia, made all the more precious by its location between the worst hotel in the world and a particularly gray Soviet block. The eye reels at the church's dazzling conceit, its mad collection of seemingly sugarcoated spires and crenellations, its utter edibility. Here is a building more pastry than edifice.

But in 1996 I did not have the wherewithal to spin clever prose. I had not yet undergone twelve years of four-times-a-week psychoanal-ysis that would make of me a sleekly rational animal, able to quantify, catalog, and retreat casually from most sources of pain, save one. I beheld the tiny scale of the church; the photographer had framed it between two trees, and there was a stretch of potholed asphalt in front of its diminutive entrance. It looked vaguely like a child overdressed for a ceremony. Like a little red-faced, tiny-bellied failure. It looked like how I felt.

I began to master the panic attack. I put the book down with sweaty hands. I thought of the girl that I loved at the time, that not-so-gentle censor of my bookshelf and my tastes; I thought about how she was taller than me and how her teeth were gray and straight, pur-poseful like the rest of her.

And then I wasn't thinking of her at all.

The memories were queuing. The church. My father. What did Papa look like when we were younger? I saw the big brows, the near-Sephardic skin tone, the harried expression of someone to whom life had been invariably unkind. But no, that was my father in the present day. When I imagined my early father, my preimmigrant father, I always bathed myself in his untrammeled love for me. I would think of him as just this awkward man, childish and bright, happy to have a little sidekick named Igor (my pre-Gary Russian name), palling around with this Igoryochek who is not judgmental or anti-Semitic, a tiny fellow warrior, first against the indignities of the Soviet Union and then against those of moving to America, the great uprooting of language and familiarity.

There he was, Early Father and Igoryochek, and we had just gone to the church in the book! The joyous raspberry Popsicle of Chesme Church, some five blocks away from our Leningrad apartment, a pink baroque ornament amidst the fourteen shades of Stalin-era beige. It wasn't a church in Soviet days but a naval museum dedicated, if memory serves correctly (and please let it serve correctly), to the victorious Battle of Chesme in 1770, during which the Orthodox Russians really gave it to those sonofabitch Turks. The interior of the sacred space back then (now it is once again a fully functional church) was crammed with a young boy's delight—maquettes of gallant eighteenth-century fighting ships.

. . .

Allow me to stay with the theme of early Papa and the Turks for just a few pages more. Let me introduce some new vocabulary to help me complete this quest. *Dacha* is the Russian word for country house, and as spoken by my parents it might as well have meant the "Loving Grace of God." When summer warmth finally broke the grip of the lifeless Leningrad winter and lackluster spring, they schlepped me around to an endless series of dachas in the former Soviet Union. A mushroom-ridden village near Daugavpils, Latvia; beautifully wooded Sestroretsk on the Gulf of Finland; the infamous Yalta in the

Crimea (Stalin, Churchill, and FDR signed some kind of real estate deal here); Sukhumi, today a wrecked Black Sea resort in a breakaway part of Georgia. I was taught to prostrate myself before the sun, giver of life, grower of bananas, and thank it for every cruel, burning ray. My mother's favorite childhood diminutive for me? Little Failure? No! It was *Solnyshko*. Little Sun!

Photographs from this era show a tired group of women in bathing suits and a Marcel Proust–looking boy in a kind of Warsaw Pact Speedo (that would be me) staring ahead into the limitless future while the Black Sea gently tickles their feet. Soviet vacationing was a rough, exhausting business. In the Crimea, we would wake up early in the morning to join a line for yogurt, cherries, and other edibles. All around us KGB colonels and party officials would be living it up in their snazzy waterfront digs while the rest of us stood weary-eyed beneath the miserable sun waiting to snag a loaf of bread. I had a pet that year, a gaily colored wind-up mechanical rooster, whom I would show off to everyone on the food line. "His name is Pyotr Petrovich *Rooster*ovich," I would declare with uncharacteristic swagger. "As you can see he has a limp, because he was injured in the Great Patriotic War." My mother, fearful that there would be anti-Semites queuing for cherries (they have to eat, too, you know), would whisper for me to be quiet or there would be no Little Red Riding Hood chocolate candy for dessert.

Candy or no, Pyotr Petrovich Roosterovich, that avian invalid, kept getting me into trouble. He was a constant reminder of my life back in Leningrad which was mostly spent slowly suffocating from winter asthma, but which left me plenty of time for reading war novels and dreaming Pyotr and I were killing our share of Germans at Stalingrad. The rooster was, put simply, my best and only friend in the Crimea, and no one could come between us. When the kind, elderly owner of the dacha in which we were staying picked up Pyotr and stroked his hobbled leg, muttering, "I wonder if we could fix this fellow," I grabbed the rooster from him and screamed, "You louse, you blackguard, you thief!" We were promptly kicked off the premises and had to live in a kind of underground hut, where a puny three-year-old Ukrainian boy also tried to play with my rooster, with similar consequences. Hence, the only words I know in Ukrainian: *"Ty khlopets mene byesh!"* ("You boy are hitting me!") We didn't last too long in the underground hut either.

I suppose I was a tightly wound kid that summer, both excited and confounded by the sunny southern landscape before me and by the sight of healthier, stronger bodies bouncing around me and my broken rooster in their full Slavic splendor. Unbeknownst to me, my mother was in the middle of a crisis herself, wondering whether to stay with my sick grandmother in Russia or leave her behind forever and emigrate to America. The decision was made for her in a greasy Crimean cafeteria. Over a bowl of tomato soup, a stout Siberian woman told my mother of the senseless beating her eighteen-year-old son had endured after his conscription by the Red Army, a beating that had cost him a kidney. The woman took out a photo of her boy. He resembled a moose of great stature crossbred with an equally colossal ox. My mother took one look at this fallen giant and then at her tiny, wheezing son, and soon enough we were on a plane bound for Queens. Roosterovich, with his sad limp and beautiful red wattle, remained the only victim of the Soviet military.

But whom I really missed that summer, the reason for my violent outburst against all manner of Ukrainians, was my real best friend. My father. Because all those other memories are just cue cards for an enormous stage set that has long evaporated along with the rest of the Soviet Union. Did any of this really happen? I sometimes ask myself. Did Junior Comrade Igor Shteyngart ever really huff and puff his way across the shoreline of the Black Sea, or was that some other imaginary invalid?

Summer 1978. I lived then for the long line to the phone booth marked by the word LENINGRAD (separate phone booths for different cities) to hear my father's voice crackle dimly against every technological problem the country was experiencing, from a failed nuclear test in the Kazakh desert to a sick braying billy goat in nearby Belorus-

sia. We were all connected by failure back then. The whole Soviet
Union was just fading out. My father told me stories over the phone,
and to this day I think my hearing is the most active of my five senses
because I would strain to hear him so acutely during my Black Sea
vacations.

The conversations are gone, but one of the letters remains. It is
written in my father's clumsy childish script, the script of a typical
male Soviet engineer. It's a letter that survives because so many people
wanted it to. We are not an overly sentimental people, I hope, but we
have an uncanny knowledge of just how much to save, of how many
wrinkled documents a Manhattan closet will one day hold.

I am a child of five in a subterranean vacation hut, and I am holding
in my hands this holy scribbled letter, the Cyrillic dense and filled
with crossed-out words, and as I am reading I am speaking the words
aloud, and as I am speaking them aloud I am lost in the ecstasy of
connection.

> *Good day, dear little son.*
>
> *How are you doing? What are you doing? Are you going to climb the*
> *"Bear" Mountain and how many gloves have you found in the sea?*
> *Have you learned to swim yet and if so are you planning to swim away*
> *to Turkey?*

A pause here on my part. I have no idea what these sea gloves are
and only a dim recollection of "Bear" Mountain (Everest it was not).
I want to focus on the last sentence, the swimming to Turkey one.
Turkey is, of course, across the Black Sea, but we are in the Soviet
Union, and we obviously cannot go there, either by steamship or by
doing the butterfly stroke. Is this subversive on my father's part? Or a
reference to his greatest wish, the wish that my mother relent and let
us emigrate to the West? Or, subconsciously, a connection to the
Chesme Church mentioned above, "more pastry than edifice," com-
memorating Russia's victory over the Turks?

*Little son, there are only a few days left until we meet again, do not be
lonely, behave yourself, listen to your mother and your aunt Tanya.
Kisses, Papa.*

Do not be lonely? But how could I not be lonely without him? And
is he really saying that he, too, is lonely? But of course! As if to soften
the blow, right below the main text of the letter, I find my favorite
thing in the world, better than the chocolate-covered marzipan that
excites me so feverishly back in Leningrad. It's an illustrated adventure story from my father! A thriller along the lines of Ian Fleming,
but with a few personal touches to appeal to a peculiar little boy. It
begins like so:

*One day in [the resort town of] Gurzuf [where I am presently gaining
color along my cheeks and arms], a submarine named* Arzum *sailed in
from Turkey.*

My father has drawn a submarine with a periscope approaching a
phallic Crimean mountain, covered either with trees or beach umbrellas; it is difficult to tell. The illustration is crude, but so is life in
our homeland.

*Two commandos wearing Aqua-Lungs departed the boat and swam for
the shore.*

The invaders look more like walking sturgeon in my father's broad
hand, but then the Turks are not known for their litheness.

*Unbeknownst to our border guards they headed for the mountain, for
the forest.*

The Turks—or are they really Turks, perhaps they are American
spies merely using Turkey as a staging ground (Jesus Christ, I'm not

even seven years old, and already *so many enemies*!) — are indeed climbing the beach-umbrella-covered mountain. One thought: "*our* border guards." A sleight of hand, on my father's part; he has devoted the previous thirty years of his life to hating the Soviet Union, much as he will devote the next thirty to loving America. But we haven't left the country yet. And I, militant worshipper of the Red Army, red Pioneer neckties, just about anything bloody red, am not allowed to know yet what my father knows, namely that everything I hold dear is untrue.

He writes:

> *In the morning the Soviet border guards saw fresh trails on the beach of the "Pushkin" sanatorium and called on the border guard, who summoned their search dog. She quickly found the two hidden Aqua-Lungs under the rocks. It was clear—an enemy. "Search!" the border guards commanded the dog, and she immediately ran in the direction of the International Pioneers Camp.*

Oh, what I would give for a doggie, the adorable fuzzy kind my father's pen is now deploying against those overweight American Turks. But my mother has enough troubles managing me, let alone a pet.

Story to be continued—at home.

To be continued? At home? How cruel. How will I know if the brave Soviet border guard doggie and her heavily armed human masters will discover the enemy and do to the enemy what I wish to be done to the enemy? That is, the infliction of a slow, cruel death, the only kind we're comfortable with here in the USSR. Death to the Germans, death to the fascists, death to the capitalists, death to the enemies of the people! How my blood boils even at this ridiculously young age, how infused I am with helpless anger. And if you fast-forward to the virgin futon in my roach-infested Brooklyn studio, to the drunken downtown resettlement agency, to the annex of the Strand bookstore, circa 1996, believe me, I am still full of vile, unanalyzed, de-Oberlinized rage. A quiet, thoughtful child on the outside, garrulous and funny, but scratch this Russian and you will find a dozen Tatars, give me a rake and I will rush against the enemy hidden in the village bales, I will flush them out like a border collie, I will rip them to the shreds with my own teeth. Insult my pet mechanical rooster, will you! And so: anger, excitement, violence, and love. "Little son, there are only a few days left until we meet again," my father writes, and these words are truer and sadder than any in my life. Why a few days more? *Why not right now?* My father. My hometown. My Leningrad. The Chesme Church. The countdown has already begun. Each moment, each meter of distance between us, is intolerable.

• • •

It's 1999. Three years after my panic attack at the Strand Book Annex. I've returned to my Petersburg, née Leningrad, née Petrograd, for the first time in twenty years. I am twenty-seven years old. In about eight months, I will sign a book deal for a novel no longer called *The Pyramids of Prague.*

But I don't know that yet. I'm still operating on the theory that I will fail at everything I try. In 1999 I am employed as a grant writer for a Lower East Side charity, and the woman I'm sleeping with has a boyfriend who isn't sleeping with her. I've returned to St. Petersburg to be carried away by a Nabokovian torrent of memory for a country that no longer exists, desperate to find out if the metro still has the comforting smells of rubber, electricity, and unwashed humanity that I remember so well. I return home during the tail end of the Wild East days of the Yeltsin era, when the president's drinking bouts vie for the front pages with spectacular acts of urban violence. I return to what, in looks and temperament, is now a third-world country in steady free fall, every childhood memory—and there were fates worse, far worse, than a Soviet childhood—soiled by the new realities. The accordion-style bendy bus on the way from the airport has a hole the size of a child between its two halves. I know this because a small child nearly falls out when the bus lurches to a halt. It takes me less than an hour after landing to find a metaphor for my entire visit.

By day four of my return I learn that my exit visa—foreigners in Russia must have a permit both to enter and *leave* the country—is incomplete without a certain stamp. A good third of my homecoming is spent hunting for this validation. I find myself boxed in by gargantuan Stalin-era buildings in the middle of Moskovskaya Ploshchad, Moscow Square, the exact neighborhood where I lived as a child. I am waiting for a woman from a questionable visa service so that I can bribe a hotel clerk with a thousand rubles (about thirty-five dollars at the time) to have my visa properly authenticated. I am waiting for her in the scruffy lobby of the Hotel Mir, "the worst hotel in the world," as I will call it in my *Travel + Leisure* article a few years later. The Hotel Mir, I should add, is exactly down the street from the Chesme Church.

And without warning I can't breathe.

The world is choking me, the country is choking me, my fur-collared overcoat is pressing down on me with intent to kill. Instead of Tony Soprano's "ginger ale in my skull" I am subject to an explosion of seltzer and rum across my horizon. On my seltzer-and-rum legs I wobble over to a new McDonald's on the nearby square still crowned with Lenin's statue, the square where my father and I used to play hide-and-seek beneath Lenin's legs. Inside the McDonald's I try to find refuge in the meaty midwestern familiarity of this place. *If I am an American—hence invincible—please let me be invincible* now! *Make the panic stop, Ronald McDonald. Return to me my senses.* But reality continues to slip away as I put my head down on the cold slab of a fast-food table, weak third-world children all around me dressed in party hats celebrating some turning point in little Sasha's or Masha's life.

Writing about the incident in *The New Yorker* in 2003, I surmised: "My panic [attack] was an off-shoot of my parents' fear twenty years ago: the fear of being refused permission to emigrate, of becoming what was then called a *refusenik* (a designation that brought with it a kind of jobless state-sanctioned purgatory). Part of me believed that I would not be allowed to leave Russia. That *this*—an endless cement square teeming with unhappy, aggressive people in awful leather jackets—would be the rest of my life."

But now I know that was not the truth. It wasn't about the visa stamp, the bribe, the refusenik status, any of it.

Because as the world spins around me at the McDonald's there's one thing I'm trying not to think about, and it's the Chesme Church nearby. Its "sugarcoated spires and crenellations." I'm trying not to be five years old again. But why not? Just look at me and my papa! We've launched something between those church spires. Yes, I'm remembering it now. It's a toy helicopter on a string, buzzing between them. Only now it's stuck! The helicopter is stuck between the spires, but we are still happy because we are better than this, better than the country around us! This must be the happiest day of my life.

But why am I panicking? Why is the oval of Ativan disappearing beneath my fake white built-in American teeth?

What happened at the Chesme Church twenty-two years ago?

I don't want to go back there. Oh, no, I do not. Whatever happened, I must not think of it. How I want to be home in New York right now. How I want to sit over my flimsy garage-sale kitchen table, press my American teeth into Mother's $1.40 Kiev-style chicken cutlet, and feel the disgusting buttery warmth all over my stupid little mouth.

The nesting doll of memory collapses into its component pieces, each leading someplace smaller and smaller, even as I get bigger and bigger.

Father.

Helicopter.

Church.

Mother.

Pyotr Petrovich Roosterovich.

Turks on the beach.

Soviet lies.

Oberlin love.

The Pyramids of Prague.

Chesme.

The book.

I am standing there once again in the Fulton Street Strand, holding *St. Petersburg: Architecture of the Tsars,* the baroque blue hues of the Smolny Convent Cathedral practically jumping off the cover. I am opening the book, for the first time, to page 90. I am turning to that page. I am turning to that page again. The thick page is turning in my hand.

What happened at the Chesme Church twenty-two years ago?

• • •

No. Let us forget about that. Let us leave me in Manhattan, for now, as I turn the page at the Strand, innocent and naïve in my nine-to-five shirt, with my dickish liberal arts ponytail behind me, my novelist dreams in front of me, and my love and anger burning as crimson as ever. As my father wrote in his adventure story:

To be continued—at home.

2.

ENTER THE SNOTTY

The author is told that the breadline does not, in fact, deliver.

CERTIFICATE OF BIRTH
———————

IGOR SHTEYNGART

5 July 1972

Dear Parents!
We cordially congratulate you and share your joy at the birth of a new human being—a citizen of the Union of Soviet Socialist Republics and a member of the future Communist Society.

We wish your family health, much love, friendship, and harmony.

We are certain that you will raise your son to be a conscientious toiler and a loyal patriot of our great motherland!

Signed,
Executive Committee of the
Leningrad City Council of Workers' Deputies

• • •

I AM BORN.

My pregnant mother crosses a Leningrad street and a truck driver honks at her, because scaring pregnant women is the thing to do. She grabs her stomach. The water breaks. She rushes to the Otto Birthing House on Vasilyevsky Island, an important floating appendage to the map of Leningrad, the same birthing house where she and her two sisters have come into the world. (Russian children are not born in full-fledged hospitals as in the West.) Several weeks premature, I drop out of my mother, legs and ass first. I am long and skinny and look a bit like a dachshund in human form, except that I have a fantastically large head. "Well done!" the orderlies tell my mother. "You've given birth to a good *muzhik*." The *muzhik,* the sturdy, brawny Russian man, is the last thing I will ever become, but what rankles my mother is that the orderlies are using the informal form of address with her (*ty* versus *vy*). My mother is sensitive to these distinctions. She is from a good family and not merely another Jewess (*yevreika*) you can informally insult.

The Otto Birthing House. For a "member of the future Communist Society," this Art Nouveau–ish building is as fine a place to be born as any in the city, perhaps the country. Beneath my mother's feet, an exquisitely tiled floor bearing the motif of waves and butterflies; above her, chrome chandeliers; outside, the enormous Petrine buildings of the Twelve Colleges of Leningrad State University and a calming burst of Russian evergreens within the subarctic landscape. And in her arms, me.

I am born hungry. Ravenous. I want to eat the world, and I can never be satiated. Breast, condensed milk, whatever you have I will suck on it, bite it, swallow it. Years later, under the tutelage of my beloved grandmother Polya, I will become a fatso, but for now, thin and lean and hungry is how I'll go.

My mother is twenty-six, and by the standards of the time she is old to be a mother. My father is thirty-three and is already halfway into his existence as far as the local life expectancy for men is concerned. My mother teaches piano at a kindergarten; my father is a mechanical engineer. They own an apartment of about five hundred square feet, with a balcony, in the center of Leningrad, which makes them privileged; in relative terms, far more privileged than we will ever be in the United States, even when a minor colonial in Little Neck, Queens, is added to our portfolio in the late 1980s.

What is also true, and what will take me most of my life to understand, is that my parents are too dissimilar to marry successfully. The Soviet Union is supposed to be a classless society, but my father is a village boy, from difficult stock, and my mother is from the Petersburg cultural class, a class that has its own problems but whose miseries are laughably minor by comparison. To my mother, my father's kin are savage and provincial. To my father, hers are pretentious and false. Neither of them is entirely wrong.

My mother looks half Jewish, which, given the place and time, is too Jewish by half, but she is beautiful in a compact, practical way, a modest beehive of hair sitting atop a worried face and a turtleneck, always a smile ready at the corners of her cheeks, a smile reserved mostly for family. Leningrad is her city, much as New York will soon be hers as well. She knows where the occasional chicken cutlets are sold and the pastries bursting with clotted cream. She holds on to every kopeck, and when the kopecks become cents in New York, she will hold on to them even more. My father is not tall, but he is handsome in a gloomy Levantine sort of way, and he takes care of his physique—indeed, for him, the physical world is the only salvation from a mind constantly churning away at itself. At my own wedding many years later, more than one person will jokingly remark that it is odd that such a good-looking couple could have produced me. I think there is truth to that. My parents' blood did not mix well within me.

• • •

Fathers are not allowed into the Otto Birthing House, but for the ten days we are separated my father is struck by the sharp (if not terribly unique) feeling that he is no longer alone in the world and that he needs to be next to me. In my first years on earth he will express these feelings, let's call them love, with great skill and single-mindedness. The other aspects of his life, a generally uninspiring career engineering large telescopes at the famous LOMO photography factory, his dashed dreams of becoming a professional opera singer, will fall away as he tries to fix the broken child in his arms.

He will have to do it quick!

Swaddling is still merrily practiced at the Otto Birthing House, and the dachshund-shaped me is tied with a giant blue bow (*bant*) around my neck. By the time the taxi from the birthing house arrives at our apartment, my lungs are nearly empty of air and my comically large head is nearly as blue as the bow strangling me.

I am revived, but the next day I start sneezing. My anxious mother (let us count the number of times "anxious" and "mother" appear in close proximity throughout the rest of this book) calls the local polyclinic and demands a nurse. The Soviet economy is one-fourth the size of the American one, but doctors and nurses still make house calls. A beefy woman appears at our door. "My son is sneezing, what do I do?" my mother hyperventilates.

"You should say, 'Bless you,'" the nurse instructs.

• • •

For the next thirteen years—until I don a husky suit for my Bar Mitzvah at Congregation Ezrath Israel in the Catskills—I will be sick with asthma. My parents will be scared witless, and often I will be, too.

But I will also be surrounded by the strange, unbidden beauty of being a sickly child, the homeyness of it, the safety of lowering myself into a fort of pillows and duvet covers and comforters, oh those madly thick Soviet comforters that are always bleeding their Uzbek cotton interiors. There's ghetto heat coming off the radiators, but also my own musty child warmth reminding me that I exist as more than just a container for the phlegm in my lungs.

Is this my first memory?

The earliest years, the most important ones, are the trickiest. Emerging from nothingness takes time.

Here is what I *think* I can remember.

My father, or mother, awake through the night holding my mouth open with a tablespoon so that I don't suffocate from asthma, so that the air will get into my lungs. Mother, gentle, worried. Father, gentle, worried, but sad. Scared. A village man, a short but tough *muzhik,* set before a malfunctioning creature. My father's solutions to most problems involve jumping into a cold lake, but here there is no lake. His warm hand is at the back of my head brushing the fine hairs with sympathy, but he can hardly hold back the frustration when he says to me, *"Akh, ty, Soplyak."* Eh, you, Snotty. In the years hence, as we realize that the asthma will not go away, the anger and disappointment in that statement will become more pronounced, and I will see the curl of his thick lips, the sentence broken up into its constituent parts:

Eh.

Sigh.

You.

Shake of the head.

Snotty.

• • •

But I'm not dead yet! The hunger is strong inside me. And it is strong for meats. "Doctor's kolbasa," a soft Russian mortadella substitute; then, as my teeth grow in complexity, *vetchina,* or Russian ham, and *buzhenina,* dangerously chewy cold baked pork, a taste of which will linger on the tongue for hours. These foodstuffs are not easy to arrange; even the prospect of stinking week-old fish will draw hundreds of people into a queue stretching around the corner beneath the flat, pink morning sky. The optimism of the post-Stalin leader Nikita Khrushchev's "thaw" is long over, and under the increasingly sclerotic rule of the comically doddering Leonid Brezhnev, the Soviet Union is beginning its swift descent into nonbeing. But how I hunger for my meats along with several teaspoons of *sgushchyonka,* condensed milk, in the iconic blue cans. "Milk, whole, condensed, with sugar" might be the first five words I try to read in Russian. After the heady nitrites of the kolbasa, I am blessed by a touch of this sweet, dispensed by my mother. And each circle of love binds me closer to her, to them, and every subsequent betrayal and misjudgment will bind me even closer. This is the model of the cloyingly close Russian Jewish family, but it is not peculiar to our ethnicity alone. Here in the USSR, with our freedoms circumscribed and the doctor's kolbasa and condensed milk in short supply, it is only amplified.

I am a curious child, and nothing is more curious to me than the electric outlet. The height of experience for me is to stick my fingers into those two shabby holes (Freudians, you're welcome) and feel the jolt of something more alive than me. My parents tell me that inside the outlet lives *Dyadya Tok,* or Uncle Electric Current, a bad man who wants to do me harm. *Dyadya Tok,* along with my meat vocabulary (*vetchina, buzhenina, kolbasa*) and *Soplyak* (Snotty), are some of the first words I learn in the mighty Russian tongue. There is also my savage cry of "*Yobtiki mat'!,*" a childish mispronunciation of *Yob tvoyu mat',* or "Go fuck your mother," which, I suppose, provides a nice overview of the state of relations between my parents and their two families.

My hunger and curiosity are evenly matched by worry. It will take five more years before I formulate death as an end to life, but my inability to breathe gives me a good preview. The lack of air is making me nervous. Isn't this elemental? You breathe in, and then you breathe out. It doesn't take a genius. And I try. But it doesn't happen. The machinery is creaking inside me but to no effect. I do not know other children, there is no basis for comparing myself with them, but I know that, as a boy, I'm all wrong.

And how long will the two creatures holding my mouth open with a tablespoon continue to do so? I can tell that it is hurting them terribly.

There is a photograph of me at one year and ten months taken at a photo studio. Wearing a pair of children's jogging pants with their outline of a cartoon bunny on one of the front pockets, I hold a phone in my hand (the photo studio is proud to exhibit this advanced Soviet technology), and I am getting ready to bawl. The look on my face is that of a mother in 1943 who just received a fateful telegram from the front. I am scared of the photo studio. I am scared of the telephone. Scared of anything outside our apartment. Scared of the people in their big fur hats. Scared of the snow. Scared of the cold. Scared of the heat. Scared of the ceiling fan at which I would point one tragic finger and start weeping. Scared of any height higher than my sickbed. Scared of Uncle Electric Current. "Why was I so scared of everything?" I ask my mother nearly forty years later.

"Because you were born a Jewish person," she says.

Perhaps. The blood coursing through my veins is mostly Yasnitsky (my mother) and Shteyngart (my father), but the nurses at the Otto Birthing House have also added 10, 20, 30, 40 cc's of Stalin and Beria and Hitler and Göring.

There is another word: *tigr*. My infancy is not graced by toys or what they now call educational tools, but I do have my tiger. The common gift for a young mother in Russia in 1972 is a stack of cotton diapers. When my mother's coworkers find out that she lives in the fancy new buildings by the Neva River—today these buildings look like something from a declining part of Mumbai, with varicolored, slapped-on wooden balconies—they realize diapers won't do. And so they gather the eighteen rubles needed to buy a luxury gift, a stuffed tiger. Tiger is four times larger than I am, and he is orange in just the right way, and his whiskers are as thick as my fingers, and the look on his face says, *I want to be your friend, little Snotty*. I can climb across him with as much acrobatic skill as a sick boy can muster, just as I will climb across my father's chest for many years to come, and, as with my father, I will pull at Tiger's round ears and squeeze at his plump nose.

There are more memories here I would like to capture and display for you, if only I were faster with my net. Under the care of my paternal grandmother Polya, I fall out of a baby carriage and land headfirst into asphalt. This may create learning and coordination difficulties that persist to this day (if you see me driving down Route 9G, please be alert). I learn to walk, but without any particular confidence. In neighboring Latvia, on summer vacation at a local farm, I stumble into a coop with my arms outstretched and bend down to hug a chicken. Tiger has always been kind to me, how much worse can this colorful smaller animal be? The Latvian chicken shakes its wattle, steps forward, and pecks me. Out of political consideration perhaps. Pain and betrayal and howling and tears. First, it's Uncle Electric Current; now it's the Baltic poultry. The world is harsh and inconsiderate, and you can rely only on your family.

And then the memories begin to flood in. And then I become who I was always meant to be. Which is to say: someone in love. Five years old and completely in love.

His name is Vladimir.

But that will have to wait.

3.

I AM STILL THE BIG ONE

A FAMILY ALBUM

The Ukraine, 1940. The author's father, bottom row, second from left, being held by the author's grandmother. Just about everyone else is going to die soon.

THANKSGIVING 2011. A three-story minor colonial in Little Neck, Queens. What a class-obsessed Britisher might call middle-middle-*middle* class. My small family is gathered around a reflective orange mahogany table—product of Ceauşescu's Romania, dragged against all common sense from Leningrad—on which my mother will soon serve a garlicky, wet turkey kept gurgling beneath a sheet of plastic wrap until the moment it is presented and a dessert made out of a dozen matzohs, a gallon of cream and amaretto liqueur, and a tub of raspberries. What I believe my mother is aiming for is a mille-feuille, or, in Russian, a *tort Napoleon*. The result is a vaguely Passover-based departure from pastry reality. In deference to its point of origin, she likes to call it "French."

"But the best part is the raspberries which I grew myself!" my father shouts. In this family, points will not be awarded for quiet or solemnity; in this *mishpucha* everyone is always angling for a turn at Mr. Microphone. Here we are, a tribe of wounded narcissists, begging to be heard. If there's only one person actually *listening* it is me, and not because I love my parents (and I love them, too, oh, so terribly), but because it is my job.

My father rushes up to my cousin and mock punches him in the stomach, shouting, "I am still the big one!" Being the big one is important to him. Several years ago, drunk off of turning seventy, he took my then girlfriend (now wife) to his vegetable garden, where he handed her his biggest cucumber. "Here is something to remember me by"—he winked, adding—"I am big. My son is small."

Aunt Tanya, my mother's sister, is ranting about Prince Chemodanin, who, she is convinced, is one of our progenitors. A *chemodan* is a suitcase in Russian. Prince Suitcase, according to Aunt Tanya, was one of old Russia's illustrious figures: a faithful correspondent to his fellow prince Leo Tolstoy (although Tolstoy rarely wrote back), a thinker, an aesthete, and also, why the hell not, a groundbreaking physician. My cousin, her son, who is always about to go to law school (as I was always about to go to law school at his age), whom I actually *like* and also worry about, is talking excitedly about the prospects of libertarian candidate Ron Paul in perfect English and confusing Russian.

"We're a good, normal family," my mother suddenly announces to my fiancée.

"And of course Prince Suitcase was also a brilliant doctor," Aunt Tanya adds, assaulting my mother's "French" with a teaspoon.

I join my father on the couch in the living room, where he is seeking shelter from the extended family. Every few minutes Aunt Tanya bursts in with her camera, shouting, "Come on, get closer! Father and son, okay? Father and son!"

LITTLE FAILURE

[29]

My father seems depressed and aggrieved, more so than usual. Today I know that I am not the full source of his unhappiness. My father is very proud of his physique and, conversely, critical of mine, but on this Thanksgiving he does not look as rod thin and athletic as usual. He is gray-bearded and small, not fat by any means, bearing as much weight as a seventy-three-year-old man who is not a Burmese peasant should bear. Earlier, the father of my cousin Victoria's husband, one of the few Americans that have thankfully diluted the all-Russian cast of my family, had poked him in the stomach saying, "You storing food away for the winter, Semyon?" I knew my father would swallow that insult whole, then, in the space of two hours, metabolize it into rage ("I am still the big one!"), the rage and humor that are our chief inheritance.

The ethnic cable is on, advertisements for shady Brooklyn dentists and new Queens wedding halls struggling to pump out the joy. I feel my father's stare needling my right shoulder. I can calculate his stare from almost any distance on earth.

"I'm not afraid of death," he says apropos of nothing. "God is watching out for me."

"Mmmm," I low. A new Russian soap opera set in the Stalin era comes on, and I hope that it can move our conversation in a different direction. When we had just arrived in America, my father used to take me for long walks around leafy Kew Gardens, Queens, trying to teach me the history of Russian-Jewish relations through a series of vignettes he liked to call *The Planet of the Yids*. Whenever I sense him falling down the rabbit hole of depression, preceded by him acting out something violent or phallic (cue the cucumber), I like to move us back to the past, where neither one of us is guilty of anything.

"This is interesting," I say of the show in my best American "Hey, let's be friends" kind of voice. "What year was this filmed, do you think?"

"Don't mention the names of my relatives in the book you're writing," my father says.

"I won't."

"Just don't write like a self-hating Jew."

Loud laughter from the dining room: my mother and her sister in their natural mirth. Unlike my father, an only child, Mama and Aunt Tanya come from a relatively large family of three daughters. Tanya can be overly sweet and has a strangely American conviction that she is somehow special, but at least she does not come across as depressed. My mother has the best social skills of the bunch, always knowing when to bring people into her orbit and when to push them aside. Had she been born in the American South in the proper era, I think she would have done well.

"Da, poshyol on na khui!" Tanya, the youngest, is shouting over the din of the television. *Well, let him go to the dick!* And my mother is laughing a naughty middle child's laugh, so happy that her sister is here in America and she has someone to say *khui* and *yob* and *blyad* with. Their seven-year separation—Tanya was allowed to emigrate from Russia only after Gorbachev took power—was unbearable for my mother. And because I spent my youth as a kind of tuning fork for my parents' fears, disappointments, and alienation, unbearable for me as well.

"I don't have any friends," my father says in response to the laughter from the dining room. "Your mother doesn't allow them here." The first part is certainly true. I am curious about the second.

"Why not?" I ask.

He doesn't answer. He sighs. He sighs so much I think he inadvertently practices his own form of Kabbalistic meditation. "Well, God be with her."

Lying next to my father is a VHS tape entitled *Immigration: Threatening the Bonds of Our Union: Part II: Treachery and Treason in America,* produced by an outfit called American Patrol in Sherman Oaks, California. (Why does the extreme right wing like colons so much?) I'm wondering what the trigger-happy members of the American Patrol would make of my father, a Social Security–collecting Osama bin Laden–looking Semite sitting on a couch in an ethnic Queens neighborhood, his dining room stinking of immigrant fish, his house flanked by a Korean family on one side, an Indian clan on another.

"We are living different lives," my father says, astutely. "And it makes me sad."

It makes me sad, too. But what can be done? I used to be more forthcoming with my father, and, consequently, I used to hate him. Now I know just how much pain I can inflict, and do inflict, with each book I publish that does not extol the State of Israel, with each National Public Radio pronouncement that does not bind me in covenant with his famous God. Would it kill me, I think, to tell him right now: *You are still the big one, Papa?*

I am the small one, forever, and you are the big one.

Would that make it right between us? There he was at the dinner table before his depression set in, still high on family feeling and a little bit of vodka, rushing over to serve me first, ladling in the mushroom soup, extra heavy on the onions, that he makes special for me. "Sour cream?" he asks me. "Yes, please." "Bread? Vodka? Cucumber?" Yes, yes, and yes, Papa. The rest of the table might as well not exist for him.

"He loves you so much," a girlfriend I brought to the family table once told me, "but he doesn't know how to express it. Everything he does and says comes out wrong."

I want to stay with him and make him feel better. I want to finish watching the Russian show on TV. Finish off the cucumbers and the soup choked with the mushrooms he has picked himself in a dense upstate forest. "Forty dollars each mushroom would cost in the store!" my mother is yelling at my cousin who is failing to partake of the dense fungus. "And still he won't eat it!"

I want to have a family. I want to laugh, and also be awed by Aunt Tanya's postmodern let's-get-it-over-with-and-really-start-drinking Thanksgiving toast: "God bless America *whatever.*"

I want to be there when my mother, usually so in control, has cut herself three times in the course of preparing her "French." Are her hands shaking? Is her eyesight failing? She looks so tired today. Will she recover in time for the manic burst of cleaning and worrying that will accompany her into the night? Is God watching out for us?

I want to close my eyes and feel a part of the cornucopia of insanity swirling around the table, because that insanity has alighted on my shoulders as well.

· · ·

But I also want to go home. To Manhattan. To the carefully constructed, utterly inoffensive apartment that I have wrought to show in part that the past is not the future, that I am my own man. This is the creed I have made for myself: Day Zero. A new start. Keep the rage in check. Try to decouple the rage from the humor. Laugh at things that are not sourced from pain. You are not them. He is not you. And each day, with or without my parents' presence, my creed proves to be bullshit.

The past is haunting us. In Queens, in Manhattan, it is shadowing us, punching us in the stomach. I am small, and my father is big. But the Past—it is the biggest.

· · ·

Let's start with my surname: Shteyngart. A German name whose insane Sovietized spelling, eye-watering bunching of consonants (just one *i* between the *h* and *t* and you got some pretty nice "Shit" there), and overall unattractiveness has cost me a lot of human warmth. "Mr., uh, I can't pronounce this . . . *Shit* . . . *Shit* . . . *Shitfart*?" the sweet Alabama girl at reception giggles. "Is, uh, a single bed okay for you?"

What do you think, honey, I want to say. *Do you think a Shitfart gets to* share *a bed?*

All my life I've tried not to think of that misspelled "Shteyngart" as a pungent waste product of history. The correct name had to be Steingarten, or Stone Garden, which is as beautifully Zen as a German Jewish name can get, a name offering the kind of serenity and peace that none of my Hebrew ancestors had surely ever experienced in their short, explosive lifetimes. Stone Garden. As if.

Recently I found out from my father that Shteyngart is not our name at all. A slip of the pen in some Soviet official's hand, a drunk notary, a semiliterate commissar, who knows, but I am not really Gary Shteyngart. My family name is—Steinhorn. Meaning "Stone Horn." Though I was born Igor—my name was changed to Gary in America so that I would suffer one or two fewer beatings—my Leningrad birth certificate should have welcomed into this world one Citizen Igor Stone Horn. I have clearly spent thirty-nine years unaware that my real destiny was to go through life as a Bavarian porn star, but some further questions present themselves: If neither Gary nor Shteyngart is truly my name, then what the hell am I doing calling myself Gary Shteyngart? Is every single cell in my body a historical lie?

"Just don't write like a self-hating Jew," my father is whispering into my ear.

• • •

The Stone Horns inhabit the Ukrainian town of Chemirovets, where my father's paternal grandfather was killed for no good reason in the 1920s. My father's grandmother was left to fend for herself and a family of five children. There was not enough to eat. Those who could went up to Leningrad, Russia's former imperial capital and second most important city once the Bolsheviks crowned Moscow as the capital. There, they mostly died, too. They were a deeply religious clan, but the Soviets took that from them as well, before they took what little else remained.

On the maternal side of my father's family, the Millers lived in the nearby Ukrainian village of Orinino, population about one thousand souls. My father visited Orinino once in the 1960s, where he found a handful of hospitable Jews to talk genocide with, but I've never been on a *shtetl* pilgrimage. I envision a town that isn't down on its luck, because it never had any luck to begin with; a postagricultural, post-Soviet village, clapboard houses missing large sections of, well, clapboard, women bearing tubs of yellowish water from a local pump, a man pulling a South Korean TV/VCR combo in a donkey cart, a dazed rooster stumbling along some main thoroughfare—inevitably

Lenin or Soviet Street—toward that little hill just outside of town where all the Jews lie safely in a nice long burial mound, never to bother anyone with their alien Yiddish, their dour garb and kosher butcheries. But this is just an author's imagination. Perhaps it's nothing like that. Perhaps.

In addition to the Millers and the Stone Horns, the other surnames to track in this family drama are Stalin and Hitler. As I march my relatives onto the pages of this book, please remember that I am also marching them toward their graves and that they will most likely meet their ends in some of the worst ways imaginable.

But they don't have to wait for the Second World War to start. The good times are already rolling in the 1920s. While my great-grandpa Stone Horn is being killed in one part of the Ukraine, Great-grandpa Miller is being killed in another part. The Millers are not a poor family. Their main source of income is one of the largest houses in town, which they have turned into a coach inn. Farmers and merchants coming to the local fair shelter their horses and oxen with my great-grandparents. They are probably as rich as anyone on that side of my family has ever been, until nearly a hundred years later, in 2013, I lease myself a Volvo. One bitter Eastern European night, Great-grandpa Miller is riding home with a great deal of Jewish money in his saddlebag, when one of the many criminal bands roaming freely across the Ukraine in the chaos following the 1917 Revolution murders him. The Millers are ruined.

• • •

In order for me to be born, all four branches of my family have to end up in Leningrad, trading in their tiny towns and villages for that somber, canal-laced cityscape. Here's how it happens.

In 1932 Stalin decrees that the inhabitants of the Ukraine should pretty much fucking starve to death, leading to the elimination of an estimated six to seven million citizens, Christians, Jews, anyone who has a stomach that can't be filled with rye. My great-grandmother sends her starving seven-year-old daughter, Fenya, to an orphanage in

Leningrad. Fenya and my grandmother are among the three Miller siblings out of nine who will survive World War II. Some will die fighting at the front against the invading Germans; some will die at the hands of the SS and their Ukrainian colleagues; at least one will, poignantly, "lose her mind," according to my father, and die before the war even gets properly started.

Polina, or Babushka (Grandma) Polya as I knew her, arrives in Leningrad in the 1930s when she is fourteen years old. In three novels I have written about the immigrant experience in the final years of the twentieth century with a sense of righteous ownership. But my parents came to this country stuffed with advanced degrees and keen to master the universal language of English. As for me, I was merely seven and expected to succeed wildly in a country we thought of as magical but whose population did not strike us as being especially clever.

But back in the 1930s my grandma Polya is a true immigrant. She comes to Leningrad as a Yiddish- and Ukrainian-speaking teenager, without knowledge of Russian or city life. Somehow, she gets herself admitted to the Teacher's Technical College, a two-year school, where a kindly instructor takes pity on her and helps her master the tongue of Pushkin and Dostoyevsky. I always thought that both of my grandmothers struggled against the despised Jewish accent, the *Ghhhh* sound in place of the strong Russian *RRRRRR,* but when I bring it up with my father, he says emphatically: "Your grandmother *never* had a Jewish accent." Still, whenever I try to flaunt my hard-perfected English, whenever my new language comes pouring out of me, I think of her.

• • •

After finishing the teachers college, Grandma is sent to work in an orphanage, known euphemistically as a children's home (*detskii dom*), in a Leningrad suburb. Stalin's Great Purge, a political bloodletting with few equals in human history, is hitting its peak, and some of the Soviet Union's finest people are being shot outright or packed onto trains and sent eastward to the labor camps. Other fine people are allowed to starve to death in their homes. The children of the tortured and the dead are often sent to the "children's homes" that dot the land, and Grandma Polya, by age seventeen, is already employed as a teacher and disciplinarian. By the age of twenty she is the deputy director of the orphanage. She is murderously tough as only the daughter of a murdered Jewish coach-inn owner can be, but if I, her grandson, can attest to one fact that I know is true beyond all others, it is this: She loved children.

As my grandmother is settling into life in the big city, the great Jewish express from the Ukrainian countryside delivers up to Leningrad my grandfather, Isaac Stone Horn, who has by now been rechristened Shteyngart. Grandpa Isaac is from a village close to Grandma Polya's, and the humid ties of Judaism bring them together in the cold imperial capital in 1936. Some fifty-five-odd years later I am at a seminar table at Oberlin College. Our small class, with its combined $1,642,800 of annual tuition and fees, is dutifully discussing the travails of that mysterious but glorious working class we've heard so much about, but what I'm not quite realizing is that my grandpa Isaac was an honest-to-goodness common worker, and I, by extension, am the grandson of an honest-to-goodness common worker.

In the late 1930s Isaac is toiling at a leather factory in Leningrad, making soccer balls, volleyballs, and belts. He's self-educated, a socialist, loves singing and books and Grandma Polya. Out of that love, my father, Semyon, is born in 1938, a year and ten days before the Molotov-Ribbentrop Pact is signed between the Soviet Union and Nazi Germany.

The world surrounding new Soviet citizen Semyon Shteyngart is about to set itself on fire.

"*Oni menya lyubili kak cherty,*" my father says of those fleeting few years when both his parents were alive. *They loved me like devils.* It's an inelegant statement from a man who can veer between depression and anger and humor and joy with Bellovian flair. It's an unverifiable statement as well. After all, how could he remember? So let's say this: It's a belief, and a near-holy belief at that. And whatever grace was imparted to him in those few years before the first German Panzer Division crossed the border, I want to believe in it, too.

"If the war hadn't happened," my father says, "my parents would have had two, three children." Rarely, but sometimes, the differences between us collapse as quickly as the Soviet Union's defenses on June 22, 1941. Like my father, I am also an only child.

"Your mother and I should have had another baby," my father says of that absence. "But we didn't get along in America."

· · ·

Hitler betrays Stalin and invades the Soviet Union. Stalin is horrified by this breach in schoolyard-bully etiquette and holes up in his tree house outside Moscow, where he suffers a nervous breakdown. He is about to fuck up so completely that it will take twenty-six million Soviet death certificates to save civilization from collapsing. At least two of those death certificates will bear the last name of Shteyngart.

The Germans are advancing upon Leningrad. My grandfather Isaac is sent to the front to hold them back. For 871 days, the siege of that city will take 750,000 civilian lives, its starving residents forced to feast on sawdust; their pets; at worst, one another. Here my story almost ends. But as with so many of us foreigners clogging the subways of Queens and Brooklyn, a single twist of fate keeps our kind shuffling along. Before the Germans surround the city, Grandma Polya's Children's Home is evacuated from Leningrad. She, along with my three-year-old father, Semyon, and his cousins, is sent to a dark, freezing village called Zakabyakino in the Yaroslavl Region, some four hundred miles to the east of Leningrad. To the Russian ear "Zakabyakino" has the ring of "Hicksville," and to this day, my father will refer to all remote, farcical places—e.g., the Catskill Mountains, the state of Ohio—by that name.

The first memory of my father's life? The evacuation from Leningrad, with the German air force in hot pursuit. "We were on a train and the Germans would bomb us. We would hide under the train wagons. The Messerschmitt planes had this sound, ZUUUUU . . . WOO . . . WOO." My father, an emotive speaker, raises his hand, his knuckles dusted with fine hairs, and drops it in a slow but decisive arc to mimic the bombing run as he does the Messerschmitt sound. ZUUUU . . .

In Zakabyakino, the survivors of the Messerschmitt bombings, my father included, are met with relative good fortune: They do not starve. There is milk and potatoes in the village. There are also fat country rats, which crawl in with my father and cousins with the intent of eating the slim Leningrad children as they sleep on the stove. To escape them, one of my aunts jumps out of a second-floor window.

My aunt jumping out of the window to flee the rats is my father's second childhood memory.

My father has a best friend his age. A non-Jewish kid named Lionya. When he is three years old, my father's best friend dies of some unspecified war-related disease. This is my father's third memory: Lionya's funeral. My father tells me of Lionya's existence during the spring of 2011. "Lionya," short for "Leonid," is a fairly unremarkable Russian name, but in my first novel, published in 2002, the childhood friend of the novel's hero, Vladimir Girshkin, happens to be Lionya, and indeed, he is one of the few truly sympathetic people in the book (together Vladimir and Lionya share a batch of Little Red Riding Hood candies given by Vladimir's mother and fall asleep side by side on a Soviet kindergarten mat). In my third novel, published in 2010, "Lionya" is the Russian name of one of the two main characters, Lenny Abramov. Without knowing who he was, I have spent half my life honoring Lionya in prose.

The fourth memory: February 1943, the news arrives from the front, my father's father, Grandfather Isaac, has been killed near Leningrad. The Soviet troops, my grandfather among them, make several attempts to break the blockade of Russia's second city, but they are outgunned, their most talented officers having already been shot dead during Stalin's purge. It is unknown how Isaac Semyonovich Shteyngart died. For decades I was told he died in a tank, burned alive in a gruesome but heroic gesture to stop the Germans, but that is untrue. My grandfather was an artillerist.

After her husband is killed, Grandmother Polya buries herself in work at the Children's Home and refuses to acknowledge her husband's death. Like so many women with death certificates, she continues to wait for him until after the war.

At age five, my father is one of the millions of Russian children who cannot fully comprehend the man missing from the household. A few years later when the war is over he finally *does* understand. He hides under the couch, and he cries and thinks of a man he does not know. Later, when he discovers classical music, when he hears Tchaikovsky, he will cry to that, too. Under the couch, he listens to Tchaikovsky through his tears and hatches plots that will allow him to go back in time and assassinate Hitler. Still later, Grandmother Polya is remarried to a man who will all but destroy my father's life and make me into whatever it is I am today.

My life begins with a much-mimeographed piece of paper: "To Citizen Shteyngart P. [Grandma], NOTIFICATION, Your husband Sergeant Shteyngart Isaac Semyonovich, fighting for the Socialist Motherland, true to his military oath, evincing heroism and courage, was killed 18 February 1943."

Somewhere in distant Yaroslavl, little Lionya is buried.

My grandfather's body lies in a soldier's grave near Leningrad, which is to say, closer to home.

And the Germans, they are always massing. And Stalin, he is still cowering at his tree house near Moscow. And the Messerschmitt pilots, they know their targets well. ZUUUUU . . . WOO . . . WOO.

. . .

Father.

What are you doing?

What are you saying to me?

Who is speaking through you?

"I read on the Russian Internet that you and your novels will soon be forgotten."

Staring ahead at me like an angry, wounded child, then laying his gaze down, as if scared of it, on his prix fixe dish of something truffled. We are at the View, the revolving restaurant of the Marriott Marquis in Times Square. Dinner at the Marriott plus a $200 gift certificate to T.J.Maxx, the inexpensive clothing store, is my mother's dream birthday gift.

"Yes," my mother says, "I read that, too. It was _____." She cites the name of a blogger. My parents have not read my latest book, but they know the name of the blogger in Samara or Vologda or Astrakhan or Yaroslavl who says I will soon be forgotten.

Do you want me to be forgotten, Father? Do you want me closer to you? But I do not say the obvious. "Look." I turn to my mother. "It's the Hudson River. And beyond it, those lights—New Jersey."

"Really?" My mother cranes her neck. Her ability to be fascinated by things is her best gift to me. Each time I see her now, her hair is younger and spunkier, sometimes bobbed, sometimes teased, and her pretty face stands up to the sixty-seven years it has known with youthful bluster. She will not let go of life as easily as my father will.

"That's Four Times Square," I say, trying to deflect my father's crooked stare. "The Condé Nast Building. *The New Yorker*'s offices are there, as well as many other magazines."

"A ranking of New York writers came out on the Internet," my father says. "You were ranked thirty, and David Remnick"—*The New Yorker*'s editor—"was eight positions ahead of you. Philip Gourevitch"—one of the magazine's brilliant staff writers—"was ranked number eleven. They are both ahead of you."

"Semyon, stop," my mother says.

"What?" my father says. "*Ya shuchu.*" I am joking.

"*Shutki!*" he says, loudly. Jokes.

"No one understands your *shutki*," my mother says.

Aunt Tanya, ready to ingratiate herself with me, has her own opinion. "Yes, they say you will soon be forgotten, but many writers aren't acknowledged until after their death."

My father nods. His work here is almost finished. "And tell Remnick that if he doesn't stop writing bad things about Israel, I will be forced to write a letter to *The New Yorker*."

"Look," I say, pointing at a skyscraper just coming into view. "That eagle! It's Barclays Bank. Remember how our first bank checks in America had that eagle on them?"

My father's gaze is upon me. Trying to gauge my reaction; trying to figure out what to say next.

Let me stop for a moment. What is it like to be him right now? What does he see through his brow-heavy stare? His son. A stranger. Ordering truffled things from the menu. With his Obama and his Remnick, the haters of Israel. My father has been to Israel for only seven days, but he loves it as obediently as anyone who doesn't understand his young lover, who sees only her slinky dark shape, the curve of her settlements. In the third-floor attic where my father lives—the spacious second floor has long been surrendered to my mother—life is punctuated by the boom of the classical records and the drone of extremist rabbis on the radio. How did his son travel so far from there? Isn't it his duty to stay by his father?

After each teardown, after each discussion of Internet rankings and blogs, after each barrage of insults presented as jokes, my father finishes with, "You should call me more."

My son. How could he leave me?

I am looking down to see part of the floor moving around the restaurant's core. A dullard at physics, I don't understand how this works exactly: why this part of the floor is gently turning and the other part is perfectly still. I picture a team of sweaty, harnessed immigrant men in the basement of the Marriott making the skyborne restaurant revolve. "The soprano Galina Vishnevskaya has died," my father says.

"Ah."

"I went to the same musical school in Leningrad as her. They ruined her voice, and they ruined my voice, too. They made me a bass instead of a baritone."

It's about him now. About his opera career, the one he gave up to become, like most Soviet Jewish men, a mechanical engineer. It's not about me. I breathe easily. At another recent dinner my father had put his arm around me, his face so close to mine that the whites and grays of his goatee nearly touched the grays of my stubble, and said: "I burn with a black envy [*chyornaya zavist'*] toward you. I should have been an artist as well."

. . .

The weekend after the Marriott dinner, I call them from the rural house where I spend half the year, trying to work. "The French Internet says your book is one of the best of the year!" they shout.

"They love you in France!" my father says.

I don't want to hear anything about the Internet, bad or good, but suddenly we're laughing. We're talking about my father's design work on what would become the world's biggest telescope in 1975, a telescope that, like most Soviet products big and small, died on arrival. "Oh, how many Hero of Socialist Labor awards were given for that damn thing, and it didn't work!" my father says. This is our little world, Soviet satire, failed empires, ridiculous dreams. I am filled with longing for them, for their company. I'm smiling and snug under the covers, the first dusting of December snow out my window, thick, clean country snow.

Down and up. Up and down. I am forgotten. I am remembered. I am number thirty. I am beloved in France. What is this? This is parenting. The parenting he knew, the parenting he gave. It is familiar and safe. Safe for some of us.

A few weeks before, at another family gathering, my father leans over the small woman who is now my wife and begins one of his "life on the farm" monologues. "When I was young, I kill sheep. Girls say, 'No! Is so cute.' But I slice, slice." He makes a slicing motion across the imaginary animal's throat. I lean into my wife, for support, although she is too strong to need it. "Then there is too much cat in village. So I take kitten and I drown. Drown, drown." The dunking motions are articulated. "And then, of course, chicken comes and—"

Before the hen's neck can be wrung, my wife and I look at each other with understanding. He is trying to assert himself. And to scare her. But beneath the blood of the martyred animals—for no good reason, I remember the Hebrew term for sacrifice, *korban*—lies a more prosaic truth. I am married now and even further apart from him. Someone else has come between us.

The Sheep Killer wants his son back.

· · ·

"My first memory of when I was eight is that when I heard classical music, especially violin, I would cry sometimes," my father says. "I would hide under the table and listen to the music and feel sad and cry. This is when I started to think about my father. I didn't have memories because I didn't really know him, but the sadness of not knowing him was tied in with the music. There was something about my father that I couldn't remember. I started to buy records in a neighboring village, not a big assortment, but my first record was Caruso when he was singing his final aria from *Tosca*." With a furrowed brow, with all the sadness and empathy he can muster, my father begins to sing in Russian: *"Moi chas nastal . . . I vot ya umirayu!"*

The hour is gone . . . And I, desperately, die!

There is a photograph of my father at fourteen or fifteen, dressed in a full tsarist general's uniform and wig, his eyes ablaze with the peaceful sadness I don't think I have ever found outside of a handful of Russian novels or after a volley of strong cocktails. He has been cast as Gremin in the school production of Tchaikovsky's *Eugene Onegin*. It is a difficult part for a young bass, but my father is known around his small village as Paul Robeson, after the African American singer barnstorming across the Soviet Union with his "Ol' Man River." "In my school I was a celebrity," my father says. "Almost like you now."

In an alternate universe, Russia is a kind and sympathetic democ-

racy, my father is the famous opera singer he wished to become, and I
am his adoring son.

• • •

Back at the modest three-story colonial in Little Neck, Queens, the
Thanksgiving dinner is winding down. I think of something my father had told me when I interviewed him last. He was speaking of the
war, of being a tiny kid who had just lost both his father and his best
friend, Lionya. "I fed a dog somewhere," he said. "You shouldn't write
that because people were dying in Leningrad, but I remember how I
fed a dog with a butter sandwich my mother had given me, which I
guess means I wasn't starving."

"Papa," I say, "why don't you want me to write that story?" Around
the table, the family smiles and gives collective encouragement. It's a
fine story.

"I was ashamed because people were starving and I had a sandwich," my father says. "But, yes, I guess you may put that in."

My father sits at the head of a table before the carcass of an enormous American turkey. What he is ashamed of is the one act of de-
cency I have yet encountered in all the tales of our family's past. A
young boy with a dead father and a dead friend bends down before a
country dog and feeds it his butter sandwich.

And I know that sandwich. Because he has made it for me. Two
slices of that dark, unbleached Russian bread, the kind that tastes of
badly managed soil and a peasant's indifference to death. On top of it,
the creamiest, deadliest of American butter, slathered in thick feta-like
hunks. And on top of that cloves of garlic, the garlic that is to give me
strength, that is to clear my lungs of asthmatic gunk, and make of me
a real garlic-eating strong man. At a table in Leningrad, and a table in
deepest Queens, New York, the ridiculous garlic crunches beneath
our teeth as we sit across from each other, the garlic obliterating whatever else we have eaten, and making us one.

4.

MOSCOW SQUARE

To become a cosmonaut, the author must first conquer his fear of heights on a ladder his father has built for that purpose. He must also stop wearing a sailor outfit and tights.

HIS NAME IS VLADIMIR. Never Volodya, the diminutive, always Vladimir. Some may say he is not a handsome man, but he is a serious one. Maybe he laughed once, but I've never seen him laughing. You do not cross Vladimir. You do not trifle with his ideas. His full name is Vladimir Ilyich Lenin, and I love him.

Vladimir came to our Leningrad from a town on the Volga River. An excellent swimmer, he was a model for youths from the start. When he first came to Leningrad, Vladimir played a lot of chess. The tsar exiled him to Siberia, but he ended up in Munich and London and then Geneva and Finland. You can never tell with Vladimir Ilyich Lenin. You think you've got an angle on him, but boom!—he's like the wind. Vladimir was a Bolshevik, and he hated Mensheviks, because he didn't like the liberal bourgeoisie and they did. Vladimir's interests included ice-skating and creating an alliance of workers and peasants with which to overthrow the tsar. Everyone in Russia was very happy when Vladimir and his best friend, Joseph, came back to our town, ran out the tsar and later shot him, making life joyful for little children like me. Today Vladimir lies in a mausoleum in Moscow, but I can hardly believe that when there are signs all over our town that say LENIN WILL LIVE FOREVER! I should know, because recently my family moved to Moscow Square, which is on the road to the airport, and here the biggest statue of Vladimir in all of Leningrad towers over me and reminds me that I am not alone.

• • •

Moscow Square. *Moskovskaya Ploshchad*. This is where my life really begins. My recall of these years is attuned, vibrant, and frighteningly perfect. My brain has been slapped around enough so that entire volumes of data from college to marriage have been erased, but here there are no gaps. Except for one.

Moscow Square. It is built up in the grandiose Stalinist Soviet Imperial style to make the populace forget about the baroque trifles of olde tsarist St. Petersburg a few kilometers to the north. But the damn citizens, the *Leningradtsy,* they stubbornly refuse to forget.

Moscow Square: Its geometry is cold, its colors are muted, its size is gigantic, and there are occasional colonnades and assorted Greek flourishes to make the place seem timeless and inevitable. The square is so vast it seems to have its own microclimate, a clap of oily rain will slick down its hectares of brick and marble, and in the summer violets are known to burst out amid all the ideology.

Here is my frozen King Kong–sized Lenin, my love, nearly jumping in the direction of nearby Finland, with his hand pointed emphatically at the horizon, with his coat sexily unfurling in the wind. Indeed, there is so much movement atop his granite pedestal that some locals have dubbed him "the Latin Lenin," as if any second he may launch into a salsa or, better yet, a proper Cuban rumba. Taking pride of place behind Lenin is a grandiose box of a building whose facade features workers, peasants, and soldiers marching solemnly toward the bright socialist future. This was destined to be a House of the Soviets, Leningrad's equivalent of city hall, during the Stalin era, then became a top secret facility in which at least two American defectors (both part of the Julius and Ethel Rosenberg spy ring) were reputed to work on military projects, and today is a sad, listless place where you can get a photocopy of your passport or certificate of military service done for a few rubles. The square's dramatic Stalinist impact has further been cut short by the Citibank branch down the street, the Ford dealership a little farther down, the ad hoc slot machines around the corner, and the intermittent fruit stand hawking bright imported oranges, ethereal red peppers, and glossy pears from a distant galaxy. One of St. Petersburg's 4.8 million McDonald's (one for each citizen) hums along at the southwest corner.

But when I am growing up there is none of that! There is Lenin, there is the Top Secret Building for Defectors and Spies, and across the street is a marble-like structure of equally imposing size that contains another important aspect of Soviet life: the *gastronom*. To call a *gastronom* a supermarket would be to insult supermarkets everywhere. Rather it is a uniquely precapitalist space in which ham at times appears and then very rapidly disappears. The ham is often not precisely ham, but the fat around the ham. My mother wages a weekly battle with the *gastronom* staff to make sure they cut her the rosy, edible part of my favorite snack. On one fateful occasion, right before we emigrate, my mother begins to shout at the woman, "Why are you giving me nothing but fat?"

The year is 1978, when Soviet Jews are finally allowed to leave for Israel and, more happily, for the United States or Canada. My moth-

er's enemy in the stained white smock appraises her nose and dark hair
and shouts back: "When you move to Israel they'll slice the ham for
you without fat!"

"Yes," my mother answers. "In Israel I'll have the fatless ham, but
all *you* will ever have is the fat." One can comment on the unkosher
absurdity of this conversation, but in truth these are possibly the first
brave and truthful words my mother has spoken in thirty years of
careful Soviet life, the first time she has stood up for herself in front of
"the system," and the *gastronom* is the system at its most elemental.

But I'm getting ahead of myself.

• • •

Moscow Square. Statue of Lenin, Top Secret Building for Defectors
and Spies, *gastronom*. And to the left of Lenin, a small copse of *yolki,*
or spruces. When I am well enough from the asthma, Papa and I
chase each other beneath the spruces, playing hide-and-seek. I am a
tiny vertical dachshund and can slot myself in behind the thinnest
tree, and Papa will pretend not to see me for the longest time, while I
breathe in, *fully breathe in,* the rich green piney smell of the little arbo-
real fellow next to me. Rumor around the neighborhood has it that
some drunk cut down one of the spruces to make himself a New
Year's tree and was sentenced to ten years in a penal colony for the
crime. The fool! You don't chop down a spruce in front of Vladimir
Ilyich Lenin.

And here I am shuddering with excitement behind a tree while the
big papa is hunting for me, he really can't find me! And above me,
Lenin is gesturing acquisitively toward Finland, his dome balder than
my father's, which is still fringed with some hair between the temples.
I am hiding behind a spruce, and my father is singing, "*Synochek, Igor-
yochik, gde ty?*" (Little son, Little Igor, where are you?), and I am inhaling one forbidden icy spruce breath after another.

The sun is setting on us and Lenin and the House of Spies, and
soon the game will be called off on account of cold. There is a theory
floating around that I will become overheated from playing and that

my hot bare neck will combine with the autumn frost to make the sickness return. Like Fermi's Paradox this theory is difficult to prove one way or another, but generations of Russian women have worked it out in their kitchens, factories, and offices.

I do not want the game to stop. You know what, I *still* don't want the game to stop. Not even today, May 25, 2012. Because my father is bigger than me. He is still the big one. And I can see him among the spruces in his light coat (which smells, as everything else does around here, of steaming cabbage) and his brightly colored, possibly irradiated, plaid scarf. And he is looking for me. Here is Father, above me, and here is Lenin above him, and this is my family and this is my country. Am I feeling this or am I thinking it? Both, I am sure. I already understand how easily a feeling can become a thought and the other way around.

"I've lost him, I've lost my son," my father is wailing. "I've lost my little Igor. Where is he? I simply cannot find him."

Is he kidding or is he seriously worried?

And I want to jump out and say, "Here I am! You haven't lost me at all!" But this is against the rules of the game. Isn't all the fun in *staying hidden*? You're supposed to feel scared when the papa who's looking for you gets closer, is about to find you, but instead I feel sadder when he seems to lose my scent. And then when he approaches I feel scared again. Sad, scared. Scared, sad. Is that what I've been looking forward to for so long in my sickbed? No, it is this: Suddenly Papa jumps out from behind an adjoining spruce, screams "Found you!" and I scream with joy and try to escape. He scoops me up in one easy gesture, hoists me onto his shoulders, and we walk past the Lenin, who is also happy that I've been found, toward our apartment one gigantic Stalinist block away where Mother is making cabbage soup, hot and tasteless.

• • •

We live on Tipanov Street, House 5, Apartment 10. A sign at the mouth of the street informs us that ALEXANDER FYODOROVITCH

TIPANOV (1924–1944) WAS A BRAVE DEFENDER OF THE CITY OF
LENIN. IN 1944, HE SHIELDED HIS TROOPS WITH HIS BREAST
AGAINST ADVANCING FIRE, ALLOWING HIS COMRADES A SUC-
CESSFUL CHARGE FORWARD. THE FEARLESS WARRIOR WAS
POSTHUMOUSLY AWARDED THE TITLE HERO OF THE SOVIET
UNION. I like to think that my grandfather Isaac, my father's father,
who also died in the war at a ridiculously young age, performed a
similar feat, even if he wasn't a Hero of the Soviet Union. Oh, how I
would love to put my own breast in front of some artillery fire so that
my comrades could charge forward and kill Germans. But first I will
have to make a friend or two my own age, and that equally heroic feat
is still years away.

As my father carries me from the hide-and-seek spruces by the
Lenin statue to Tipanov Street, House 5, Apartment 10, we pass by
the other important institution in my life, the pharmacy.

One of the most frightening words in the Russian language is
banki, which nominally refers to the plural of a glass or a jar but which
the Oxford Russian-English dictionary also helpfully describes as
"*(med.)* cupping glass." I'm not sure about the *med.* part, because I've
yet to meet any sufferer of asthma, pneumonia, or any other bronchial
disaster that this insane form of peasant remedy has ever cured. The
local pharmacy carries few useful medicines, but the least useful of
them is *banki.* The application of said "cupping glass" to the soft white
back of a wheezing Leningrad boy in 1976 represents the culmination
of three thousand years of not-so-great medical intervention beginning with the traditional practices of the Greeks and the Chinese and
ending here at the pharmacy on Tipanov Street.

This is what I remember all too well. I'm lying on my stomach. The
banki are produced; they are little glass jars, greenish in tint, each
probably the size of my child-foot. My entire back is rubbed with
Vaseline by my mother's strong hand. What follows is frightening
beyond words for any sane adult, let alone an anxious child. A pair of
tweezers wrapped in cotton is soaked in vodka or rubbing alcohol and
set on fire. The flaming pincers are stuck into each glass cup, sucking

out the air to create suction between the cup and the skin. The cups are then clamped along the length of the patient's back, supposedly to pull the mucus away from the lungs but in reality to scare the little boy into thinking his parents are raving pyromaniacs with serious intent to hurt.

Let me close my eyes now. I'm hearing now a long match struck against the matchbox by my mother—*ptch*—then the flames of the pincers as orange and yellow as the polluted Leningrad sunset, then the whoosh of air being sucked out as if by a neutron bomb, just like the one the American imperialists are threatening on television to use against us, then the sting of the warm glass against my back. And then ten minutes of lying as still as a dead October leaf at the bottom of a pool, lest the *banki* pop off my tortured back and the whole procedure is to be repeated again.

The first step of our multipart emigration to America will involve a weeklong stop in Vienna, before we move on to Rome and, finally, New York. I will be six years old and breathless from asthma per the usual and will have to be taken to a Viennese medical clinic. Herr Doktor will take one look at my black-and-blue-bruised back and prepare to call the Austrian police forces with a fresh report of child abuse. After my parents nervously explain that it was merely "cupping," he will laugh and say: "How old-fashioned!" or "How idiotic!" or "You crazy Russians, what will you do next, huh?" He will give me something I have never encountered back in the USSR: a simple steroid-fueled asthma inhaler. For the first time in my life, I will enjoy the realization that I do not have to choke to death every night.

But right now there is no such solace. And both my father and I know that the fun we just had running among the spruces beneath the Lenin in Moscow Square will exact a price. Tonight I will be sick. In fact, I know even as we walk past the pharmacy with its bold, ugly APTEKA sign, I am already instructing my lungs to shut down. Another thing we do not realize in 1979: Asthma is, at least in part, what they call an "emotional disease," triggered by stress and fear.

But fear of what?

Sweaty me is carried into the warm, cabbagy apartment and my mother is screaming at my father: "How could you stay out so late? How could you let him run in the cold? He's overheated! Now he will be sick!"

And he starts screaming back at her, "Oy, yoi, yoi! She knows everything! A fucking doctor she is!"

"Don't swear"—*Ne rugaisya matom*—"the child is here."

To me: "Igor, *ne povtoryai*." Don't repeat our cursing.

"You're the one who swears."

"Me? You know what? Go to the dick!" *Poshol na khui.*

"Fuck your mother!" *Yobtiki mat'*. I record and mispronounce the bad words inside myself.

My mother loses her Russianness and retreats into the primordial Yiddish of her late grandmother from the Belorussian shtetl of Dubrovno: *"Gurnisht! Abiter tsoris!"* You're a nothing! A bitter misfortune!

My breathing grows shallow. What language will they sink to next? Aramaic? I take off my pajamas and dutifully lie down on my stomach. My parents, still screaming at each other in two languages, prepare the cupping kit, getting the rubbing alcohol ready to feed the flames. A mere decade later I will find a new space to fill with alcohol.

And so I am cupped.

· · ·

After cupping I cannot sleep. My back is covered in circular welts, and the asthma has only been exacerbated. I am on the living room couch that serves as my bed, wheezing. I pick up an illustrated children's book about a young boy and girl who are (for reasons that now escape me) shrunk down to miniature size and then attacked by a swarm of gigantic mosquitoes. On one of the pages of the book, a spot of jam has coagulated to form what looks like the crushed remains of a particularly vile insect (in swampy Leningrad, the mosquitoes are the size of Lenins). A sleepless, suffering child exists in a kind of fourth dimension, where language runs unbidden through the tiny but growing mind and the external senses are primed to receive a flood of information. Hence: fictional mosquito, coagulated jam, vile insect, the heavy embrace of the sagging couch, patterns of the wall rug hanging above it forming real Arabic numbers and unreal Tibetan words (I have recently visited the Museum of Ethnography), Mama and Papa in the next room, sleeping after their latest fight, oblivious to all the action inside my head.

The northern sun clambers atop its perch with what can only be described as resignation, radiating pink across the tops of birches and the heavy architecture. A pink that, to the sleepless young eye, is filled with ribbons of life, amoeba shapes that float and twirl across the landscape and beyond it, a fifth dimension to the already busy fourth one I have described above. And to my old man's wheezing is added amazement. I have been cupped, true, but I have lived through another night. The sagging couch, which I have long ago rechristened the *Imperial Snotty,* an eighteenth-century Russian frigate just like the one that lives in the nearby Museum of the Battle of Chesme, formerly the Chesme Church, where Papa and I like to launch our toy helicopters among the church spires, has made its way through the foggy night. The pressure of falling asleep has lifted, there is nothing to fear and nothing worth struggling for, and with that easing of expectations comes the unexpected. I fall asleep in the morning, the city bright and alive around me, Lenin with his outstretched hand greeting the schoolchildren in their uniforms, the workers and soldiers and sailors in theirs. Outside the window, two neon signs gently flicker on as I rumble into sleep. MEAT, one of them says. And then: PRODUCE.

. . .

Words. I hunger for them even more than the MEAT and PRODUCE they claim to advertise. The next day, if I am well, we will walk past my Lenin to the Moscow Square metro station, and there will be more words for me to eat.

Velikii moguchii russkii yazik. The Great and Mighty Russian Tongue

is how my first language bills itself. Throughout its seventy-year ten-
ure, bureaucratic Sovietspeak had inadvertently stripped the language
of Pushkin of much of its greatness and might. (Try casually saying
the acronym OSOAVIAKhIM, which denotes the Association for
Assistance of Defense, Aircraft, and Chemical Development.) But in
the late 1970s the beleaguered Russian tongue can still put on quite a
show for a five-year-old boy in a Leningrad metro station. The trick is
to use giant copper block letters nailed to a granite wall, signifying
both pomp and posterity, an uppercase paean to an increasingly low-
ercase Soviet state. The words, gracing the walls of the Technological
Institute station, read as follows:

1959—SOVIET SPACE ROCKET REACHES THE SURFACE OF THE
MOON

Take that, Neil Armstrong.

1934—SOVIET SCIENTISTS CREATE THE FIRST CHAIN REAC-
TION THEORY

So that's where it all began.

1974—THE BUILDING OF THE BAIKAL-AMUR MAIN RAILROAD
TRUNK HAS BEEN INITIATED

Now, what the hell does *that* mean? Ah, but Baikal-Amur sounds
so beautiful—Baikal, the famous (and now famously polluted) Siberian lake, a centerpiece of Russian myth; Amur (*amour?*) could almost
be another word Russian has gleefully appropriated from the French.
(It is, in fact, the name of a region in the Russian Far East.)

I'm five years old, felt boots tight around my feet and ankles, what
might be half of a bear or several Soviet beavers draped around my
shoulders, my mouth open so wide that, as my father keeps warning

me, "a crow will fly in there." I am in awe. The metro, with its wall-length murals of the broad-chested revolutionary working class that never was, with its hectares of marble vestibules, is a mouth opener to be sure. And the words! Those words whose power seems not only persuasive but, to a kid about to become obsessed with science fiction, they are indeed extraterrestrial. The wise aliens have landed and WE ARE THEM. And this is the language we use. The great and mighty Russian tongue.

Meanwhile, a metro train full of sweaty comrades pulls into the station, ready to take us north to the Hermitage or the Dostoyevsky Museum. But what use is there for the glum truth of Rembrandt's returning Prodigal Son or a display of the great novelist's piss pots, when the future of the human race, denuded of its mystery, is right here for all to see. SOVIET SCIENTISTS CREATE THE FIRST CHAIN REACTION THEORY. Forget the shabby polyester-clad human element around you, the unique Soviet metro smell of a million barely washed proletarians being sucked through an enormous marble tube. There it is, kid, in copper capital letters. What more do you want?

• • •

I decide to become a writer. Who wouldn't, under the circumstances?

My living and sleeping space in the living room is divided into three broad categories. One part is the Technological Chest of Drawers, upon which rests a fancy new rotary phone that I am learning to pick up with great skill ("Mama, *telefon*!") and a potbellied Signal television set. The television set is an object of great consternation among Soviet citizens because it regularly explodes. At one point, 60 percent of the house fires in Moscow are said to be caused by poorly assembled exploding television sets. As an infant I had already become aware of the perfidy of Uncle Electric Current and am now learning about the dangers of Cousin Television Set.

In an opposite part of the room is the Athletic Corner. Here my father has built me a simple wooden ladder that reaches to the ceiling and is designed both to give the housebound patient some exercise and to cure one of my greatest fears, the fear of heights. He has begged the workmen at his factory to carve out every sleek wooden bar, and the resulting ladder is possibly the most gorgeous thing in our apartment. It is also one of the scariest. Every month I try to scale one more of the dozen bars until, dizzy and dry mouthed, I am flying as high as four feet off the ground! Just a little more effort, just a little less asthma, and I will be what every Soviet boy aged three to twenty-seven wants to become: a cosmonaut.

But I have other plans. The third part of the living room is the Culture Couch. This is where Culture happens and also where I sleep. (To this day, I work in bed, three pillows under my back, and have no use for desks, lecterns, and other distractions.) Culture is very important. My father dreamed of becoming an opera singer. Could one of my earliest memories involve him bellowing at me from *The Queen of Spades,* my head turned quizzically to the side, my mouth opened asthmatically, a smile growing on my lips? My mother plays the piano. Aunt Tanya, her sister, is a violinist. My beautiful cousin Victoria, daughter of my mother's older sister, Lyusya, only five years older than me but already fully in control of her lithe and elegant body, can hop atop the Culture Couch and pirouette like the ballerina she is training to become. If I am to have anything to do with this family, I must become a *kulturnyi chelovek,* a cultured person.

And so I put on my little sailor's outfit, knot the collar in the front, and pick up a child's violin. Aunt Tanya teaches me how to strike the stringy thing, the what-do-you-call-it, against the body of the instrument. The pad against my cheek feels velvety and nice, and the sailor's outfit, with its white tights and little shorts, is equally pleasant, but honestly I have no idea what the fuck I'm doing. The violin will give way to a less-esteemed instrument, the three-stringed Russian balalaika, which will eventually find its way into a dusty corner. In America, an elderly Russian gentlewoman, living next door to my grandmother, will try to inflict the piano upon me for five American dollars a lesson. None of it will leave an impression.

• • •

No, what I want to do is quite different. The violin's dulcet wheezing is not for me (I have my own violin inside me, thank you), I cannot move my body like Cousin Victoria or holler from *The Queen of Spades* like my father: "Whaaaat is our life? A gaaaame!" If anything, I am more likely to explode like our Signal television set. I'm becoming a pathological reader. The first book, as I've mentioned above, concerns two children, a boy and a girl, who are shrunken down to the size of a kopeck and have to fend for themselves against giant mosquitoes and the like. The second book, the one responsible for everything else that has ever happened to me, is called *The Wonderful Adventures of Nils and the Wild Geese.* In the book, Nils, a bad boy prone to hitting the animals on his farm, is also magically shrunk down to a kopeck and then has to brave an adventurous life with the wild geese who carry him all over Sweden, to Lapland and back.

The Wonderful Adventures of Nils by Selma Lagerlöf—incidentally, the first woman to win the Nobel Prize in Literature—is a Swedish book, much loved in that country. It is no coincidence that the two books from which I learned how to read were both about small children shrunk to even smaller size and then forced into a hostile world. The lesson, at least to me, was clear: Bad boys don't grow. And according to the *All-Soviet Guide to Boys' Development,* which my mother studies religiously, with its diagrams of naked drawn boys of ever-ascending size with their ever-enlarging nutsacks, I am also not growing very well, in either corpus or sack. In every respect, I am a small *thing* full of limitations. When my aunt Tanya brings me my favorite ice cream, I get up and very seriously declare: "Thank you, but no. I am not allowed to eat it."

In the Soviet Union *The Wonderful Adventures of Nils* is a fine book for a five-year-old, although in the United States the dense one-hundred-sixty-page volume would likely be assigned in fifth grade and, in some states, in college. The biggest regret of my childhood is missing the television airing of the 1950s Soviet adaptation of the book, called *The Enchanted Boy*. It is the first time I take a pencil to paper and, with the help of my father, write a letter to the broadcaster, Channel One, on the devilishly tiny-squared, graph-paper *tetradka* that every Russian child knows well.

> *Respected Channel One,*
> *I am a Leningrad boy, age 5. Last week you showed* The Enchanted Boy. The Wonderful Adventures of Nils and the Wild Geese *is my favorite book. I have read it so many times I have to use masking tape to hold it together. I cried when I found out you have already shown* The Enchanted Boy. *Please, please show it again. I really want to see it.*
> > *With respect,*
> > *Igor Shteyngart, City of Leningrad*

My father and I walk past the pharmacy, past the Lenin, to drop the letter into a mailbox. I feel very close to my father at the moment. Holding his hand, I am jumping up and down with excitement, even though I might get sweaty and sick from all the jumping. When we get to the mailbox, my father folds the piece of paper bearing my childish scrawl in half and throws it in, without postage or address. At the time, I both know *and don't know* that the letter will never reach Channel One in Moscow. I am both hopeful *and* I know better than to be hopeful. But what does my father know? That the paramount state broadcaster will not reair the story of Nils and the geese just because a five-year-old boy with an insufficient nutsack demands it? Or that soon we will leave the country for good, and there will be no Channel One in the free world; there will be, eventually, seven holy channels in the New York metro area—channels 2, 4, 5, 7, 9, 11, and 13—and even more if we purchase a UHF bowtie.

Back on the Culture Couch in 1977, I am rereading Nils asthmatically, letting enough air into my lungs so that I may hear the actual words spoken aloud by me, imagining that they are being spoken aloud on the television set. My grandmother Galya joins me. I have two grandmothers. Grandma Polya, on my father's side, likes to sit with me on our favorite bench in Moscow Square and feed me various meats. She will come with us to America and be my best friend for a long time. Grandmother Galya, unbeknownst to me, is slowly descending into vascular dementia. She is the main reason my mother doesn't want to emigrate, and she will die in the Soviet Union in the late 1980s, barely sentient and in great pain. My aunt Tanya will stay behind and take care of her, a debt my mother will try to repay for the rest of her life.

Grandmother Galya used to work as a journalist and an editor at *Evening Leningrad* (*Vechernii Leningrad*). She knows of my love of *Nils and the Wild Geese;* she's seen the lovingly applied masking tape holding together every volume of children's literature I own. One day while babysitting me, she proposes: "Why don't *you* write a novel?"

And so it begins. I am five years old with a thick, stubby pencil in my hand and a graph-paper *tetradka* waiting to be scribbled on. Grandmother Galya is smart. She raised herself up from the shtetl, took a gold medal in the local gymnasium, and schlepped her way to Leningrad to become a cultured person. She knows what every good editor knows well. You can't just command "Write!" to your charges. There must be a reward system. Grandma Galya does not have access to the cold baked pork I love so well, but she does possess another important staple: cheese.

It is thick, hard, yellowish Soviet cheese, a poor relation of the megatons of orange lactose that the United States government will drop on my grandma Polya three years hence in Rego Park, Queens. But it establishes a pattern of exchange, goods for words, that has seen me through to the present day. Grandma Galya slices the cheese into dozens of pale yellowish squares. "For every page you write," she says, "you will get a piece of cheese. And for every chapter you complete, I will make you a sandwich with bread, butter, and cheese."

The resulting novel probably cost my grandmother a hundred pieces of cheese and at least a dozen cheese-and-butter sandwiches. No trace of it remains, but my childhood masterpiece likely began with these words:

Odin den', utrom rano, Vladimir Ilyich Lenin prosnulsya.
One day, early in the morning, Vladimir Ilyich Lenin awoke.

Lenin is awake and alive in Leningrad! He has stepped off his pedestal in Moscow Square, and now it's time for payback. At one point, before launching the October Revolution, he was hiding in a hunter's cabin made of branches and straw (a proper Russian *shalash*) in Finland. And to this day, Finland, while officially neutral, stubbornly remains outside the Union of Soviet Socialist Republics. In my sprawling novel, *Lenin i ego volshebnyi gus'* (*Lenin and His Magical Goose*), this will be remedied forthwith.

After getting off his granite pedestal, Lenin meets a sympathetic talking goose, enormous in size, likely flying in from Georgia or Azerbaijan or Armenia or wherever else the dark men who sell flowers in the market come from. Lenin and the goose become best friends. Together, they make a pact: *We will invade Finland!*

Lenin gets on top of the goose, and they fly over the border into what will one day become the European Union, and Lenin begins bombarding the hapless Finns with our thick Soviet cheese from above. When not bombing the Finns, Lenin and the goose huddle together in their *shalash* and talk in capital letters, the goose saying things like "Have you heard, Vladimir Ilyich, that THE BUILDING OF THE BAIKAL-AMUR MAIN RAILROAD TRUNK HAS BEEN INITIATED?" Such a homey time Lenin and his fowl friend are having enclosed in those thick green branches, spruce branches from Moscow Square, naturally. But Vladimir Ilyich can bomb only so many Finns with cheese, because, you see, he has asthma!

It's a little-known fact. He's supposed to be so athletic, that Lenin, always swimming and ice-skating and so vibrant at chess, but, no, he is a fellow sufferer! All is proceeding according to the five-year plan, the Finns are almost ready to capitulate, when the talkative goose, probably a Menshevik, betrays Lenin to the Finnish secret police. The goose knows that Lenin is at his most vulnerable when he is having a raging asthma attack, so he lays Lenin down on his stomach, starts cupping him with *banki,* and then calls in the evil Finns. It's almost curtains for the greatest genius of mankind, but Lenin manages to throw off the *banki* and break free of the Nordic swine. He captures the treacherous goose, cooks him in a big red pot, and enjoys a delicious goose feast with his newly converted socialist comrades.

Finis.

• • •

I am regurgitating everything in my oxygen-starved brain, from the low art of *Nils and the Wild Geese* to the high schlock of Soviet iconography. But it's a crueler story than anything Selma Lagerlöf, Nils's creator, could have made up in her democratic Sweden. The lesson of *Lenin and His Magical Goose* is: Love authority but trust no one. There's also this. I am writing the novel for my grandmother, a Communist for most of her life, and I am saying, *Grandmother: Please love me.* It's a message, both desperate and common, that I will extend to her and to my parents and, later, to a bunch of yeshiva schoolchildren in Queens and, still later, to my several readers around the world.

• • •

It is almost time for the Shteyngarts to leave Moscow Square.

Every few weeks, the asthma gets so bad that an ambulance comes screaming into our peeling courtyard. Dr. Pochevalova, whose presence has me so scared I can conjure neither her face nor form, is remembered only by the ugly, disgustingly ugly, words floating off her stern lips. "Inflammation of the lungs" (*vospaleniye lyogkikh*) and "mustard compresses" (*gorchichniye kompressy*).

On television they will not reair *The Enchanted Boy,* but I do see a show called *Planet Andromeda,* a crude Soviet attempt at *Star Trek* genius. The one scene that stays with me: Men—cosmonauts, I suppose—are being bombarded by some kind of solar ray against a black backdrop. The cosmonauts are screaming and withering in agony.

In the courtyard of our building there is a children's slide that is affixed to a playground space rocket. I climb along the rusted metal ribs of the rocket, which I think of as the Good Rocket, and cautiously slide down the frozen incline, twenty kilograms of child, thirty kilograms of coat. The Good Rocket may be rusty, but it contains all the hopes and dreams of a nation that first catapulted a satellite, then a dog, then a man, into the void above us, into the void that *is* us.

The Bad Rocket is a grimy Dickensian steam pipe (oddly rocket shaped, with a wide bottom, a tapered body, and a capsule-like cone) that stretches up all five stories of our building and hums and vibrates in the night, as if it, too, has asthma. After watching *Planet Andromeda,* I convince myself that something evil is about to happen, that we are about to be bombarded with solar rays against a black backdrop, that the Bad Rocket will take off for the stars, that it will rip off a part of our building and drag me and Papa and Mama with it. I begin to sketch out ideas for a new book, *Vladimir Ilyich Lenin Conquers Andromeda.* Even the far-flung galaxies must be made safe for socialism.

Unbeknownst to me, the Soviet Union is falling apart. The grain harvests have been terrible; there is hardly enough grain to feed the masses or keep them fully drunk. Meanwhile, in the United States a grassroots movement to free Soviet Jews from their polyester captivity has gained momentum. And so, the American president Jimmy Carter has reached a deal with the Russians. In exchange for tons of grain and some high technology, presumably television sets that won't explode with such regularity, the USSR will allow many of its Jews to leave. Russia gets the grain it needs to run; America gets the Jews it needs to run: all in all, an excellent trade deal.

My parents have surrendered their jobs, sold our five-hundred-square-foot apartment, and are using the remaining rubles to ship our glossy Romanian furniture and our Red October upright piano across the Black Sea, across the Mediterranean, across the Atlantic, across any body of water that will float this strange, superannuated cargo. My mother's increasingly senile mother, Grandma Galya, has signed the documents that will permit her daughter to emigrate (another humiliating requirement of the system: parental consent). The right visas have been placed in my parents' passports, the rare *exit* visas that allow Soviet citizens to do the unthinkable—to get on an airplane and exit the best country in the world, the country of workers and strivers. We are about to take off for the stars, and Grandma Galya and her cheese will be left behind, so all that will remain is the memory of a thick old woman in a floral skirt and the sound of the big pencil against graph paper, her smile as she proofread my childish ravings. And there will be no more walks to Chesme Church to launch toy helicopters into the spires as my father, that predigital Wikipedia of a man, gestures at the architecture and lectures me sweetly in my mother tongue: "The first well-known church designed as a departure from the Byzantine style is the Cathedral of St. Sophia in Novgorod, built between 1045 and 1050 A.D."

And another dear someone will be left behind.

• • •

Lenin, my goose, my fierce bloody friend, my dreamer. What do you dream of now, on your pedestal at Moscow Square, in your mausoleum in actual Moscow?

Do you ever, would you ever, dream of me?

5.

ARTICLE 58

The author's mother at age eleven, with the worried adult gaze he will grow to know well. Note the pretty bow in her hair. The year is 1956, and the place is the Soviet Union.

"IT SEEMS LIKE you don't really know me.

"You see me through your father's eyes.

"And sometimes I think I do not know you."

It is my mother's birthday, and we are in the rotating restaurant atop the Marriott Marquis. My father and Aunt Tanya, my mother's younger sister, have sat down at our table awaiting their truffle soup and steak medium to medium well, but my mother wants ten minutes alone with me. We are sitting by the ladies' toilet in the restaurant's

nonrevolving core, watching women pass by in their piquant suburban outfits, so much flesh on a freezing December night.

My mother's line of thought confuses me. I know she is anxious
about the memoir I am writing. They both are. "Tell us, how many
more months do we have to live?" my father will ask about the impending publication date. But how can she say we do not know each
other? We have spent eighteen years living in such close proximity
that any non-Jewish, non-Italian, non-Asian American exposed to
even an hour of such closeness would raise up her blond locks to the
sky and cry, "Boundaries!"

Do I really not know my mother? She was my friend when I was a
little boy. I was rarely allowed any others, because she deemed them
disease carriers who could aggravate my bronchial illnesses. Cousin
Victoria, the ballerina—I remember staring at her through glass back
in Leningrad, the two of us smudging the square pane of a French
door with our palms, coating it with our breath. How we wanted to
reach out and hold hands. She was also an only child.

And so, mother and son alone, trudging through lines to get water
for their underground vacation hut in Crimea, to marvel at the Swallow's Nest Castle near Yalta, walking hand in hand through innumer-
able trains, train stations, town squares, mausoleums—and always
talking to each other, because my Russian was advanced and curious,
and she could use an advanced and curious companion. In those days,
I eased her anxiety instead of provoking it.

And as for seeing her through my father's eyes? For so long, I have
adapted his world-weariness, his sarcasm, his *shutki* (jokes). I have
tried to be him, because I was a boy and he was meant to illustrate the
next step in my evolution. "Whom do you love more, your mother or
your father?" was the unfair question foisted upon me by my parents
in Leningrad. Unfair, because I needed my mother, needed her company and her dark hair to braid during the moments when I was too
tired of reading a book. But I *felt* the explosive nature of my father's
love for me, the centering role I was to play in his difficult life. You

can either run toward such love or run away from it. Only recently have I chosen to do neither, to stand still and watch it take its course.

But as I have grown older I have chosen my mother's life. The endless calculations, the worries, the presentiments, and, most of all, the endless work. The sunrise-to-sundown work, even in retirement, that keeps you from fully settling up with the past. The chicken cutlets she sold me for $1.40 a piece after I had graduated from college have given birth to a thousand such cutlets, a hundred thousand, a million, each clearly marked with a price tag. The fanatic attention to detail I'm sure my father never had, not as an opera singer, not as an engineer, I now call my own. As well as the attendant worry, the fear of getting it wrong, the fear of authority. As I stroll around the grounds of an upstate historic site, the mansion of FDR's cousin-mistress, I am already preparing that all-important question for the elderly woman behind the counter: "I've bought tickets to the guided tour, but could I use the bathroom now, before the tour starts?"

My mother, her ambition stifled, channeled away by history and language, has given birth to my own. The only difference is: I have no God, no family myth, to cling to, no mythmaking abilities beyond the lies I tell on the page.

"Ours was such a nice family compared to your father's," my mother says. "We always used diminutives with each other, Ninochka, Tanechka. We had season's tickets to the symphony." When announced with such regularity, the Song of the Enlightened Loving Family, triumphing over adversity and despair, begins to sound like my father's Song of Israel, which is always holy, always incapable of wrong. Am I mad to think that love is not so easy? Or am I missing the right gene for easy love?

"And sometimes I think I do not know you," my mother says.

I have written close to twelve hundred pages of fiction, all of it translated into Russian, and hundreds of pages of nonfiction, much of it about the experience of being a Russian child in America, some of it trapped between the pages of this very book. Even if the fictional parts were not entirely autobiographical, shouldn't they have served as

at least a partial explanation for who I am? Or were the more important parts obfuscated by the *shutki*? Or perhaps, scarier still, the cogni-
tive gap between mother and son is too great; the distance from here
to there, from Moscow Square to my apartment near Union Square
to this revolving restaurant in Times Square, cannot be closed with
words alone.

Is hers but a less angry, more bewildered version of my father's *My
son, how could he leave me?*

As we walk over to the table, my father already itching to discharge
his own *shutki* at me—the ten minutes I have spent alone with my
mother have raised his jealousy and his ire—I think: What if it didn't
have to be like this? What if I were born to American parents instead?

It is not an altogether idle question. It almost happened. In a way.

. . .

My mother comes from two very different breeds of inhabitants of
the mighty Rus. On her father's side, the Yasnitsky clan is descended
from twelve generations of Russian Orthodox churchmen hailing
from the godforsaken Kirov Region lost somewhere in Russia's vast-
ness, somewhere between Helsinki and Kazakhstan. Photographs of
my great-grandfather, a deacon, and his brother, the archpriest of a
tiny village, offer a funny contrast to my Semitic features: Each looks
as if the Holy Spirit has long decamped within his transparent blue
eyes; each looks beautiful and content and so far removed from the
acid baths of horror in which the rest of my ancestry used to take their
morning dips. The cross hanging from Archpriest Yasnitsky's neck
could have been used to crucify a medium-sized animal like a fox ter-
rier or a young capybara. The only physical features tying together my
disparate ancestry are the full-blown rabbinical beards that both
churchmen are sporting.

My mother's half Jewishness often raises a pause among literary
interviewers from Israeli and American Jewish publications. "And,"
they ask, "Jewish on which side?" The subtext here is that Judaism is a
matrilineal religion; hence if my mother's mother were to be a gentile,

I would be a "Jewish writer" in name only. I like to dawdle for a bit, to allow the worst to cross (quite literally) the minds of my Hebraic interlocutors, before revealing to everyone's relief that it was my grandfather who was the big gentile and my mother's mother was of Jewish stock.

• • •

And was she ever.

The Nirman family hails from the small town of Dubrovno in what is now the independent dictatorship of Belarus, sandwiched between Poland and Russia. The nearest city is Vitebsk, Marc Chagall's birthplace and muse. Orthodox Jews, dripping with prayer shawls and mysticism, once graced both sides of the Dnieper River, which runs through Dubrovno like a minor Mississippi. Unlike my father's ancestry of laborers, the Nirmans are shtetl royalty, descendants of a long line of rabbis.

One of the Dubrovno villagers leaves for America between the wars, where, inevitably, he makes a killing in some minor trade. He comes back to Dubrovno to claim a bride, my great-grandmother Seina. They hit it off, but then the poor schmuck lights a cigar on a Friday evening in front of my rabbinical great-great-grandfather. *Thou shalt not spark up a Montecristo on the Sabbath* is yet another prohibition of our overwhelming faith. The rabbi cries "Never!" to the marriage proposal and throws the suitor out of his house.

"If not for that cigar," my mother tells me, "we could have been born in America and not had the *tsoris* [Yiddish: "trouble"] we had in that Russia."

I'm pretty sure that's not how lineages work, but perhaps if my great-grandmother Seina had emigrated to America with her cigar-chomping suitor, some strange, distant iteration of a Gary could have been cobbled together in a Chicago or a Burbank, versed in baseball lore and tax strategies. If the many-universe hypothesis that the scientists are working on is true, perhaps that Gary could meet this Gary, maybe after I've given a reading at a Jewish center in Chicagoland or

LA. Perhaps alternate-Gary would come up to me and say, "I'm Russian, too!" And I would say, *"Ah, vy govorite po-russki?"* And he would say "Huh?" and explain to me that, no, he doesn't speak Russian, but his great-grandmother was from *Dub*-something, a town near Vitebsk. And I would explain that Vitebsk's not even really in Russia, it is in Belarus, and that what alternate-Gary truly is is an American Jew or, better yet, *an American,* which is a fine enough identity that one doesn't have to add Russian or Belarusian or anything else to it. And then we would split the difference and go out for soy-crusted chicken wings at a local tapas bar, where I would learn that alternate-Gary's niece, a budding essayist, is applying to my department at Columbia.

After the American goes back to his star-spangled land with another local maiden, Great-grandma Seina takes second prize in the marital sweepstakes: She marries the village butcher. The good life ensues in a big house with a garden and apple trees and many children. My grandmother Galya, the one who fed me cheese in exchange for my first novel, is born around 1911. When she is ten years old Galya is given the task of watching over the family's youngest daughter during the night. The child falls out of the crib and dies. To compound the horror, her parents make the ten-year-old attend her sister's funeral. She never sets foot in a cemetery again. For the rest of her life, Grandmother Galya is haunted by the fear of being buried alive. For the rest of her life, my mother is *also* haunted by the fear of being buried alive. Being a modern man, I take this deeply ancestral fear and turn it into something more practical: I am afraid of being buried within a sealed metal container such as a subway car or an airplane.

• • •

Time is passing. The Jews of my mother's family are getting ready for death, or the labor camps, or a little bit of both.

As on my father's side, a similar pattern emerges: One of the children, a girl, becomes a quick study, masters Russian, the language of power (as opposed to Yiddish, which is the language of Jews).

Grandma Galya, with her gold medal from the Russian gymnasium and her dream of becoming a journalist, makes her way up to Leningrad, where she enrolls at the Printing Technical College. There, she will meet Dmitry Yasnitsky, my grandfather, son of the Russian Orthodox deacon, another hardworking provincial beaver who will one day become an economist at the prestigious Leningrad Mining Institute, even as Grandma will find an editorial perch at *Evening Leningrad*.

The daughter of rabbis is about to marry the son of priests, and my mother will soon be on her way to the ruined postwar country that awaits the first warm flicker of her eyelids. That country has a name.

. . .

"Dude, where are you from?"

I am sitting for an interview for some kind of MTV-like network, an interview that will never be aired.

"The Soviet Union," I say.

A beat. The interviewer looks out from beneath his hair. "And, like, what *is* that?"

What *is* the Soviet Union? Or, more accurately, what *was* it? This is not an outlandish question. That particular nation passed away more than twenty years ago, a millennium in our speedy times. A generation of Russians has grown up without singing "The Soviet tankmen are ready for action! / Sons of their Great Motherland" or knowing that, before yoga, waiting in line for an eggplant for three hours could constitute a meditative experience.

To explain the Soviet Union, I will tell the story of my great-uncle Aaron, on my mother's side. Conveniently enough, his travails will also lead to my mother's first memory.

. . .

When the advancing German army stopped by my grandmother's village of Dubrovno, in what is now Belarus (Grandmother Galya had long before left for Leningrad), and began herding the Jews together, sixteen-year-old Aaron's parents faced a particular problem: Their little girl, Basya, couldn't walk. The Germans shot all the invalids right away. They did not want the girl to die frightened and alone in her wheelchair. So they told their son Aaron to run away through the vegetable gardens and into the forest, while they would die quickly with Basya. Instead of just herding everyone into the ghetto, the German troops decided they could be more proactive and make a few house calls. Aaron ended up hiding in the family attic, where he watched his sister and parents being shot dead in the courtyard. His memory: the ticking of the clock as the Germans drew their rifles and, also, his fingers going numb because he was clutching a piece of wood as he watched.

After the Germans moved on, Aaron hoofed through the fields to a happy local chorus of "Run, Yid, run!" Other, more sympathetic Christians fed him, and eventually he joined up with a Belorussian partisan force in the forests around Dubrovno. At this point his major disadvantage was that he had only one shoe, the other having been lost to a sprint through the snow. He became what they called a "son of the regiment" (*syn polka*), the youngest of a ragtag band of fighters. The partisans were eventually absorbed into the Red Army proper and began to beat the Germans back toward Berlin.

And this is where Great-uncle Aaron's problems *really* began.

They began the way problems so often do in Russia, with poems.

When not busy shooting Germans, Uncle Aaron wrote poems. No one really knows what they were about, but those poems did catch the eye of the girlfriend of Aaron's superior, a corporal.

Once the corporal found out that his girl was Private Aaron's muse, the young poet was arrested and sentenced under the USSR's Article 58, counterrevolutionary activity, in Aaron's case, the praising of German technology. ("He really *was* impressed by German tanks," my mother says.)

And so the boy who watched his parents and sister slaughtered before his eyes at age sixteen, who ambushed German soldiers on the roads of Belorussia by age seventeen, came out of the war at age eighteen to collect the typical reward of the era, ten years of hard labor in a Siberian *lagpunkt,* or work camp.

My mother's favorite thing in the world growing up was sweetened condensed milk (*sgushchyonka*), a cousin of the Latin American *dulce de leche*. Among the oversweetened pantheon of Russian desserts, it would become my childhood favorite as well.

In the labor camps foodstuffs like *sgushchyonka* served as currency—a good way not to get raped or forced into the worst kinds of labor—and so my grandfather would cart up to twenty of those iconic blue cans of Soviet condensed milk to the post office to send to his brother-in-law Aaron. My mother, on the other hand, was allowed only one tablespoon of condensed milk before bedtime.

My mother's first memory: walking through the ruined streets of postwar Leningrad with her aristocratically thin, ever-ailing economist father, a cigarette stamped permanently into his mouth, as he dragged along twenty cans of *sgushchyonka* to send to her uncle, the prisoner, thinking, *How lucky Uncle Aaron must be that he gets to eat twenty cans of condensed milk!*

There is a picture of my mother at the time. She is about four years old and as chubby as I've ever seen her, smiling underneath a pleasant brown bob. Born months after the war ended to a family with decent connections and a decent flat, she will one day join that ever-ephemeral phenomenon, the Russian middle class. The picture is one of several of my mother being young and happy—at the Thanksgiving dinner she takes me to my upstairs bedroom with these photos and says, "Look how happy *my* family looked by comparison to *his*," meaning my father's. Indeed, there's nothing special about the photo, except that its upper-right corner has been torn off, and one can discern a crescent of needle holes. Why did someone take needle and thread to this innocent image?

This photograph was "sewn into the case file" (*podshyto k delu*) of my great-uncle Aaron when he was in the camps. At one point, my grandmother had sent a letter with the photograph of my mother to my uncle Aaron in Siberia, and the camp's administration had found the beaming face of a four-year-old important enough to sew into a prisoner's case file.

Perhaps the greatest unanswered question I have toward the entire Land of the Soviets is this: *Who did the sewing?*

In a country recovering from the greatest war humanity has ever known, with twenty-six million in their graves (my grandfather Isaac included), *who* took the time out of a starving, snowy day to carefully hand sew the tiny photo of a smiling four-year-old, my mother, into the "criminal" case file of a man—a *boy,* really, by today's standards—who had watched his family die just half a decade ago, who had fought the enemy back across the border, and who had subsequently been imprisoned for writing poetry and admiring a German tank? So much information is open to us, the past is ready and accessible and Googleable, but what I wouldn't give to know the person whose job it was to make sure my mother's photo made the rounds of Stalin's labor camps, only to end up, as Great-uncle Aaron fortunately did, in a cozy house along the Eastern Seaboard of the United States, minus the four fingers on his right hand, lost to a timber saw in Siberia during his decade of savage and pointless labor.

• • •

My mother. With her dreams of being buried alive. With her meticulous collection of family photos, some filed under the World War II subheading "Uncle Simon, Wife, Murdered Children," written in Russian in her equally meticulous script.

My mother, in the first despairing bloom of youth, looking, as she would say, *ozabochena,* a combination of worried and moody and maybe lovesick, a Soviet-era bow crowning the top of her puffy, full-lipped face as if to inform us that the woods behind her do not belong to a sunny summer camp in the Catskills. It is 1956. She is eleven years old in a striped summer dress, resembling, already, a worried young Jewish adult.

My beaming mother in her red Young Pioneer tie, ready to serve the Soviet state with the common Pioneer cheer *I am always ready!* shouted at the top of her lungs. "I never took it off," she says of the red tie. "After I got into the Pioneers, I never took it off. Even in the summer! Such a great Pioneer I was!"

My mother, serious and dreamy, behind a childhood piano. Her mother ties her to the piano bench with a towel so that she won't escape to jump rope with the kids screaming for her outside her window. Eventually the music will seep in. She will go to music school and later teach piano in a Leningrad kindergarten. She will marry a man who wants to be an opera singer, who once went to music school just like her, although she will deem his school inferior.

My mother, off camera, in our Moscow Square apartment, tossing from a nightmare in one room while I am tossing from asthma *and* a nightmare in the other. She's dreaming she left her notes at home and now the kindergarten class won't be ready for a special performance. I'm dreaming I forgot some part of me, too, a toy version of *Buratino,* the Russian Pinocchio, left on a platform in Sevastopol, Crimea, left for some lucky boy or girl.

My mother in our first American co-op apartment, dark brown curls, backless dress, playing the shiny Red October upright piano we had brought at great cost from Leningrad. Atop the piano, a golden menorah with a fake emerald at its center alongside a white vase filled with chalky ceramic flowers. My mother looks hesitant before the keys. She is already throwing herself into her American work, work that will lead her from the title of Typist to that of Fiscal Administrator for a large Manhattan-based charity. The Red October, useless now, will be given to Goodwill in return for a three-hundred-dollar tax deduction.

"Two girls," my mother says, holding up the photo of her playing the piano in Leningrad, the dreaming, distracted child, and the other of her, a single-minded immigrant mother, behind the Red October in Queens, New York. "One as I was and one as I became."

I have known only one of those girls. My dear immigrant mother, my fellow anxious warrior. The one she became. The other one I have tried to know. Through the stories, the photographs, the archival evidence, the shared love of condensed milk, the Red Pioneer tie I never got to wear but that graced her neck so proudly. I have known only one of those girls. But, please believe me, I have known her.

6.

MY MADONNACHKA

The author's beloved grandma Polya rejoins the family in Rome. She has flown in three kilograms of soap from Leningrad. A Soviet newscast has informed her of a shortage of soap in America.

T HIS WAS SUPPOSED TO READ like a Cold War spy novel. Security checks, East Berlin, Soviet customs agents.

This was supposed to read like a Cold War spy novel, but the James Bond in question, me, can't make *kaka*.

"Mama! Papa! Ooooooooo!" It is the day before our departure for Western Europe and then America, and I am sitting on my little green potty—write a hundred-page novel, sure; but use an actual grown-up toilet, I'm too scared of falling in—and I can't get the *ka-kashka* out.

Staraisya, staraisya, my parents urge me, one after the other. Try harder, try harder. *Napryagis'.* Strain yourself.

Later, I'm on the Culture Couch, my stomach still full of undigested cabbage, and I can't sleep. The suitcases are packed, the living room where I sleep is now dominated by a pair of huge army-green sacks stuffed with decades of accumulated life, specifically the thick cotton comforter beneath which I struggle to stay alive; in fact, *everything* is packed, and the fighting between my parents has reached some kind of worried détente, the usual go-to-the-dicks and fuck-your-mothers and don't-swear! replaced with gloomy, indeterminate whispers, even as the Bad Rocket belches its smoke outside, and I tremble within on the Culture Couch. I peek at the rising sun, at the signs for MEAT and PRODUCE. Everything is covered in frost. Real Russian frost. Every snowbank is a fortress on the scale of the turreted Engineers' Castle, the snow pale and bled out by the brief winter sun. Anyone who has experienced such frost will never abide its mushy Western equivalent.

Neither Mama nor Papa has told me that we are about to leave the Land of the Soviets for good. My parents are paranoid that I might blab it to some adult in power, and our exit visas will be canceled. No one has told me, *but I know.* And I have staged my own form of protest. I have brought on the worst asthma attack yet, a sputtering of helplessness so obscene that my parents consider *not leaving.*

Our apartment near Moscow Square has been sold to the son of a high-ranking party member. The party member's son and his dad are very keen to see us haul our Jewish asses out and take possession of every square foot of our former property, not to mention our explosive Signal black-and-white television. They will also get the shabby Culture Couch on which I've slept and dreamed cultured dreams, tried to play the violin and the balalaika, and, with the help of my grandma Galya, written my masterpiece *Lenin and His Magical Goose.* Also included in the price of the apartment, the floor-to-ceiling wooden ladder my father built to try to help me conquer my fear of heights and to make me into an Athlete.

Son of a Party Member stops by with his high-ranking father, who happens to have a medical degree. "We don't know what to do," my mother tells the Communist Party duo. "The child has asthma. Maybe we should stay."

Dr. Apparatchik, keen to get the apartment into his Communist son's hands, says, "My medical opinion is that you should go. There will be better care for asthma in the West."

Which is so very true.

My mother decides we should proceed with our flight. In response, my asthma gets worse. *I will not let them take me.* In the morning, I try the potty again, but nothing doing, the cabbage inside me knows our destination better than I do. It desperately wants to emigrate to the West, to end its life inside a gleaming Viennese toilet.

. . .

The last minutes on Tipanov Street are hazy. Do we sit down for a silent moment before the journey, as is the Russian custom? What's the point? This journey will have no end.

Taxi to the airport. And there the truth of the matter is revealed to me: Aunt Tanya is here and my aunt Lyusya, who will die a decade later of cancer that would be operable almost anywhere else, and her daughter, my cousin Victoria, the ballerina whose hand I touched through glass during my quarantine, who begs my mother, "I want to come with you!" Everyone is here except my grandma Galya, who is bedridden. *Nas provozhayut.* We are being "sent off," meaning this is not just a jaunt down to Crimea or Soviet Georgia. This is final. But where are we going?

Wailing before the customs line, the Jews are saying goodbye to their relatives with all the emotion they are well known for, saying goodbye forever. And there are so many Jews headed out on the Leningrad–East Berlin flight that the shores of Brooklyn and the tree-lined boulevards of Queens and the foggy valleys of San Francisco are already groaning in anticipation. Eyes still wet, all of us Snotties today, we are searched thoroughly by customs agents. A big man in full uniform takes off my fur hat and pokes around the lining, looking for diamonds we may have stashed illegally within. As a child I have never been mistreated by the system. In Russia, as in socialist China, there is a special grace accorded to children—in both countries there is usually only one little emperor per family. But I am no longer a Soviet citizen, and I am no longer worth according any special childhood privileges. I do not know it, but I am a traitor. And my parents are traitors. And if a good many people got their wish we would be dealt with as traitors.

The customs agent is plunging his thick fingers into my fur hat, and the asthmatic me is so scared he does not even have the where-withal *not* not to breathe. And so I gulp down the thick ammonia-and-sweat-scented air of the small Stalin-era international terminal of dodgy Pulkovo Airport. My parents are nearby, but for the first time in my life I am alone without them, standing before authority. The customs agent finishes fondling my hat and puts it back on my head with a combination of a smile and a sneer. I am leaving Russia, but he will never leave. If only the child-me could have the compassion to understand that monumental fact.

Down the customs line, our luggage and the two gigantic army-green sacks have been thrown open for inspection. Feathers are flying out of our prized red comforter as the pages of my mother's beige leather address book—the names and phone numbers of some relatives in Queens—are being torn out for no good reason by a sadist in uniform, as if we are spies smuggling information to the West. Which, in a sense, we are.

And then we are clear of the formalities, and clear also of our relatives. Writing today I can guess the word in my mother's mind: *tragediya*. It is a tragic day for her. My father's mother will soon join us in America, but my mother will not see her mother until 1987, right before her death, by which point Grandma Galya will be too far gone to even recognize her second daughter. Until the reformist Gorbachev takes over, traitors to the Soviet Union are not allowed to return to visit their dying parents. I suppose I am feeling her sadness, because I am, as my mother likes to say, *chutkiy,* or sensitive. But truth be told, I am not *chutkiy* enough. Because all I can see in front of us is the Aeroflot plane, the Tupolev-154. On one of his didactic trips around the Chesme Church, my father has told me that the Tupolev is the fastest civilian jet ever built, faster than the American Boeing 727! Certainly faster than the toy helicopter we are launching at the church spires along with our aeronautical cheers of "URA!"

And now we are inside this sleek, magical airplane, the one that can so decisively outfly our Cold War rival's, and rumbling past the vast airfield, past the denuded winter trees in the distance, past the acres of snow deep enough to hide a thousand children. Forget asthma. I, myself, am holding my breath before the wonder of it. Sure, I am afraid of heights, but being inside the futuristic Tupolev, the fastest civilian jet ever built, is akin to being wrapped in my father's arms.

No one has told me where we are going, but I have already prepared to be a fine representative of the Soviet race. On my breast, beneath the monumental overcoat and the monumental winter sweater, is a shirt sold only in the USSR and perhaps in the more discriminating shops of Pyongyang. It is a green wide-collared thing with blue and green vertical stripes and, between the stripes, a galaxy of yellow polka dots. The terminals of the shirt are tucked into a pair of black pants that reach up to my kidneys, ostensibly to keep them warm in transit. I have pinned this shirt with the symbol of the upcoming 1980 Moscow Olympics, a stylized Kremlin capped with a red star. The fluid lines of the Kremlin are reaching toward the star because my nation is always reaching toward excellence. Beneath the Olympic pin is situated the pin of a smiling tiger's face. This is in mourning of *Tigr,* my stuffed tiger, who is too big to make the journey to wherever it is we are going.

Which is *where* again? Mama and Papa remain silent and worried throughout the flight. My mother scans the airplane's badly sealed window for drafts. Drafts, according to Russian medical lore, are the great, silent killers.

We land with a proper thud somewhere and taxi to a terminal. I am looking out the window and *yobtiki mat'*, fuck your mother, the sign—FLUGHAFEN BERLIN-SCHÖNEFELD—is not even in Russian anymore. Inside the terminal, past the officials in their green getups, an unfortunate, umlauted language is being spoken, my first understanding that the world is not powered entirely by the great and mighty Russian tongue.

"Papa, who are these people?"

"Germans."

But aren't we supposed to kill Germans? That's what Grandpa did to them in the Great Patriotic War before they blew him up in his tank. (A childhood lie on someone's part; as I've mentioned before, he was merely an artilleryman.) And yet, even the child in me senses the difference between here and home. East Berlin is the socialist showpiece of the entire Warsaw Pact, and the airport waiting lounge seems to hover somewhere between Russia and the West. There are dashes of chrome, if I remember correctly, and exotic nongray colors, purple or mauve perhaps. The men seem to be powered by some extraordinary force, a grim ability to walk forth in a straight line and to meaningfully declare things in their strange tongue. The difference, I am too young to understand, is that the men here are not completely, debilitatingly drunk.

Fuck your mother, please, where are we going?

A writer or any suffering artist-to-be is just an instrument too finely set to the human condition, and this is the problem with sending an already disturbed child across not just national borders but, in the year 1978, across interplanetary ones. I have not had a full-blown asthma attack in twenty of the past nearly forty years, but even thinking of Flughafen Berlin-Schönefeld shortens my breath as I write this. Here we are sitting surrounded by our possessions, two army-green sacks and a trio of orange suitcases made out of *real Polish leather* that leave my hands smelling like cow. Here I am next to Mama, who has just surrendered her dying mother. Here I am next to our family's history, which I do not fully know yet, but which is every bit as heavy as our two army-green sacks. Here I am pushing my own history through East German customs, a history not even seven years old but already with its own mass and velocity. In practical terms, the army-green sacks are too heavy for a child, or a mama, to lift, but I push them forward with a kick whenever I can to help out my family. The instincts that will see me through my life are stirring for the first time: forward, move forward, keep going, keep kicking.

And then another Soviet plane, the water-bug-shaped, propeller-driven Ilyushin-18, bellies up to the terminal, and I am excited by the thought of a second plane ride in one day, even if instead of the Soviet carrier Aeroflot, its logo a hammer and sickle bracketed by a pair of enormous goose-like wings, we are seated within an East German airliner with the ugly name of Interflug and no Communist coat of arms to speak of. I am strapped in; the plane takes off for a very short (and loud and droning) flight south. Momentarily, we will land in a world unlike any we could have imagined, the one many will tell us is free.

But nothing is free.

• • •

Vienna. To this day passing through its fancy international airport is bittersweet. This is the first stop on what is becoming a regular three-part journey for Soviet Jews. First, Vienna, then Rome, then an English-Speaking Country Elsewhere. Or, for the true believers, Israel.

In addition to my Moscow Olympics pin and my homage to my *tigr,* a worn Soviet atlas accompanies me to Vienna. I love maps. With their longitudes crossing latitudes at precise ninety-degree angles, with the topographical yellows of the African veldt and the pale caviar grays of the Caspian Sea, maps will help make sense of the world spinning relentlessly beneath our feet.

The customs area at VIE is a madhouse of Russian immigrants collecting their worldly possessions. One of our swollen army-green sacks happens to burst in transit, spilling out one hundred kilograms of red compasses with yellow hammers and sickles that, unbeknownst to me, we are going to sell to Communist Italians. As Mama and Papa crawl on all fours trying to gather their wares, *yobtiki mat', yobtiki mat'*, I subdue my sweaty worry by carefully tracing the frosty expanses of Greenland in my atlas—*cold, cold, cold*—rocking back and forth like a religious Jew. The first Western person I have ever seen, a middle-aged Austrian woman in a dappled fur coat, sees me *davening* over my maps. She elegantly steps over my parents and hands me a Mozart chocolate candy. She smiles at me with eyes the color of Lake Neusiedl, one of the largest in Austria according to my map of Central Europe. If I believe in anything now, it is in the providence of that woman.

But here is another thing that I see: My parents are on their knees. We are in a foreign country, and my parents are on the floor trying to gather the flimsy goods that are to sustain us through our journey.

On that night, we are "safe" in the West. We are staying in a Viennese rooming house called Pan Bettini, which is also being used by the local prostitutes. "Such classy prostitutes!" my mother exclaims. "They ride on bikes. They dress so subtly."

"I know I'm not allowed chocolate," I say, "but can I eat the Mozart candy? I'll save the wrapper for later. It will be my toy."

"Listen, little son," my father says. "I can tell you a secret. We are going to America."

I cannot breathe. He hugs me.

Or maybe it should be: He hugs me. I cannot breathe.

Either way, we are going to the enemy.

• • •

Christmas is coming to Vienna, and few cities take the holiday as seriously. Papa and I are walking down the broad Hapsburg boulevards lost to neon and red trim and Wolfgang Amadeus Mozart's thin-

lipped visage and the occasional manger with its silent wooden Baby
Jesus. In my thickly gloved hand I am holding my own Lord and
Savior, an inhaler. My lungs are still swollen, the phlegm is rumbling
inside, but the illness has been dealt a serious setback by that miracle
of Western technology, courtesy of an ancient Viennese doctor whom
my father has charmed with his broken German ("asthma *über alles!*").

We are going to the enemy.

In my father's hand a different kind of miracle, a banana. Who has
ever heard of a banana in winter? But here in the Austrian capital, for
less than a schilling, it is possible. The shopwindows are crammed
with goods—vacuum cleaners with nozzles thin and powerful like the
snouts of aardvarks; cutouts of tall, elegant women holding aloft jars
of cream, their faces smiling like they mean it; models of healthy boys
dressed haphazardly in ensembles of woolen caps, shockingly short
winter jackets (but won't these Austrian *Jungen* catch cold?), and
gleaming corduroy pants. My father and I are walking mouths open,
so that "a crow may fly in," as the Russian saying goes. We have seen
the Opera and the Wien Museum, but what has impressed us the
most is the frighteningly fast black-and-yellow trams that zip us across
town and to the Danube in minutes.

We are going to the enemy.

Here the first moral quandary sets in. The Viennese trams operate
on the honor system. Do we use the few schillings we have to buy a
ticket, or do we take advantage of the West's generosity and buy more
bananas? A source of much discussion, but in the end Papa decides
that we better not upset the Austrians. Or you-know-what might happen again. All around us late-model Mercedeses sweep the gaily illu-
minated streets, lit to within an inch of daylight. There are thousands
of us Soviet Jews stomping our way through Christmas Vienna that
night, mouths agape, letting the pleasure and the horror of home-
leaving finally wash over all of us, wondering if we really should have
paid for that tram ticket. In our hotels, we have all been confronted
with *the shelf in the bathroom,* containing not just one but two spare

rolls of toilet paper. Before such magnificence our collective Soviet ethics yield. We grab the spare toilet paper and stuff it into the most sacred parts of our luggage, edging out all those degrees in mechanical engineering.

We are going to the enemy.

Holding our asthma inhaler and banana before us, my father and I walk up the stairs to our room in the Hotel for Prostitutes, where Mother is chastely waiting for us.

She bends down to my level to make sure the scarf has been tied correctly around my neck (any gaps, and my father will get it). "Are you breathing okay?" she asks me. Yes, Mama. I have my new inhaler.

Then to my father, "A banana! How can it be?" And not just that, my father tells her, throwing a whole bunch of bananas on the table and then reaching into his sack. *They have marinated gherkins in jars.* And also a powdered mushroom soup from a brand called Knorr. I look at the clear bright package on which the Knorr Corporation has drawn a cadre of herb-dotted mushrooms boiling themselves silly inside an octagonal bowl, and next to them an artist's rendering of the actual ingredients: the saucy little mushrooms before they were thrown into the water and all the high-level vegetables that are just creaming to jump in alongside them.

My parents are in rapture over the *marinated gherkins in jars.*

I am in rapture over the Knorr soup, although I tell myself not to get too excited. We are going to the enemy.

"Eat, eat, little one," my mother says. "While it's hot, so that it can bring up the phlegm."

"Decent soup, but not like ours back home," my father says. "*Real* white mushrooms from the forest near Leningrad cooked in butter, and then you make the soup with sour cream and with lots of garlic. There's nothing better!"

Already, the nostalgia. And the echoes of Soviet patriotism. But somehow this little packet of Knorr has produced enough mushroom soup to feed three refugees. Now there is only one thing to do. To peel the bananas and have an outrageous fruit dessert in the middle of December! One banana each, into our hungry refugee mouths, and *tphoo!*

"They are rotten! You've bought rotten bananas!"

We are going to the enemy.

• • •

The second part of the journey begins. The Israeli representatives have begged my parents to change their minds and get on an El Al flight straight to the Holy Land, where we can all be BIG JEWS together and stand up for ourselves ("Never Again!") against our enemies in their checkered Arafat-style thingies, but my parents have courageously resisted. The letters from their relatives in New York have been emphatic, if cliché: "The streets here are paved with gold. We can sell leather jackets at the flea market." Now we are boarding a series of trains that will take us to Rome and, from there, to one of the powerhouse English-speaking countries in desperate need of Soviet engineers, America or South Africa, say. The two army-green sacks and the trio of orange suitcases made out of *real Polish leather* are harnessed once more. We are on a cozy European train eating ham sandwiches and boring our way through the Alps to finally emerge on the other side. And then something inexplicable begins to happen. By which I mean: Italy.

My aunt Tanya's belief that one of our ancestors, the magnificent Prince Suitcase, was the tsar's representative to Venice may bear out in the end. Because once we reach Italy we become different people (although who doesn't?). As the train rumbles southward, I take out my atlas and trace our journey topographically past the brown ridges of the Ligurian Alps, over the spine of the Apennines, and into darkest water-fed green. *Green?* Sure, we've encountered that color in Leningrad whenever the summer's heat would disturb the winter snows for a month or two, but who could imagine green on this scale? And alongside the green, past the country's boot-shaped boundaries, the deep blue of . . . Sredizemnoye More, the Mediterranean. And, fuck your mother, it's December, but the sun is shining with atomic strength, shining early and bright in the *winter morning,* as our train pulls into Roma Termini, a train station of enormous fascist span, which, to borrow from my future best friend Walt Whitman, contains multitudes: a noisy mélange of Russians, Italians, and Gypsies, each with their own rallying cry. Yes, there will be bananas here. Better bananas. And tomatoes nurtured by the motherly figure of the Italian sun. Tomatoes that explode in the mouth like grenades.

. . .

One is cautioned by the better critics never to write about photographs. They are an easy substitute for prose, a hackneyed shortcut, and, besides, they lie like all images do. So what am I to make of the photo of my small family—Mama and Papa and me between them—sitting on a worsted blanket in a chipped, dingy apartment in Ostia, a seaside suburb of Rome? My father has his arm around my mother's shoulder, and my love is divided between his knee and her cheekbone. She is in a turtleneck and a knee-length skirt, smiling with all of her remarkably natural (for a Soviet émigrée) white teeth. He, in a white shirt and jeans, with his prominent Adam's apple, his Italian-black goatee and sideburns, is beaming in a more restrained way for the camera, the lower lip, usually set in an unhappy position, be it sadness or anger, dragooned into happiness. And between them I am rosy cheeked, aflame with health and joy. I am still the owner of the same stupid Soviet polka-dot shirt, but most of it is hidden by a new Italian sweater, its shoulders ringed with something like epaulets, so that I may continue the fantasy that I will join the Red Army someday. My hair is as long and unruly as the Italian state, and the gap between my crooked teeth is its own opera, but the rings under my eyes that have made such an underaged raccoon out of me are gone. My mouth is open and, through the gap in my teeth, I am breathing in mouthfuls of the warm, ennobling Roman air. This photo is the first indication I have of all three of us together happy, ecstatic, as a family. If I may go so far, it is the first anecdotal evidence I have that joy is possible and that a family can love each other with as much abandon as it can muster.

Five months in Rome!

We are mostly at leisure. Our pastel apartment is crumbling but cheap, rented from a small but budding Odessa mafioso, who will soon seek greener pastures in Baltimore. Our days are filled with churches and museums, Colosseums and Vaticans, and, on Sundays, the Porta Portese market in Trastevere, a rambunctious, nearly Balkan bazaar by a bend in the Tiber River. My father, a so-so mechanical engineer and unfulfilled singer ("How they used to applaud me when I sang!"), has been readying for America by becoming a minor businessman. The American Jews, guilty over their inaction during the Holocaust, have been exceedingly kind to their Soviet brethren, and most of our five-month wait in Rome—our application for refugee status in the United States is still being processed—is generously paid for by their gathered funds. But Papa has bigger ideas! Each week we pack an army-green sack with Soviet crap bound for Porta Portese. There are stacks of green East German sheet music for symphonies by Tchaikovsky and Rimsky-Korsakov. Why Italians would want to buy such artifacts is now beyond me, but it is almost as if my father, not fully convinced of the journey ahead, is saying, *I am a worthy person who has lived for forty cultured years on this earth. I am not just some Cold War loser.* He also sells a samovar to a kind Italian couple, an engineer and a music teacher, a mirror image of my father and mother, and they invite us to bowls of spaghetti so dense we become confused by the gluttony. How can anyone eat so much food? In America, we will see how.

Before we left Leningrad, the émigré party line has informed us of an interesting quirk. While half of the Eastern Bloc would likely get up and move to Missouri if given the chance, the crazy Italians can't get enough of communism. They can even get pretty violent about it. The newspapers are still screaming about the Brigate Rosse, the Red Brigades, and how an industrialist's son had recently been kidnapped and had part of his ear cut off. Still, business is business, and anything Russian is huge. A fat big-bosomed former prostitute from Odessa stalks the beaches of our seaside Ostia, shouting, "*Prezervatiff! Prezervatiff!*" as she peddles Soviet condoms to the amorous locals. Given their poor quality, I wonder how many inadvertent future Italians owe their existence to her wares. Meanwhile, our neighbor, a timid Leningrad doctor, ventures out to the pier with a bale of Soviet heart medicine. "*Medicina per il cuore!*" he croons. The local police think he's peddling heroin and pull out their *pistole*. The timid doctor, all glasses and big bald dome, runs off as the police fire warning shots after him. He is unwilling to let go of the giant umbrella he has used to shield himself from the warm Italian rain. The sight of the Jewish doctor and the umbrella escaping down the Mediterranean coast with the *carabinieri* in tow warms our hearts and provides endless conversations over the cheap chicken liver that constitutes most of our diet. (The prized tomatoes and balls of mozzarella are for once a week only.)

I am given a more lucrative, and more legal, sales line: compasses emblazoned with the yellow hammer and sickle against a red background. At Porta Portese, I walk around the perimeter of the bedsheet that defines our stake, brandishing a sample compass and hollering at passersby with my now-healthy little boy's lungs, "*Mille lire! Mille lire!*" A thousand lire, less than a dollar, is what each of the compasses costs, and the Italians, they are not animals. They see a poor refugee boy in a polka-dot-vertical-striped shirt, they will give him a thousand lire. "*Grazie mille! Grazie mille!*" I reply as the money is thrust in one hand and a little piece of Russia leaves another.

I am allowed to hang on to some of those *mille lire* notes, Giuseppe Verdi's bewhiskered *punim* winking back at me from the currency. My obsession is guidebooks. Cheap English guidebooks, their spines a glob of glue and some string, with encompassing names like *All Rome* and *All Florence* and *All Venice*. I set up a little treasure chest of books in the tiny room we share in Ostia, and I try to read them in English, with limited success. The English-Russian dictionary is introduced to my world, along with the new non-Cyrillic alphabet. And then the words: "oculus," *baldacchino,* "nymphaeum." "Papa, what does this mean?" "Mama, what does that mean?" Oh, the pain of having an inquisitive child.

The American Jews are now flinging money at us with abandon (three hundred U.S. dollars a month!), the hammer-and-sickle compasses are really paying off, so we use the proceeds to take guided bus tours of Florence and Venice and everything in between. Brimming with *All Florence* knowledge I interrupt the lackadaisical Russian tour guide at the Medici Chapel. "Excuse me," my nerdish voice rings out across the marble. "I believe you are not correct, Guide. That is Michelangelo's *Allegory of Night.* And this is the *Allegory of Day.*"

Silence. The guide consults his literature. "I believe the boy is right."

A rustle in the midst of the Russian refugees, a dozen doctors and physicists and piano geniuses among them. "That boy knows everything!" And then, most important, to my mother, "A delightful child. How old is he?"

I am lapping it up. "Six. Almost seven."

"Remarkable!"

Mother hugs me. Mother loves me.

But knowing things is not enough. And neither is Mama's love. In a church gift shop I buy a little golden medal depicting Raphael's *Madonna del Granduca.* Haloed Baby Jesus is so porky here, so content with his extra protecting layer of flesh, and Mary's beatific sideward glance drips with so much devotion and pain and understanding. What a lucky boy Jesus is. And what a beautiful woman is Mary. Back in Ostia, I develop a hideous secret vice. While my parents are off hustling Tchaikovsky sheet music or talking to the criminal Leningrad doctor and his young childless wife, I hide in the bathroom or somewhere lonely in the depths of our room. I take out the Madonna del Granduca and I cry. Crying is not allowed because (1) it's not manly and (2) it can bring on asthma with all that snot. But, alone, I let the tears drop out of me with complete hot abandon as I kiss and kiss the beatific Virgin, whispering, "Santa Maria, Santa Maria, Santa Maria."

The American Jews are paying for us, but the Christians are not content to let entire herds of confused, post-Communist Jews just wander past. There is a Christian center nearby, which we call the Amerikanka, in honor of the American Baptists who run it. They bait us in with some dried meat and noodles, only to show us a full-color film about their God. A reckless, know-it-all hippie motorcyclist is lost amid the Sahara Desert, he runs out of water, and, just as he is about to die, Jesus comes over to dispense precious water and career advice. The production values are terrific. In the bathroom of our flat I cradle the Madonna del Granduca. "I just saw your Son in the film, Santa Maria. He was bleeding so much. Oh, my poor Madonnachka."

The next week the workers at the local Jewish organization decide to up the ante. They screen *Fiddler on the Roof.*

. . .

Beloved Grandma Polya arrives from Leningrad and, with her sparse hair and country smile, accompanies me on trips across Rome, walking me up and down the Tiber in my snazzy new Italian light coat, watching the sun do things to the enormity of St. Peter's Dome or wondering at the Pyramid of Cestius rising out of the ancient ocher cityscape. "Grandma, aren't pyramids supposed to be in Egypt?" The map of Rome is so worn there are thumb-bored holes where the Colosseum and the Piazza del Popolo should be, and I have truly destroyed the Villa Borghese. Grandma, sweating in the new heat, looks around apprehensively. More than fifty years before, she was born in a stifling Ukrainian village, and now she is in the *Caput Mundi*. "Grandma, did the Romans really vomit in the Baths of Caracalla?"

"Perhaps they did, little Igor. Perhaps they did."

Grandma has other things to worry about. Her husband Ilya, my father's stepfather, is a dour worker whose own best buddies in Leningrad have nicknamed him Goebbels. By Russian standards he is not an alcoholic, meaning he is not drunk from eight in the morning until pass-out time at night. Still Grandma Polya has had to carry him off the tram more than once, and more than twice he has beshat himself in public. Since his arrival, our small rooms in Ostia are loud with battle. One day I find a treasure on the staircase of Grandma's building, a gold watch encrusted with possible diamonds. My father returns it to the Italian family living atop Grandma and Ilya, and they offer him a fifty-dollar reward. Puffed with pride, my father generously refuses the astronomic sum. The Italians counter with a five-dollar reward and a free trip to a local café for a cappuccino and some panini. "Idiot!" Ilya shouts at my father, with his little gopher-like head atremble and the perpetual web of spittle in front of him. "Good-for-nothing! We could have been rich! A diamond watch!"

"God will see my deed and bless me," Papa replies magnanimously.

"God will see how stupid you are and never send you anything else!"

"Shut your stinking mouth!"

"Go to the dick!"

"Don't swear. The child can hear."

In my bathroom with my Raphael Madonna as the adult world trembles around me: "Santa Maria, Santa Maria, Santa Maria." And then my memorized list of Roman Forum ruins: "Temple of Saturn, Temple of Vespasian, Temple of Castor and Pollux, Temple of Vesta, Temple of Caesar."

Two handsome Americans from the CIA come to interview Papa. They want to know about his previous job at the LOMO (Leningrad Optical Mechanical Amalgamation) factory, present-day makers of the hipster cameras used in Lomography, but back in 1978 manufacturers of telescopes and sensitive military technology. Of course, my father has never been anywhere *near* the sensitive military stuff. He had been known to conduct "disruptive pro-Zionist and anti-Soviet conversations" about Israel and the 1967 Six-Day War, possibly the most glorious six days of his life, until one day his boss called him in and said, "Fuck your mother, Shteyngart, you can't do anything right! Get out of here!" A stroke of luck to have a father with such a big mouth, for had he become acquainted with the factory's military technology, we would never have been allowed to leave the Soviet Union.

The enemy spooks leave empty-handed, but one day my father sits me down for a chat. My toys, at the time, in addition to my Mozart candy wrapper and my Madonna, are two clothespins with which we hang our laundry to dry in the Mediterranean heat. One is a red "Tupolev" and the other a blue "Boeing." Whenever I'm not drooling over the Sistine Chapel, I do my boy's stuff. I race the two airplanes across the quiet Ostia streets, across the cold sands of the nearby beaches, always letting the Tupolev plane win over the enemy jetliner.

The skies over Ostia are sunny and the May air is brisk, the perfect atmosphere for a U.S.-USSR jet race.

My father and I are sitting on the shabby bedspread in our apartment. I prepare my Boeing and Tupolev clothespins. And he tells me what he knows. It was all a lie. Communism, Latin Lenin, the Komsomol youth league, the Bolsheviks, the fatty ham, Channel One, the Red Army, the electric rubber smell on the metro, the polluted Soviet haze over the Stalinist contours above Moscow Square, everything we said to each other, everything we were.

We are going to the enemy.

"But, Papa, the Tupolev-154 is still faster than the Boeing 727?"

In a resolved tone: "The fastest plane in the world is the Concorde SST."

"One of our planes?"

"It is flown by British Airways and Air France."

"So. It means. You're saying . . ."

We *are* the enemy.

• • •

I am walking down the Ostia boardwalk with my grandmother. In the distance is the Luna Park's sad little Ferris wheel I am still too afraid to ride. The Tupolev and the Boeing take off, and I clatter down the wooden runway with the two clothespins in my hands above my head, circling my grandma Polya, who lumbers forward lost in her own thoughts, smiling occasionally because her little grandson is healthy and running around with two clothespins. The red pin, the

Tupolev, instinctively reaches for the sky, wants to win over the blue Boeing, just as the stylized lines of the Kremlin are reaching for the red star, because we are a nation of workers and strivers. *We.*

The goal of politics is to make us children. The more heinous the system the more this is true. The Soviet system worked best when its adults—its men, in particular—were welcomed to stay at the emotional level of not-particularly-advanced teenagers. Often at a dinner table, a male *Homo soveticus* will say something uncouth, hurtful, disgusting, because this is his teenager's right and prerogative, this is what the system has raised him to be, and his wife will say, *Da tishe!*—Be quiet!—and then look around the table, embarrassed. And the man will laugh bitterly to himself and say, *Nu ladno,* it's nothing, and wave away the venom he has left on the table.

The blue pin is overtaking the red pin, the Boeing is too fast, too well designed, to lose. I do not want to be a child. I do not want to be wrong. I do not want to be a lie.

We are crossing the Atlantic on an Alitalia Rome-JFK flight. The stewardess, as devoted and beautiful as the Madonna in my pocket—my Moscow Olympics pin is swimming in the Mediterranean—brings me a special gift, a glossy map of the world and a collection of stickers representing the various models of Boeing in the Alitalia stable. I am encouraged to pin the Boeings all over the map. Here is the vast red terra incognita of the Soviet Union, and there is the smaller blue mass of the United States with its strange Floridian growth on one side. Between these two empires lies the rest of the world.

Our plane dips its wing as it approaches, and we catch a jumble of tall gray buildings filling up the window like the future. We are approaching the last twenty years of the American Century.

7.

WE ARE THE ENEMY

One of the few photographs we have from this period. We were too busy suffering.

1979. Coming to America after a childhood spent in the Soviet Union is equivalent to stumbling off a monochromatic cliff and landing in a pool of pure Technicolor. I am pressing my nose to the window of the taxiing jetliner, watching the first hints of my new homeland passing by. Oh, that immense solidity! The sweep of what used to be JFK's Pan Am terminal with its "flying saucer" roof and, above, the expanse of sky that doesn't press down on Queens, as the Russian sky tramples Leningrad, but flows past in waves, allotting a bit of itself to each red-bricked or aluminum-sided house and to each of the lucky families that dwells within. The airliners in their bright liveries are clustering around a sea of gates like hungry immigrants trying to get in, Sabena, Lufthansa, Aer Lingus, Avianca.

The intensity of arrival will not abate. Everything is revelation. On the ride from the airport, I am shocked by my first highway overpass, the way the car (a private car bigger than three Soviet Ladas) leans into the curve hundreds of feet above the greenery of Queens. Here we are floating through air but *in a car*. And buckled into the backseat, with my parents also leaning into the airborne curve, I feel the same emotions I will experience when choking upon my first cheesy American pizza slice months later—elation, visceral excitement, but also fear. How will I ever measure up to the gentle, smiling giants strolling this land who launch their cars like cosmonauts into the infinite American sky and who live like lords in their little castles on forty-by-one-hundred-foot lots in Kew Gardens, Queens? How will I ever learn to speak English the way they do, in a way so informal and direct, but with the words circling the air like homing pigeons?

• • •

But along with the revelation of arrival is the reality of my family. It is fitting that I am wearing my Italian sweater with its epaulets. The Alitalia plane was also a troop transport. I have landed in a war zone.

There are two hateful words that will define my next decade in America. The first is *rodstvenniki;* see under "Relatives." The second is *razvod;* see under "Divorce."

Our first problems are geographic. My mother doesn't want to go to New York, which in the 1970s is known around the world as a bankrupt, polluted, crime-ridden metropolis. Channel One in Leningrad has dutifully shown us clips of the homeless *negry* on Manhattan streets choking under billows of racism and smog. We have also been told that San Francisco would be better for my asthma. (At least one fellow Russian asthmatic I know ended up in dry, sun-baked Arizona based on similar geographic principles.) But the matriarch of my father's relatives, Aunt Sonya, wants my father to sell leather jackets at the flea market with her son, Grisha.* In Rome, my mother had been petitioning the venerable Hebrew Immigrant Aid Society, the deliverer of Soviet Jews, to send us to San Francisco while in New York Aunt Sonya has been petitioning for us to come help them sell leather jackets.

Family reunification takes precedence, and we are sent to New York instead of Northern California, where so many members of my generation of Soviet immigrants are currently making a fantastical living in the Google sector of the economy. My mother, having abandoned her own dying mother in Leningrad, has been thrust into the maw of my father's family, whom she regards as *volchya poroda*.

A wolfish breed.

In addition to Grandma Galya, we have abandoned two beautiful Europeanish cities, Leningrad and Rome, for—Queens. Which is where the wolfish breed lives. We are surrounded by constellations of redbrick apartment buildings with struggling people of many races and creeds. To my mother's eye the whole setup looks like a sad approximation of what cultured European life should be.

My parents and I are housed together with Aunt Sonya in her small Forest Hills apartment. The experience of hearing the word *rodstven-niki* (relatives) slither out of my parents' mouths has soured me on the very concept of having relations, and one particular incident from the days we live together has stuck inside my memory hole. My older Distant Cousin Tima has done something bad, has incorrectly sold a leather jacket at the flea market perhaps, and his father, Grisha, strikes him in front of the whole family. There's a Russian phrase here—*dal emu po shee,* to give one across the neck. I am on the floor of Aunt Sonya's apartment with my new toy, an American pen that you can click open and shut, completely engrossed in the beautiful clicking motion, and then: the sound of open palm hitting adolescent neck. Distant Cousin Tima is a swarthy, gangly boy with a Sephardic-like outbreak of mustache, and I can see him cringe and fold into himself

---

* The names of my father's relatives have been changed.

as he's being struck. He stands there with the hurt on his neck, with everyone's eyes on him as if he were naked. My first thought is: *I'm not the one being hit!* And my second: *Tima is not going to cry.* And he doesn't. He shrugs it off, smiles bitterly, and then stores it up for some future use. This is what will separate Distant Cousin Tima, or Tima, MD, as he is now called, from a crybaby like me.

• • •

Industrious and crafty, our relatives are already making the kind of flea market money that will soon land them in one of Long Island's most storied suburbs, the kind of money that requires many strikes across the neck. In 1979, some of that money has been sunk into televisions so big (a diagonal measurement of twenty-five inches!) that I try not to play with my pen next to them, worried that if they explode in the Soviet manner they will take the entire living room down with them. Money has also been spent on *stenki*, literally "walls," a kind of mahogany-based shelving unit, lacquered to a fanatical buff, that, along with the leather jacket, is so loved by Russians. Lying on the floor, I stare at my own mahogany reflection, knowing that the lacquered "walls" and the twenty-five-inch Zenith with Space Command remote control are the utmost in human achievement. If we do everything right, if my parents learn to sell leather jackets with great cunning, someday we can live like this, too.

Through the hairy network of immigrants, my father finds an apartment in quiet and safe Kew Gardens, Queens, for the fair price of $235 per month. The one-bedroom apartment will have to accommodate three generations of us: me, Mama, Papa, Grandma Polya, and her belligerent husband Ilya, or Goebbels to his friends. With our two army-green sacks and three orange suitcases made out of *real Polish leather,* we leave one battlefield, our wolfish relatives, for closer quarters in which to nurse Old World grievances and to brew fresh New World ones.

As for the wolfish relatives themselves, I hardly see them after we get our own apartment, but I hear about them daily. They have been petitioning my father to leave my mother and find a woman of, let's say, a more flea market disposition. The more my mother cries in the living room over all those permed aunties telling Papa to leave her, the more I cry in the bathroom. Twenty-two years later, a more recently arrived relative, a middle-aged man who is also the kindest of their lot, will throw my first novel on the floor and spit on it, perhaps out of ideological considerations. When I think of my relatives, I think of this kind of emotional village excess. To throw the book on the floor, fine. To spit on it, sure. But to do both? This is not a Bollywood movie.

The apartment is off busy Union Turnpike, close to the juncture where it noisily confronts the Grand Central Parkway and Van Wyck Expressway and across from the Kew Motor Inn, a 1960s slab that we are too Fresh off the Boat to recognize as "the most famous and exotic couples-friendly motel in Queens." The Egyptian Room, yours for only forty-nine dollars an hour, looks oddly like the mirrored, lacquered, Cleopatra-friendly rooms of our relatives. All one has to do is take off the leather jacket, pay the hooker, and you're home.

Our apartment gives out onto a pleasant courtyard with a dozen oaks that are home to a handful of squirrels. I try to present these fat, bushy-tailed creatures with curvaceous peanuts, a true American marvel, just a press of middle finger and thumb and they spill out their crunchy treasure. The squirrels stare directly into my eyes, their hungry cheeks quivering, and when I lean down to throw them my treat, they are almost within reach, the fearless urban rodents. I identify a family of three of them, a perfect counterpart to my own immediate family: One seems anxious, one unhappy, and one too young to know the difference. I call them Laika, Belka, and Strelka, after the three dog cosmonauts launched into space in the 1950s and '60s. I know I shouldn't think along Soviet lines anymore, but Belka, the second dog's name, means "squirrel" in Russian, so what am I supposed to do?

• • •

The first momentous thing that happens to me in Kew Gardens, Queens, is that I fall in love with cereal boxes. We are too poor to afford toys at this point, but we do have to eat. Cereal is food, sort of. It tastes grainy, easy and light, with a hint of false fruitiness. It tastes the way America feels. I'm obsessed with the fact that many cereal boxes come with prizes inside, which seems to me an unprecedented miracle. Something for nothing. My favorite comes in a box of cereal called Honeycomb, a box featuring a healthy freckled white kid—I begin to accept him as an important role model—on a bike flying through the sky. (Many years later I learn he's probably "popping a wheelie.") What you get inside each box of Honeycomb are small license plates to be tied to the rear of your bicycle. The license plates are much smaller than the real thing, but they have a nice metallic heft to them. I keep getting MICHIGAN, a very simple plate, white letters on a black base. I trace the word with my finger. I speak it aloud, getting most of the sounds wrong. MEESHUGAN.

When I have a thick stack of plates, I hold them in my hand and spread them out like playing cards. I casually throw them on the dingy mattress my parents have hauled out of a nearby trash heap—then scoop them up and press them to my chest for no reason. I hide them under my pillow, then ferret them out like a demented post-Soviet dog. Each plate is terribly unique. Some states present themselves as "America's Dairyland"; others wish to "Live Free or Die." What I need now, in a very serious way, is to get an actual bike.

In America the distance between wanting something and having it delivered to your living room is not terribly great. I want a bike, so some rich American neighbor (they're all unspeakably rich) gives me a bike. A rusted red monstrosity with the spokes coming dangerously undone, but there it is. I tie a license plate to the bicycle, and I spend most of my day wondering which plate to use next, citrus-sunny FLORIDA or snowy VERMONT. This is what America is about: choice.

I don't have much choice in pals, but there's a one-eyed girl in our building complex whom I have sort of befriended. She's tiny and scrappy, and poor just like us. We're suspicious of each other at first, but I'm an immigrant and she has one eye, so we're even. The girl rides around on a half-broken bike just like mine, and she keeps falling and scraping herself (rumor is that's how she lost her eye) and bawling whenever her palms get bloodied, her blond head raised up to the sky. One day she sees me riding my banged-up bicycle with the Honeycomb license plate clanging behind me, and she screams, "MICHIGAN! MICHIGAN!" And I ride ahead, smiling and tooting my bike horn, proud of the English letters that are attached somewhere below my ass. Michigan! Michigan! with its bluish-black license plate the color of my friend's remaining eye. Michigan, with its delicious American name. How lucky one must be to live there.

And even here, so far away from the wonder towns of Lansing, Flint, and Detroit, something like a life is beginning for me. I have a semblance of health, the lungs are accepting and absorbing oxygen, my Soviet-o-mania is being kept at bay by Honeycomb license plates and the colorful old stash of *All Rome, All Venice,* and *All Florence* books, which I look back on as my new founding texts. I am allowed to buy a stamp album with the portrait of a jaunty pirate on the cover and also to order a thousand stamps from a stamp company in upstate New York. Some of the stamps are from the Soviet Union, to my chagrin, reminders of the ever-present upcoming Moscow Olympics, but then there are gorgeous golden stamps from Haiti bearing the images of people at work in the fields, the people we have heard so much about, that is to say, black people. (Some of the other stamps, for no reason I can now discern, are marked DEUTSCHES REICH; one features a jeep being lifted into the air by an explosion. In another, a short, uniformed man with a funny little mustache bends down to cradle the cheek of a girl holding up a basket of flowers, beneath the words 20 APRIL 1940.)

Underemployed Papa and I go to the neighborhood park down the street. At first, we are confused by the boys who like to run around a dusty field after they hit a ball with a hollow aluminum stick for no reason. So we bring *our* thing along, a European soccer ball, and some older boys join us in kicking it. I am not good at *futbol,* but then, I am not completely incompetent at it either, not with Papa by my side, being strong.

And then it all goes terribly wrong.

8.

THE SOLOMON SCHECHTER
SCHOOL OF QUEENS

A good Jewish boy smiles for his Hebrew school class photo. Notice the widely spaced teeth, the slight furrows beneath his eyes, and the Casio music wristwatch, which played both "The Star-Spangled Banner" and the Russian "Kalinka" ("Little Guelder Rose"). The author hated himself for preferring the latter.

AM STANDING amid a gaggle of boys in white shirts and skullcaps and girls in long dresses wailing a prayer in an ancient language. Adults are on hand to make sure we are all singing in unison; that is to say, refusing to wail is not an option. *"Sh'ma Yisroel,"* I wail, obediently, *"Adonai Eloheinu, Adonai Echad."*

Hear, O Israel, the Lord is our God, the Lord is One.

I'm not sure what the Hebrew words mean (there is an English translation in the prayer book, only I don't know any English either), but I know the tone. There is something plaintive in the way we boys and girls are beseeching the Almighty. What we're doing, I think, is supplicating. And the members of my family are no strangers to supplication. We are the Grain Jews, brought from the Soviet Union to America by Jimmy Carter in exchange for so many tons of grain and a touch of advanced technology. We are poor. We are at the mercy of others: food stamps from the American government, financial aid from refugee organizations, secondhand Batman and Green Lantern T-shirts and scuffed furniture gathered by kind American Jews. I am sitting in the cafeteria of the Hebrew school, surrounded first by the walls of this frightening institution—a gray piece of modern architecture liberally inlaid with panes of tinted glass—with its large, sweaty rabbi, its young, underpaid teachers, and its noisy, undisciplined American Jewish kids, and, in a larger sense, surrounded by America: a complex, media-driven, gadget-happy society, whose images and language are the lingua franca of the world and whose flowery odors and easy smiles are completely beyond me. I'm sitting there, alone at a separate lunch table from all the other kids, a small boy in already oversize glasses and the same damn polka-dot-and-vertical-striped shirt, perhaps the product of some Polka Dot Shirt Factory #12 in Sverdlovsk or, if it only existed, Shirtsk, and what I'm doing is I'm talking to myself.

I'm talking to myself in Russian.

Am I muttering long-remembered crap written in capital letters on the Soviet metro: 1959—SOVIET SPACE ROCKET REACHES THE SURFACE OF THE MOON? It's very possible. Am I nervously whispering an old Russian childhood ditty (one that would later find its way into one of my stories written as an adult): "Let it always be sunny, let there always be blue skies, let there always be Mommy, let there always be *me*." Very possible. Because what I need now, in this unhappy, alien place, is Mommy, the woman who sews my mittens to my great furry overcoat—the one that has earned me the moniker Stinky Russian Bear, or SRB in the industry—for otherwise I will lose them, as I have already lost the bottle of glue, lined notebook, and crayons that accompany me to first grade. "Mamochka," I will tell her tonight, "don't be sad. If I lost the glue today, I won't be able to lose it tomorrow."

One thing is certain—along with Mommy and Papa and one sweet kid, the son of liberal American parents who have induced him to play with me—the Russian language is my friend. It's comfortable around me. It knows things the noisy brats around me, who laugh and point as I intone my Slavic sibilants, will never understand. The way the gray-green stone of the Vorontsovsky Palace in Crimea, where we used to take our summer vacations, matches the mountains and forests around it. The way you get frisked at the Pulkovo Airport in Leningrad, the customs guard taking off your hat and feeling it up for contraband diamonds. The way SOVIET SCIENTISTS CREATE THE FIRST CHAIN REACTION THEORY in 1934.

Teachers try to intervene. They tell me to get rid of the great furry overcoat. Trim my unkempt, bushy hair a little. Stop talking to myself in Russian. Be more, you know, *normal.* I am invited to play with the liberals' son, a gentle, well-fed fellow who seems lost in the wilderness of eastern Queens. We go to a pizza parlor, and, as I inhale a slice, a large string of gooey mozzarella cheese gets stuck in my throat. Using most of my fingers, I try to pull the cheese out. I choke. I gesture about. I panic. I moo at our chaperone, a graceful American mama. *Pomogite!* I mouth. Help! I am caught in a world of cheap endless cheese. I can see a new placard for the Leningrad metro. 1979—FIRST SOVIET CHILD CHOKES ON CAPITALIST PIZZA. When it's all over, I sit there shuddering, my hands covered with spittle and spent mozzarella. This is no way to live.

• • •

I am not good with others. In Leningrad, I had been too sick to go to preschool. My mother worked as a music teacher at a kindergarten, and she brought me there on several occasions when my grandmas were not around to babysit. Invariably, I would stand up in front of the class, in front of all those pretty Slavic girls with their white bows, in front of all the xylophones arranged ceremoniously beneath the requisite portrait of musical Lenin, and announce in my self-important Mama's Only voice to the older children: "I have something to say to you! I will not participate in any activities today. I will only sit and watch."

But in Hebrew school, unless I am choking on a pizza, I am too ashamed to say anything.

There is one exception. The school bus is taking the Hebrew school kids back to our homes, and before the bus can get into the tonier parts of Forest Hills and beyond, we pass our five-story apartment building. "Ober zer!" I cry. "Ober zer! Loook at eet! Eet izt mai haus!"

And for the first time I am not the weirdo at the lunch table, and no one is laughing at me and making crazy cuckoo signs around their temples. "That's your house?" the kids shout. *"You live in that whole place?* You must be so rich! Why do you have to wear my Green Lantern T-shirt from summer camp?"

As I get off the bus I finally begin to understand the miscommunication. The children think the entire building, all fifty apartments, is my home.

· · ·

In the tight kitchen of our "mansion" my father and my mother are going at it with drunk Step-grandfather Ilya. There are family fights that I can now perceive only as colors—a searing yellow-green across my vision whenever I see an elderly bald man clench his fists. No one can curse with the depth and volume of Step-grandfather Ilya. Everyone is going to the dick tonight, and everybody's mother will be fucked.

I plop on the army cot that is my new bed, a piece of furniture that's been donated by two young neighborhood Jews—their amazing-sounding names are Michael and Zev—who for all their kindness seem to me like a second incarnation of the woman in the

Vienna airport, the one who gave me the Mozart candy with its prized wrapper. Around our table, Michael and Zev's democratic and Democratic voices ring out countered by my father's adventurous Republican English, as our new American friends support the departing Georgia peanut farmer presently in the White House and my father pines for the California actor, and in the end all is settled by the gift of a candy (Milky Way!), which I'm not allowed to eat on account of asthma, or more useful items we lack, hangers, a steam iron. For the rest of our furniture ensemble, we have selected a sofa from a nearby garbage dump and bunched up sheets to use for pillows.

When I feel sad from Hebrew school, I turn to my Soviet atlas and an Eastern Air Lines toy plane my mother bought for half a dollar on Fourteenth Street, the boulevard of discount dreams in faraway Manhattan. Using my atlas, I plot out the flight time to Rome, then to Vienna, then to East Berlin, then back to Leningrad. I memorize the coordinates of the important airports. I launch my plane down the runway of our cluttered apartment, then I sit there with the plane in my hand for the eight and a half hours it takes to get to Rome, humming to myself the sounds of the jet engine: "*Zhhhh . . . Mmmm-mmm . . . Zhhhhh . . . Mmmmm . . .*" Finally I land the plane on the green army cot (also known as Leonardo da Vinci Airport) and the next day resume the journey to Leningrad.

Soviet refugees do not freely use the diagnosis obsessive-compulsive disorder. All I know back then is that my plastic plane must *never* touch the floor until it is time to land, else all the passengers, my whole family, will die. When my asthma reappears and I can no longer *zhhhh* and *mmmm* I will tie the plane to a string hanging from the army cot so that it is technically still in the air, then sit there and watch it like the obedient child that I am, while family life takes off and crashes all around me.

My travels become more complex. I go through Paris, Amsterdam, Helsinki, then back to Leningrad. Then through London, Amsterdam, Warsaw, Moscow, Leningrad. Tokyo and Vladivostok. I become an expert on flight times and the names of important world cities.

Around this time my father begins a difficult spiritual quest. He has found an Orthodox synagogue two blocks away from us. He does not have a proper yarmulke but does possess a multicolored baseball cap with a sea bass on it. One Sabbath he decides to walk down to the shul and sits in a pew in the back. The worshippers at first think he's "a drunken Spanisher from the street." But when they realize he's one of the mythical Russian Jews they've heard about on TV, one of their long-lost coreligionists, they shower him with unadulterated love. One of them, a follower of the ultranationalist Rabbi Kahane, gives him ten American dollars. It is the Sabbath and handling money is verboten, but making sure a Jew has enough to eat takes precedence. When my father gets his first job and makes a little cash himself, he will give two hundred dollars to Kach, Rabbi Kahane's soon-to-be-outlawed organization in Israel—driving the Arabs into the sea a central plank of their platform. And when it is time for us to buy our first apartment, another congregant who happens to be the local mailman will lend us four hundred dollars, no questions asked, toward the down payment. I guess this is what people mean when they say "community."*

The next Shabbat and almost every Friday thereafter, I am brought into the tiny yellow building of Young Israel, where I can rock and sway along with the cheaply attired but kind men (the women are sent to a balcony above us) who seem to accept me and don't think I'm crazy when I accidentally spit out something in Russian or casually molest the English language with my tongue.

When the congregants of Young Israel learn that my mother was a pianist in Russia and my father used to sing opera, they invite our family to give a concert. After months of anonymity in a foreign country, my father's bass reverberates across the small, crowded sanctuary as my mother accompanies on piano. Papa sings the expected Chaliapin ditty "Ochi Chyornye" ("Dark Eyes") and the Yiddish stan-

---

* Eventually the State Department will add Kach to its list of foreign terrorist organizations, and the rabbi himself will be assassinated in New York in 1990.

dard "Ofyn Pripetchek" ("Learn, children, don't be afraid / Every beginning is hard").

My exploits with the Soviet atlas and the nine-hour flights to Stockholm have not gone unnoticed. And so, *I* am presented as the final act—the seven-year-old refugee who can name any world capital! The worshippers shout out, "Belgium!" "Japan!" "Uruguay!" "Indonesia!" Nervous yet excited, I answer those four right but flub the last: Chad. As cosmopolitan as my travels are, I have never flown my plastic Eastern Air Lines jet to N'Djamena. Despite my humiliation, we are given $250 by the congregation for our performance, which we turn into a size 2 Harvé Benard business suit. My tiny mother fills it just in time for her first successful clerk-typist job interview.

The worshippers at Young Israel suggest I attend Solomon Schechter, a conservative Hebrew day school on a sad stretch of nearby Parsons Boulevard. My father wants very much to be a practicing Jew. My mother, half Jewish, sometimes prays in the Christian manner, palms clasped together, to the God of Good Health and Steady Raises at the Queens watch factory where she now slaves away, rejoicing when the boss gives out free ice cream instead of air-conditioning.

There are decent public schools in Queens, but we are scared of blacks. If you put together two Soviet immigrants in Queens or Brooklyn circa 1979, the subject of *shvartzes* or "the Spanish with their transistor radios" would come up by the third sentence, after the topic of asthma inhalers for little Igor or Misha is exhausted. But listen carefully to those conversations. There's hatred and fear, sure, but just a little down the line, laughter and relief. The happy recognition that, as unemployed and clueless as we are, there is a reservoir of disgust in our new homeland for someone other than ourselves. We are refugees and even Jews, which in the Soviet Union never won you any favors, but we are also something that we never really had the chance to appreciate back home. We are white.

Over in the leafier parts of Kew Gardens and Forest Hills, the tribal hatred of blacks and Hispanics stands out partly because there aren't really any blacks or Hispanics. My mother's one encounter with "criminality" on Union Turnpike: A big white cracker in a convertible pulls up to her, takes out his penis, and shouts, "Hey, baby, I have a big one!"

Still, everyone knows what to do when you encounter a dark-skinned person: You run.

Because they want to rape us so very badly, us in our jackets made of *real Polish leather.* And "the Spanish with their transistor radios," you know what else they have, other than the transistor radios? Switchblades. So if they see a seven-year-old Russian boy walking down the street with his asthma inhaler, they'll come over and cut him to death. *Prosto tak.* Just like that. The lesson being you should never let your seven-year-old boy out alone. (In fact, until I turn thirteen, my grandmother will not allow me to walk down a quiet street in peaceful Forest Hills *without holding her hand.* Eyes darting one hundred meters in every direction, she is ready to cover my body with hers lest one of those animals with the switchblades comes near.)

Oh, and if you save up enough money for a Zenith television set with a Space Command remote control, a strong black will surely come by, hoist it onto his shoulder, and run down the street with it. And then a Spanish will run down the street after the black with his transistor radio for accompaniment, playing his *cucaracha* music. One of them will slip the Space Command into his pocket, too, and then you'll really have nothing.

And so, the safety of our own kind.

And so, the Solomon Schechter School of Queens.

Or *Solomonka,* as we Russians like to call it.

Only they'll be beating the shit out of me in *Solomonka,* too.

• • •

I can't speak English too good, so I'm demoted by a grade. Instead of starting in second, I am sent to the first. In every grade through senior year of college I will be surrounded by boys and girls one year younger than I am. The smarter kids will be two years younger. In the annual class photo I will find myself handed down from the top row with the tallest kids to the bottom row, because even as I grow older I somehow grow relatively smaller.

How can I be so stupid (and so short)? Aren't I the kid who knows the difference between *The Allegory of Day* and *The Allegory of Night* in the Medici Chapel? Aren't I the author of *Lenin and His Magical Goose,* a masterwork of socialist realist literature, written before I learned to properly make *kaka* atop a toilet bowl? Don't I know the capitals of most countries except for Chad? But here, at age seven, begins my decline. First through the wonders of Hebrew school, then through the tube of American television and popular culture, then down (or should I say *up?*) the three-foot bong of Oberlin College, the sharpness of my little boy's intelligence will diminish step by step, school by school. The reflexive sense of wonder, of crying over a medal of the Madonna del Granduca and not knowing why, will be mostly replaced by survival and knowing perfectly well why. And survival will mean replacing the love of the beautiful with the love of what is *funny,* humor being the last resort of the besieged Jew, especially when he is placed among his own kind.

• • •

SSSQ, I write, worriedly, on the upper-right corner of every notebook for the next eight years. The Solomon Schechter School of Queens. The shorthand is imprinted on my mind, SSSQ. The *S*'s are as drunk as Step-grandfather Ilya, and they're falling all over one another; the *Q* is an *O* stabbed between the legs at an angle. Often I forget the *Q* entirely, leaving just the quasi-fascistic SSS. *Please work on your penmanship,* every teacher will dutifully write. *Pen* I know because it is my main toy. *Man* is someone like my father, strong enough to lift a used American air conditioner he has just bought for one hundred dollars. *Ship* is like the cruiser *Aurora* docked in Leningrad, the one that fired the fateful shot that started the October Revolution. But *pen-man-ship?*

SSSQ is my world. The hallways, the staircases, the rooms, are small, but so are we. Four hundred kids, grades kindergarten through eight, marching in two lines, boys and girls, height order. There's one Hebrew teacher, Mrs. R, middle aged, in large owlish glasses, who likes to make us laugh as she leads us, sticking two hands in front of her nose, making a little flute, and singing, "*Troo-loo-loo-loo-loo.*" Other than dispensing mirth to scared children, her task is making sure that every boy is wearing his yarmulke. The first, and nearly last, words of Hebrew I learn: *Eifo ha-kipah shelcha?* (Where is your yarmulke?) That's the sweet part of the day, being taken to class by Mrs. R. But in class with Mrs. A–Q and S–Z, not so much. Because I don't know what I'm doing. With my missing scissors and my missing glue and my missing crayons and my missing yarmulke and my missing shirt, the one with the insignia of a guy on a horse swinging a mallet, a *polo* shirt, I learn much too late, I am also missing. In fact, often I am in the wrong room, and everyone cracks up over that, and I, in my untied shoes, stand up and look around, mouth open, as Mrs. A through Q or Mrs. S through Z goes out to get Mrs. R. And Mrs. R with her light Israeli accent will stand with me out in the hall and ask me, "*Nu?* What happened?" "I—," I say. But that's about all I know: "I." So she'll bend down to tie my shoelaces while we both think it over. And then she'll take me to the right room, and the familiar faces of my classmates will fill up with a new bout of laughter, and the new Mrs. A to Z (but not R) will shout the word that is the official anthem of Solomon Schechter: *Sheket!* In English, "quiet." Or, more plaintively, *Sheket bevakasha!* "*Please* be quiet." And everything will fall into its usual state of entropy, students who can't be quiet, and teacher who can't teach, as Hebrew, the second language I don't know, the one that doesn't even appear on boxes of Honeycomb, bonks me on the head, coconut style. And I sit there, wheezing myself into an asthma attack that won't come until the weekend, wondering what possibly can happen to me next, as my shoes magically untie themselves, and then it's recess time, and Mrs. R takes us outside with her sweet *troo-loo-loo* past hallways with maps of Israel drawn years before the one my parents call "that *farkakte* Carter" and his Camp David Accords gave the Sinai Peninsula away to the Egyptians, and the walls filled with children's thank-you notes in bright Magic Marker, thank-you notes to the one who watches over us, the one whose name can't even be written out fully, he's so special, the one they call G-d or, sometimes, just to add to the confusion, Adonai. As in *Sh'ma Yisroel, Adonai Eloheinu, Adonai Echad.*

Recess. Out in the school yard, beneath a nearby sign that says VULCAN RUBBER (two words that will become significant, the first one in my teens, the second one, unfortunately, only in my twenties), the girls play hopscotch and the boys run around with their noisy selves and I sit by the side trying to occupy myself with a ladybug if it's warm, and my mittens if it's not, and my cold fingers if I've already lost my mittens for the day. I still can't differentiate the boys and girls by name. They are just one large mass of *Am Yisroel,* the Jewish nation, the darker, more aggressive ones from Israel, the lighter, happier ones from Great Neck. The liberal kid whose parents bring me over to play with him walks by on his own accord. His house in Kew Gardens is something I lack the vocabulary to describe. First of all, the whole building is his *own* house, and there is grass in front of it, and there is grass in back of it, and grass on the sides, and there are trees that belong to him, which are his personal property, so he can even cut them down if he wants to and he won't go to a labor camp. And inside the house, such games there are! Board games about taking over four railroads and entire neighborhoods and also "action figures" from *Star Wars,* which I don't know what it is. But someone kind has given me something from the *Star Wars,* and what it is is a tall, very hairy monkey, with a white bandolier around its naked body and a scowl on its face. Sometimes, when I'm especially alone, I'll take the monkey out, and the kids will shout "Chewie!" I guess that's Monkey's name. And then they'll laugh because Chewie is missing half his right arm, so you can't even stick in his black rifle with the bow attachment. So it's both good that I have Monkey and it's not good, because he's deficient. I also have my pen that goes click, but nobody wants any part of that.

Anyway, out at recess, the liberals' son comes over and says, "Gary, you want to play airplanes?" And first I look past him, because who would want to talk to me, and then who is this Gary anyway? And then I remember: It's me. We've thought it over as a family, and Igor is Frankenstein's assistant, and I have enough problems already. So we take IGOR, and we move around the *I, G, O,* and *R.* So there's GIRO (which would have been great for the last decade of the twentieth century) and ROGI (perfect for the first decade of the twenty-first), and GORI. That one's nice, it's the city where Stalin was born in Georgia, but still not perfectly right. But then there was that actor, Cooper, what's his name? And so two vowels are traded for two others, and GARY I am.

"I want to play airplanes," I say. More like shout: "I want to play airplanes!" Actually, why stint here? "I WANT TO PLAY AIRPLANES!" Because this is my chance to win over new friends. "To Jakarta," I shout, "you fly Gonolulu, Gawaii,* or Guam, short rest, put benzene into wings, then Tokyo, stop Jakarta."

The children look at me with keen American indifference or burning Israeli anger, the takeaway being *sheket bevakasha,* or maybe just *sheket.* In any case, *Shut up already, you crazy freak.*

The game of airplanes is as complex as every other interaction at SSSQ. The boys run around going "*ZHUUUUUUUUU*" with their arms outstretched, and then they knock one another down with those arms. I do not make it to Jakarta. I do not even make it as far as nearby Philadelphia Airport, at 39°52'19" N, 75°14'28". Someone bonks me on the head, and down I go, all passengers on the manifest dead.

· · ·

There's a movie theater on Main Street, and my father is excited because they are showing a French movie, and so it must be very cultured. The movie is called *Emmanuelle: The Joys of a Woman,* and it will be interesting to see how joyful these Frenchwomen actually are,

---

* In Russian, the *H* is often rendered as a *G,* hence the famous university Garvard in Massachusetts and my future alma mater, the somewhat-less-famous one in Oberlin, Ogio.

most likely because of their exquisite cultural patrimony. ("Balzac, Renoir, Pissarro, Voltaire," my father sings to me on the way over to the theater.) The next eighty-three minutes are spent with Papa's hairy hand clasped to my eyes, the Herculean task before me: getting it unclasped. The less explicit parts of *Emmanuelle: The Joys of a Woman* are set in a Hong Kong brothel or a Macao girls' boarding school, and then it's all downhill from there. Despite my father's best efforts I see about seven vaginas on the big screen that day, seven more than I will see for a very long time. Of course, we have to sit through the whole thing, since we have already paid for the tickets. And one of the male characters, a radio operator, is named Igor (*"OH, Igor, OUI!"*), my former name, so there's that.

My father and I walk silent and dazed back to our apartment. *"Nu?"* my mother asks.

Silence at first, uncharacteristic silence.

"Nu?"

"Every three minutes there was a love scene!" my father shouts. "Every which way, they did it! Like this . . . And then like that. And then they turned her over and—" I hope that, at the least, my mother and father scrounged up the four dollars to see the movie by themselves and faithfully followed the series through *Emmanuelle's Perfume* (1992) and *Emmanuelle in Venice* (1993) to its logical science fiction made-for-cable-TV conclusion, *Emmanuelle in Space* (1994). They deserved as much, the hardworking immigrants.

• • •

I'm not sure what to do with the knowledge gained at the soft French (actually, Dutch) hands of Emmanuelle. I am a little boy. But I know something is up, something hairy between the legs. Not between my legs, not yet, but between the legs of others.

At SSSQ, I find a book in English about Harriet Tubman, the former slave who rescued dozens of African Americans from a terrible place called Maryland. Maybe the Hebrew school librarian thought Tubman was Jewish (her moniker was Moses).

It's a tough book because it's in English, but there are many thrilling pictures of Tubman and her rescued slaves running through the awful Maryland on their way to Canada. And I am so angry at slavery, at this horrible *thing,* as angry as the people around me are at the blacks, so angry, in fact, that we've heard the new president, Ronald Reagan, is really going to give them one "across the neck." Lying on my army cot, Emmanuelle in the back of my mind, Harriet Tubman out front, I conjure an imaginary friend, a black boy or a girl just fled from Maryland. I am still ecumenical on the subject of gender, so s/he is lying next to me, his/her arms around me, my arms around him/her, and I just say over and over something I picked up on the street, "It's all going to be okay, Sally, I promise."

• • •

The fastest way to fly to N'Djamena, Chad, is through Air France's hub in Paris. Under optimal conditions, it can be done in sixteen hours and thirty-five minutes. I am flying there still.

9.

AGOOF

The Russian card game is called Durak, or The Fool. The object is to get rid of all of one's cards, lest one be labeled The Fool. In this photo, my father's hand is stronger than mine.

THE NEXT YEAR I get the present every boy wants. A circumcision.

At Solomon Schechter I have been given an appropriately sacrificial Hebrew name: Yitzhak, or Isaac. And so the knife is drawn at Coney Island Hospital, Orthodox men davening out a blessing in the adjoining room, a sedation mask placed over my mouth (perfect for an asthmatic boy with an anxiety disorder), and then the public hospital walls—green on green on green on green—disappear to be replaced by a dream where the horrible things lovingly perpetrated upon Emmanuelle in a Hong Kong brothel are done to me by the men in black hats.

And then the pain.

Mama, Papa, where are you?

And then the layers of pain.

Mama, Papa, help.

And then the layers of pain and humiliation.

My mother has cut a hole in my underwear so that my broken penis will not have to touch polyester. I have been transferred from my army cot to my parents' bed. I lie there with my ruined genital exposed to the outside world, and shockingly enough people come to visit, all of my relatives come to see the awful thing I have between my legs. "*Nu,* how do you feel?" they ask wolfishly.

"*Bol'no,*" I say. It hurts.

"*Zato evreichik!*" they cry in approval. But you're a little Jew now!

I cover up with the book I have at my side, *All Rome,* making a little tent over myself. What I've been staring at since coming home from the hospital is one of Pietro da Cortona's oils, *Rape of the Sabine Women.* The women are not being raped in the contemporary sense, of course, but rather being abducted by the first generation of Roman men, their little children weeping at their feet, parts of their breasts exposed à la *Emmanuelle in Hong Kong.* And these men in their tunics and their helmets, they are as strong and swarthy as my father. And I am as pale and helpless as—

I'm not suggesting what I seem to be suggesting here. Only that it has all come full circle to this. The Stinky Russian Bear, the second most hated boy in first and soon to be second grade of Hebrew school (I'll get to the *most* hated boy shortly), is lying, his crotch exposed, in his parents' bed with what feels like razor blades cutting through his penis, over and over again. (It goes without saying that the *procedure* at the public hospital did not go well.) There will be creatures in horror movies in my near future, the softshell crabs of Ridley Scott's *Alien* the most visually accomplished ones, but *this* baroque chiaroscuro of dried blood and thread will never find equal. And, to this day, whenever I see a naked blade, I shudder because I know what it can do to a boy of eight.

We've all done what we've had to since coming here. My mother has slaved in an overheated watch factory in Queens, my father has studied English and the other languages of the day, COBOL and Fortran, painstakingly. Our apartment is littered with IBM punch cards from my father's computer classes, which I handle with the same awe as I do the free Honeycomb license plates, intrigued as much by their crisp, beige, American feel as by the words and phrases my father has written upon them, English on one side, Russian on the other. I remember, for some reason, the following words: "industry" (*promyshlennost'*), "teapot" (*chainik*), "heart attack" (*infarkt*), "symbolism" (*simvolizm*), "mortgage" (*zaklad*), and "ranch" (*rancho*).

Still, we didn't come to this country just to one day get a *zaklad* for our *rancho,* did we? It wasn't *all* about the money. We came to be Jews, right? Or at least my father did. I didn't really have any feeling on the subject one way or another. And now there has to be *simvolizm.* And that's why I've been cut so brutally, to be more like the children who hate me so much at school, who hate me more than I will ever be hated for the rest of my life. They hate me because I come from the country our new president will soon declare to be the "Evil Empire," giving rise to the endless category of movies beginning with the word "Red"—*Red Dawn, Red Gerbil, Red Hamster.* "Commie!" they shout, with a jolly push into a soft Hebrew school wall. "Russki!"

But I got cut down there for you! I want to shout back at them. *I left Latin Lenin in Moscow Square just to get this circumcision. I'm a Jew like you, and doesn't that matter more than where I was born? Why won't you share a sticky Fruit Roll-Up with me?*

It is hard to question the choices my parents made during the long and strange days of immigration, and I think they mostly did all right given the circumstances. But allow me to travel up to the ceiling of our Kew Gardens one-bedroom, the way I frequently did during asthma attacks when I felt myself lifted out of my deoxygenated body, allow me to look down at the boy with his little toy, Chewie from *Star Wars* missing his right arm, and then his other little toy, the one so broken and deformed that for two years every act of urination has to be done through gritted teeth, the one framed by a genital-sized hole in his underwear, and allow me to ask the pertinent question: *What the fuck?*

And I know the answer, the fairly reasonable one, that my parents have to questions of this caliber: "But we didn't know."

Or, a more pathetic refugee one attributed to my mother: "We were told to do it."

Or a less reasonable one, the one I would attribute to my father: "But you have to be a man."

And now Yona Metzger, chief Ashkenazi rabbi of Israel: "It is a stamp, a seal on the body of a Jew."

• • •

In school, my penis is trying to put on a brave face. It can't tell anyone what happened or they'll make fun of its owner, Igor, or Gary, or whatever. But if they push The Refugee Formerly Known as Igor penis-first into the wall on the line to the lunchroom, well . . . *ouch*.

I'm trying to put a brave face on myself, too. I begin to write out my first lies in the new language.

GARY SHTEYNGART   SSS [SOLOMON SCHECHTER SCHOOL]
April 31 [sadly, there are only thirty days in April], 1981   Class 2C

Essay: SPRING

Spring is here   The weather is warm an rainy Birds come From south and sing songs In spring I play soccer baseball with my friends [lie] I ride my bike [the asthma is returning from all the stress, so mostly I don't] happy spring And I go fishing [with my father, who gets very upset if I don't bait the hook right] I like spring [relatively speaking] I hate winter [because I am even sicker than in spring].

Games in spring that I play baseball [lie, a drawing of me hitting a ball with what looks like a chain saw] bike [drawing of me and what looks like my circumcised penis, a swollen third leg, on top of a bicycle] friesbee [sic, lie, a drawing of me throwing a Frisbee at a boy's neck], soccer [lie, in another drawing, a boy is shouting at me, "Don't throw it to (sic) high," and I am shouting back, "Why I listen should?"]

Oh, who is this sportsman, I ask you? This tough-talking soccer-baseball-Frisbee hero with the tons of friends, whose every response borders on the insouciant: *Why I listen should?* Left behind by a year, he's still not mastering any English, that's for sure. Putting together a report on his beloved Italy, he describes the Colosseum fairly concisely as *Had roof not any more.* Summoned down to the office of the principal: "I do samsing bad?" "No, sweetheart," the dear secretaries say, "no, *asheine punim,*" "nice face" in Yiddish. They present me with bags from places called Gimbels and Macy's, filled with batches of their children's old clothes, more T-shirt appearances by the man who turns into a bat and his masked young slave, the Boy Wonder. Upstairs, back in class, with the sacks of clothes at my feet, the kids whisper at me.

"Whatchoo got there?"

"Dzhas samsing."

"More *new* T-shirts? Ooh, let's see!" Laughter.

"Dzhas samsing for my mazer."

Mrs. A–Z, not R: "*Sheket! Sheket bevakasha!*"

"Your *mazer* goes to Macy's?"

"Dzhas samsing for my mazer zey geeff daun ze stairs."

More laughter, except from the liberals' son and one other source. The kid who is hated even more than I am.

• • •

His name is Jerry Himmelstein (no, it's not). He was born in the U.S.A. to a set of American parents with all the rights and privileges

entailed therein. And yet: He is the most hated boy in all of Schechter. I know that I must study him hard and avoid certain behaviors if I am to maintain my position as the second most hated.

It is Shabbat, one of the boys has been chosen to be the *Abba* (the Father, Hebrew), usually gentle Isaac or Yitzhak. (Every other boy here, myself included, is given the Hebrew name of Yitzhak; all we're missing are the corresponding Abrahams, our fathers.) A girl, equally gentle Chava (Eve), is the *Imma,* or Mother. She is singing in a sweet preadolescent voice over the candles, *"Baruch atah Adonai . . . Le'hadlik ner shel Shabbat."* We are all salivating over the braided challah bread and the sour-sweet Kedem "wine" and the promise of two Hershey's chocolate candies to signal the end of the ritual. The Israeli kids in the back are inducting us into the world of adulthood. *Zain,* one of them says and grabs his crotch, then makes a challah shape with his hands. *Kus,* he says and sticks his fingers down an imaginary vagina (I know what that is! Oh, Emmanuelle!), then brings three or four fingers up to his nose and smells them. *Mmmm . . . kussss.* Even as Chava and Isaac are kosherizing the candles and the bread and the "wine" and the Hershey's Kisses for Shabbat, we boys in the back are smelling our fingers with a far more religious expression, until Jerry Himmelstein breaks out in this explosion that he does, the one that sounds like: *AGOOF!*

"Sheket!" Mrs. A–Z yells. *"SHEKET, YELADIM!!!"* Quiet, children!

"It was Jerry! It was Jerry!" everyone tattles at once.

"Jerry, *shtok et-hapeh!"* Shut your mouth!

And everyone is laughing, even me, because that's Jerry for you.

• • •

Agoof is Jerry Himmelstein's rallying cry and identity statement; it is half spoken and half sneezed, and it means: (1) I think this is funny; (2) I'm confused; (3) I don't know where I am; (4) I want to be one of you; (5) please stop hitting me; (6) I don't know how to express this yet because I am eight years old, and my family is troubled, and the world in the way it is presently configured does not treat me as a human, does not afford me all the freedoms promised in the Declaration of Independence that hangs on the wall of class 2C, and I do not understand why it has to be that way.

Does *agoof* also mean "I have goofed"? Is it apologetic in nature? I will never know.

Jerry Himmelstein has both shirttails hanging out of the front of his pants like little dicks, while I normally only have one. "Jerry!" Mrs. A–Z will say, pointing at his shirttails. *"Agoof!"* Jerry Himmelstein's shoes are untied like mine, but sometimes when he's nervously swinging his little Jerry legs up and down in class, a shoe will fly up in the air and it will hit someone in the head who, if it's a boy, will hit Jerry in the stomach by return mail. *"Agoof!"* Jerry's brown hair descends down his head as if an Italian had emptied a kettle of his favorite food upon it, and his teeth are as yellow as egg yolks. His face darts back and forth looking for potential enemies. A web of spittle will attach to his face when he's in full breakdown *agoof* mode. This will usually happen at a birthday party, let's say his own. An SSSQ girl will tell him, in one way or another, that he's not a person. *Agoof!* Then a boy will knock him down into the dirt or smush him with the leftovers of a magical Carvel Cookie Puss cake onto his pasta head. *Agoof!* Then it's time to be picked for Wiffle ball, and I'll be picked second to last and he will be picked last. *Agoof!* Then instead of hitting the Wiffle ball with the Wiffle bat he will clock himself with it, and then he'll be lying down on the "plate" clutching at his own chin. *Agoooooooof!* Then another girl, in OshKosh overalls or, later, in a Benetton sweater, will come over and, instead of administering help, inform him once more that he is not a person. And now all these *agoof*s have added up, as they must, and he sits there, hand to his jaw, hand to his stomach, hand to his face, hand to whatever part has been offended, and he's wailing like something out of the Torah, like something before Abraham even, like when the earth was exploding into place in Genesis. *Adonaaaaaaaaaai! Yaaaaaahweeeeeh!* And the more he wails, the more we laugh, the girls and boys of SSSQ, because it's pretty wonderful, his pain, pretty wonderful as far as these things go.

• • •

I take the role of Jerry Himmelstein's second-in-command seriously. I must be humiliated and hit, too. It is understood that anyone can hit me. That's what I'm there for, to absorb the sunlit, nascent-mustachioed hatred of the future homeowners of eastern Queens. In a school without excessive discipline, without excessive leadership, without excessive *education,* speed bumps must be provided so that the whole enterprise can run smoothly. The Stinky Russian Bear, the Red Gerbil, will rise to the occasion!

In the back of the school bus, my friend, another Yitzhak, is punching me in the stomach. Yitzi is only several steps up the totem above me: He's not from Forest Hills or Ramat Aviv, in the fancy north of Tel Aviv; he's from Soviet Georgia, and there's only his mother to care for him, the father I don't know where he went. I like Yitzi quite a lot, because he can hit me in my own language, and when I cry out *Bol'no!* (It hurts!), he'll know what it means. He also must know about my brand-spanking-new circumcision, because he never hits below the belt. His apartment is across the street from my grandmother, who watches me after school, and we'll go there to play a handheld electronic game called Donkey Kong after the school bus drops us off. He won't really hit me after we're out of sight of the other boys, so I think this is probably just a way to assert his place. In a combination of Russian and English we try to discuss ways to move ahead in the ranks of SSSQ, me the impressionable Boy Wonder to his Batman, while his mother serves us delicious Georgian-style dumplings heavy on the onion.

He's not a bad boy, Yitzi (one day, he'll grow up to be a wonderful man). He's just trying to become American, trying to get ahead. To that end, he has an amazing leather jacket with zippers, not made of *real Polish leather* but out of something much cooler, James Dean, for all I know. Years later, in the back of a crowded minibus huffing its way onto Moscow Square in what is now St. Petersburg, I am reintroduced with *major prejudice* to that Yitzi smell, the combination of leather and onion and the back of a bus. I cry out, "Excuse me! Excuse me!" fighting my way out of the packed vehicle and into the broken sunlight. "But you've just paid," the incredulous driver will say. "I forgot something," I say to him. "I forgot something at home." Which is the opposite of what I mean.

. . .

Tot kto ne byot, tot ne lyubit, my father likes to say.

He who doesn't hit, doesn't love.

Or is it: *Byot, znachit lyubit*? He hits, therefore he loves. Said "jokingly" of violent husbands in Russian marriages.

Essentially he's got it down. If you want to make someone love you, a child, say, you should hit him well. If you've come home from your new engineering job at a national laboratory on Long Island, exhausted and angry, because you don't speak the language well and the Jewish boss was gone and you had to deal with the evil German one and the stinking Chinese one, and the Portuguese and Greek engineers who are often your allies didn't intervene in your favor, and your wife's a *suka* with her fucking *rodstvenniki* in Leningrad, her dying mother, and her sisters to whom she's just sent three hundred dollars and a parcel of clothes, the money you will need not to starve if the German boss finally fires you, and your child is underfoot crawling in the shag carpet with his stupid pen or his Eastern Air Lines plane, you should give him one across the neck.

The child is shuddering beneath your hand. *"Ne bei menya!"* Don't hit me!

"You didn't do the math, nasty swine (*svoloch' gadkaya*)." You've assigned the child math problems out of a Soviet textbook that's more age-appropriate than the bullshit they teach at his Hebrew school, pictures of 4 + 3 − 2 Great Danes and then how many doggies do you have?, instead of

$$f''(x) = -4 * [\cos(x)\cos(x) - \sin(x)(-\sin(x))] / \cos^2(x).$$

And the bitch wife whom your wolfish relatives tell you you should really divorce pops out of the kitchen. *"Tol'ko ne golovu!"* Just don't hit his head! *He has to think with the head.*

"Zakroi rot vonyuchii." Shut your stinking mouth.

Really, *suka,* can't you see that love is in the air?

And then off you go, a smack across the left of the head, now the right, now the left. And the child is holding tight to the dizzying smacks, because each one is saying *You're mine* and *You'll always love me,* each one is a connection to the child that can never be broken. And what else is registering in that head being whipsawed left to right, right to left? The thing Mrs. R is singing in Hebrew as she's marching the kids down the corridor. *Yamin, smol, smol, yamin,* left, right, right, left, *troo-loo-loo-loo.*

• • •

My mother has it all wrong when it comes to love. She barely hits. She is the expert on the silent treatment. If I don't eat the farmer's cheese with canned peaches (eighty-nine cents: Grand Union), there will be no communication. Go find your love somewhere else. To this day, my mother will launch into a particular childhood aria of mine. Apparently during one especially long period of making me unexist, I started screaming to her, "If you won't speak to me, *luchshe ne zhit'!"* *It is better not to live!* And then I cried for hours, oh how I cried.

Luchshe ne zhit'! my mother likes to replay dramatically at Thanksgiving dinners, her hands spread out like Hamlet giving a soliloquy, perhaps because, in addition to being funny in her mind, the two-day-long silent treatment did what it was supposed to do. It made the child want to commit suicide without her love. *It is better not to live!* she cries out over her juicy Thanksgiving turkey and her "French" dessert. But I disagree with the efficacy of this technique. Yes, I don't want to live without her love and attention and fresh laundry for a while, but the sentiment passes quickly. Noninteraction does not have the same tried-and-true result as a pummeling. When you hit the child you're making contact. You're contacting the child's skin, his tender flanks, his head (with which he will eventually have to make money, true), but you are also saying something comforting: *I'm here.*

I'm here hitting you. I will never leave you, don't you worry, because I am the Lord, thy father. And just as I was pummeled, so I shall pummel you, and you shall pummel yours forever, *ve imru Amen.* Let us say Amen.

The danger is crying, of course, because crying is surrender. You have to get away from the blows and lie down someplace quiet and then cry. You have to think of what will happen next. Which is this: The pain will turn dull, then disappear, and when the weekend comes you will play a game called War at Sea with your father, rolling the dice to see if your British heavy cruiser can get out of the way of his German U-boat fast enough or if the entire course of World War II will have to be rewritten. There is no particular segue from the beating to the game, from the explosive weekday to the quiet sausage-and-kasha rhythms of the weekend. On Saturday, your father is calling you "little son" and "little one" and any UN observer sent to this armistice would take off his helmet, get back in his jeep, and make his way back to Geneva with a happy report.

But there's something about the tissue of the ears. Maybe a medical doctor can comment here. When you've been hit across the ears by your father, there's a stinging, a shameful stinging, that not only keeps your ears red seemingly for days but makes your eyes moisten, as if from allergies. And then, against your will, you will bring your hand up to your ear and sniffle. And then your father will say the one thing you don't want to hear, although he'll say it in a kind weekend way: "Eh, you. Snotty."

• • •

A year or so into my thirties I was honored to meet the remarkable Israeli writer Aharon Appelfeld. Our little turboprop had made the flight between Prague and Vienna, between two literary festivals, the first time Appelfeld had touched down on German-speaking soil since he had survived the camps in his teens. Waiting for our luggage at VIE, the airport where my family had first encountered the West, the seventy-something Appelfeld told me of his brief time among the Red Army after his camp had been liberated. One of the giant Russian soldiers described to Appelfeld his treatment at the hands of his superiors: *I byut i plakat' ne dayut*. They hit and they don't let me cry after.

On the day of the beating, in my little corner I am careful with the crying, a sniffle here, a spring shower of tears there, because otherwise the asthma attack will come. But maybe I want it to come. And soon enough, my father and mother are hovering over me as if nothing had happened an hour before, and perhaps nothing has. Father bundles the red comforter around my snotty chest, and my mother readies the inhaler: "One, two, three, *breathe in!*"

. . .

Night falls; my parents are living through their nightmares in their bed. The relatives buried alive by the Germans in Belorussian fields are rising through the alfalfa of modern American life. The inhaler's steroids have flooded my body. In the wood-paneled closet a man composed entirely of little pinpricks of light, The Lightman, is assembling himself. This is not a fantasy. This is not the SS or Stalin's henchmen or even the customs agent at Pulkovo Airport in Leningrad, the one who took off my fur hat. The Lightman may have been a human being once, but now he's just made of little shimmering dots of energy—like the nuclear energy they have inside the scary silver-domed reactor at my father's lab—and where his eyes should be are just the white sclera, minus the iris and pupil. In Russia I would open my eyes at night and find the room flooded with bursts of light, amoeba shapes that would expand and then falter like domestic supernovas, briefly outshining even the strange phosphorous nighttime glare of the explosive Signal television set. But here, in America, what used to merely keep me awake is coming together to destroy me. The pinpricks of light have achieved humanity. The Lightman is assembling himself over and over, making himself, unmaking himself, biding his time. He slots himself inside my closet and breathes his sickly adult breath all over my shirt and my pair of pants. Because he is made almost entirely of light he can travel from beneath a door jamb; he can scamper up the walls to the ceiling in no time. And I spend the whole night watching him advance slowly but monstrously toward me, my back stiff as a board, my slapped red ear pinging for him like a homing signal. I cannot tell my parents about the Lightman because they will think I'm crazy, and there's no room for crazy around here. It would be easier if the Lightman came up to me and did his worst, but once he's within inches of me he disassembles himself, becomes just a bunch of floating light specks and a pair of eyeless eyes, as if he knows that once he's fully revealed himself I'll have nothing to fear.

· · ·

The next day, there I am, sleepless and angry. Everything we do here at the Solomon Schechter School of Queens is, in a way, an exchange of ideas. Jerry Himmelstein sees me coming; the spittle is arching from his lips and blowing in the wind. He looks at me with dull unhappiness. This is how it must be, and there is no return from what we must do.

I punch him in the stomach, the soft American plushiness of it.

He takes two steps back and breathes out.

"Agoof."

10.

WE HAVE ALREADY WON

*The garden apartment (second floor, right) where
the author grew short, dark, and furry.*

THE TERRIBLE THING about the major belief systems (Leninism, Christianity) is that too often they are constructed along the premise that a difficult past can be traded in for a better future, that all adversity leads to *triumph,* either through the installation of telegraph poles (Leninism) or at Jesus' knee after physical death (Christianity). But the past is not simply redeemable for a better future. Every moment I have ever experienced as a child is as important as every moment I am experiencing now, or will experience ever. I guess what I'm saying is that not everybody should have children.

• • •

But in 1981 triumph is at hand. An official letter arrives in our mail-box. MR. S. SHITGART, YOU HAVE ALREADY WON $10,000,000.00!!! Sure, our last name is misspelled rather cruelly, but cardstock this thick does not lie, and the letter is from a major American publisher, to wit the Publishers Clearing House. I open the letter with shaking hands, and . . . a check falls out.

PAY TO THE ORDER OF S. SHITGART
TEN MILLION AND 00/100 DOLLARS

Our lives are about to change. I run down the stairs into the court-yard of our apartment complex. "Mama, Papa, we won! We won! *My millionery!*" We are millionaires!

"*Uspokoisya,*" my father says. *Calm down.* "Do you want an asthma attack?" But he is nervous and excited himself. *Tak, tak. Let us see what we have here.*

Around the glowing surface of the orange dining table imported from Romania we spread the contents of the voluminous packet. For two years we have been good new citizens, watching X-rated movies, getting jobs as engineers and clerk-typists (my mother's pianist's fin-gers will finally be put to meaningful use), learning to Pledge Alle-giance to the Flag of the United States of American, And For the Something For Which That It Stands, Unavoidable, With Money For All.

"*Bozhe moi,*" my mother says, *my God,* as we look at the pictures of a Mercedes flying off the deck of our yacht toward our new mansion with an Olympian swimming pool. "Oy, does it *have* to be a Mercedes? *Tphoo,* Nazis." "Don't worry, we can trade for a Cadillac." "*Bozhe moi.* How many bedrooms does this house have?" "Seven, eight, nine . . ." "You said the kids at school have houses like this?" "No, Papa, this one, *ours,* will be bigger!" "Hm, the way I understand it, the house doesn't come with the prize. The prize is just ten million, and then we buy the house separately." "*Tphoo,* they always say here 'sold separately.'" "You can forget about the yacht, it's dangerous." "But I know how to swim, Mama!" "How do you keep the pool open in the winter? Snow will get in." "Look, there are palm trees! Maybe it's in Florida." "Florida won't be good for your asthma with all that humidity." "I want to live in Miami! Maybe there aren't Hebrew schools in Miami." "Everywhere in America there are Hebrew schools." "We could have been in San Francisco already, if not for your wolfish relatives." "San Francisco? With the earthquakes?" "For ten million we can live in two places!" "Remember we have to pay taxes, so it's more like five million." "Oy, those welfare queens will get our other five million, like President Reagan said." "*Tphoo,* welfare queens."

We sit down and, using our collective four-hundred-word English vocabulary, begin to unravel the many documents before us. If we take the ten-million-dollar check to the bank tomorrow, how long before we can buy a new air conditioner? Wait, it says here that . . . Yes, we *have* already won the ten million dollars, no disputing that, but a *panel of judges* still has to award the money to us. First we must fill out the winner's form and select five national magazines that will be sent to us free, or at least the first issue of each will be free, and then the Americans will likely send us the rest of the money. Fair enough. First we must acclimate to our new wealth, expand our literacy. I am proud of Papa's new car, a bulbous 1977 Chevrolet Malibu Classic with only seven million miles on the odometer, but it is time to get acquainted with the finer autos, so I order *Car and Motor, Motor and Driver, Carburetor and Driver, Muffler and Owner.* And for the last selection, something that maybe has my *Star Wars* Monkey, Chewy, in it: *Isaac Asimov's Science Fiction Magazine.*

We sign everywhere we need to, even places we probably don't need to. We sign the fucking envelope. "Write neater!" Mama shouts at Papa. "No one can understand your signature!" "Calm yourself, calm yourself." "Get the stamps!" "Wait with your stamps already, what does it say. *No postadzh necessary.*" The Publishers Clearing House has even taken care of that little detail. Classy.

I walk solemnly to the mailbox and deposit our claim on the future. *Adonai Eloheinu,* I say to our new God, please help us get the ten million dollars so that Mama and Papa will not fight so much, and there will be no *razvod* between them, and let us live somewhere far away from Papa's wolfish *rodstvenniki* who cause all the trouble and let them not yell at Mama when she sends the money Papa says we don't have to her sisters and Grandma Galya in Leningrad who is dying still.

That night for the first time in months the Lightman without the pupils and irises does not appear in my wood-paneled closet. In my first sleep in weeks, *in my actual dreams,* I walk into SSSQ a multimillionaire, and the pretty girl with the big teeth who's always tanned from Florida vacation kisses me with those big teeth (I haven't gotten the mechanics of kissing down yet). The kids make fun of Jerry Himmelstein, but I say, *He's my friend now. Here is two dollars. Buy us both the Carvel flying saucer cookie ice cream. And keep the change, you* gurnisht! You nothing.

• • •

We find out the truth quickly and brutally. At their respective workplaces, my parents are told that the Publishers Clearing House regularly sends out the YOU HAVE ALREADY WON TEN MILLION DOLLARS missive and that these are routinely thrown in the trash by the savvy native-born. Depression settles over our nonmillionaire shoulders. In Russia the government was constantly telling us lies—wheat harvest is up, Uzbek baby goats give milk at an all-time high, Soviet crickets learn to sing the "Internationale" in honor of Brezhnev visit to local hayfield—but we cannot imagine that they would lie to our faces like that *here* in America, the Land of the *This* and the Home of the *That.* And so we don't give up hope entirely. The judges are probably reading our application right now. Maybe I should write them a letter in my burgeoning English. "Dear Publishers Clearing House, Spring is here. The weather is warm and rainy. Birds come From south and sing songs. My mothers pianist fingers hurt very much from the typing and she has only one suit for work. Please send the money soon. We love you, Family Shteyngart."

Meanwhile *Car & Parking* and the other Publishers Clearing House magazines are starting to pile up, taunting us with many hot naked centerfolds of the new Porsche 911, the official sports coupe of Reagan-era excess. We reluctantly begin to cancel our subscriptions to all of them, except for *Isaac Asimov's Science Fiction Magazine,* a small, square little number with the drawing of an exciting molting space creature on the cover hugging a boy in its claws.

Our dreams of being instantly rich are finished, but we are moving up nonetheless. We are saving every kopeck that comes our way via my father's junior engineering job and my mother's typing. I have my Eastern Air Lines plane, my pen, my broken Monkey, my Nazi stamp collection, my circumcised penis, the Mozart candy wrapper from the Vienna airport, the secret medal of Raphael's Madonna del Granduca (will they throw me out of Hebrew school if they find out?), *All Rome, Florence,* and *Venice,* my Soviet atlas, and a bunch of donated T-shirts. My mother has the size 2 Harvé Benard business suit. My father has made a fishing rod out of a stick. Pounds of disgusting marked-down farmer's cheese and kasha will feed us until we die of sadness, and if I don't clear my plate of that warm soggy shit the thunderclap of Papa's hand rings against my temple (Mama: "Just don't hit the head!") or Mama's silence will make me consider taking my own life to everyone's laughter.

Who are we?

Parents: *My bedniye.* We are poor folk.

Why can't I have the Monkey with both hands?

Parents: We are not Americans.

But you both have jobs.

Parents: We have to buy a house.

Yes, a house! The first step to Americanism. Who needs two-handed Monkey when we will soon have our own quasi-suburban home? And I don't fully understand the importance of these "action" figures anyway, when my pen and my Eastern Air Lines jet can fly all over the world if I only close my eyes and let it be so. *"Zhhhh . . . Mmmmmmm."* How much more *action* do you want? But at lunchtime the SSSQ boys do like to take out their Lukes and Obi-Wans and Yodels and set them on their desks to demonstrate just how much property falls within their purview. They talk in their already raspy Jewish voices: "I threw out my old Yodel because the paint on his ears was falling off and then I got two new ones and a Princess Lay-uh just so Ham Solo could *do* her."

Me: "Vow."

But before you can show off your Monkey and Yodel, indeed before you can have anyone "over," you need to have a proper house, not some cheap refugee craphole with folding army cots and drunk Stepgrandfather Ilya with a patched-up, oozing hole in his stomach from some insane surgery.

Only it can't be a whole house, because a *whole* house in the truly white sections of eastern Queens—Little Neck, Douglaston, Bayside— costs around $168,000 (roughly $430,000 in 2013 dollars), and that nut is too big to crack with our small Soviet rodent teeth. But kindly Zev, the young Kew Gardens Jew who acts as our unofficial adviser, tips us off to a development off the Long Island Expressway in Little Neck called Deepdale Gardens, sixty acres of affordable garden apartments built in the 1950s for returning servicemen. As me and Mama and Papa have been fighting in the Cold War since birth, we are entitled to one, too.

The savings begin in earnest. What am I talking about? For our bloodline, the savings have been in earnest since two thousand years before Christ. A three-bedroom apartment in Deepdale Gardens will cost $48,000, and 20 percent of it—$9,600—has to be tendered in cash. Everyone is conscripted to help. Our local mailman, whom we know from Young Israel synagogue, will chip in $400 without interest. My parents' Russian friends help out, $1,000 here, $500 there, usually at 15 percent interest per annum. This is how the system works, they lend to you, eventually you lend to them, until everyone has a home away from the minorities. On the back of an address book my parents keep the sums, and I follow along with them. March 12: $6,720. $6,720 divided by $9,600 = 70 percent. We're more than two-thirds of the way there! When my parents come back from seeing their friends I await them with the address book and the question: *"Odolzhili nam?"* Have they lent us money?

Sadly, our first address—252-67 Sixty-Third Avenue, Little Neck, Queens, 11362—is mostly numerical; there is no "Oak Harbour Lane" or "Pine Hill Promontory" or "Revolutionary Road." But because each address contains just two apartments, a lower and an upper unit, there is no need to add "Apt. 2." Which means that whenever we have to write our addresses out in SSSQ, I make sure the other children see it, hoping they will think this is an entirely private house, like the one belonging to the liberals' son with the front and back yards.

The beauty part is that the apartment does have a second level, an attic, which is accessed by a splintery, retractable wooden ladder that scares me to death, inciting memories of the special ladder my father had built me in Leningrad to help me conquer my fear of heights. Up in the musty, woodsy attic I close my eyes and pray over the intense Republicanism that is the birthright of every Soviet Jew in the time of Reagan. This attic that is above our living quarters, this dank storage space with its creaky floorboards, belongs to us and to no one else. I close my eyes and feel the power of ownership.

Ours, ours, ours.

We are climbing upward! Past the welfare queens, past the Span-ishers with their transistor radios, up to the working-class white Cath-olics with the Yankees pennants who populate our courtyard. *Adonai Eloheinu,* one day let us climb up to the Solomon Schechter Jews in how much money we have, so that those Jews can be our friends, too, and we will all own station wagons together and talk about which foods are K(osher)-Pareve and which are not. We didn't win the ten million from the Publishers Clearing House. They lied to us and maybe we should even "sue" them. But we got even in our way. We bought our own cooperative garden apartment, and now even the peaked attic roof above my head is ours.*

Let me tell you what else is ours. There is a living room with a cottage-cheese ceiling and a small closet with a bookshelf built *directly* into the closet door! You can store Papa's fishing stick inside the closet and put books on the outside of it. Here we display the trashier American novels we find on the street curb with the pictures of women and men kissing each other on horseback and a special hardcover copy of Leon Uris's *Exodus*. The furniture will be the Romanian ensemble we brought from Russia: the already mentioned dining table, with an extra leaf for when kindly Zev and our other American supporters come over. There is a credenza, equally orange and glowing, upon which two Jewish menorahs are placed when visitors come, one in front of the other, one borrowed from a perch atop my mother's Red October piano, as if to say that here Chanukah is a yearlong proposition. Beneath our feet there is a red shag carpet upon which I like to play with my pen. The problem is that the carpet is ragged, and there are many nails sticking out. Often, I will tear off a small piece of my arm during play, and I begin to mentally map the living room floor, careful to avoid major injury. What's missing from this living room ensemble?

The Television. Except for Leon Uris and his tales of Israeli derring-do, our house is Russian down to the last buckwheat kernel of kasha. English is the language of commerce and work, but Russian is the language of the soul, whatever that is. And television, it is clear—by the screaming, honking, spoiled American kids around us—is death. After we come to the States, many of my more adaptable fellow immigrants quickly part ways with their birth languages and begin singing the opening tune to a show about a black man with an aggressive haircut named Mr. T. The reason I still speak, think, dream, and quake in fear in Russian has to do with my parents' dic-

---

* Technically, the roof belongs to the Deepdale Gardens Cooperative.

tum that only Russian be spoken in the home. It's a trade-off. While I will retain my Russian, my parents will struggle with the new language, nothing being more instructive than having a child prattle on in English at the dinner table.

Not to mention that after borrowing $9,600 for one floor of 252-67 Sixty-Third Avenue we cannot afford a television, so instead of *The Dukes of Hazzard,* I turn to the collected works of Anton Chekhov, eight battered volumes of which still sit on my bookshelves. Without television there is absolutely nothing to talk about with any of the children at school. It turns out these little porkers have very little interest in "Gooseberries" or "Lady with Lapdog," and it is impossible in the early 1980s to hear a sentence spoken by a child without an allusion to something shown on TV.

"NEEEEERD!" the children scream whenever I try to welcome them into my inner life.

And so the Red Nerd finds itself doubly handicapped, living in a world where it speaks neither the actual language, English, nor the second and almost just as important language, television. For most of its American childhood it will have the wretched sensation that fin de siècle Yalta with its idle, beautiful women and conflicted, lecherous men lies somewhere behind the Toys"R"Us superstore and the multiplex.

And now let me show you my private quarters. The garden apartment has three bedrooms, which is three bedrooms more than what we had when we got off the Alitalia jet at JFK just two years ago. USA! USA! I suppose. Most Russians do not breed well in captivity, and anyway my parents do not seem to like each other very much, so I have no siblings. This works out well by me. From a school essay entitled "I'm Worth Writing About": "I like my position in the family. If I had a bigger brother he would boss me around call me names and punch me and kick me and beat me up."

My parents have taken the big bedroom, where we lie together in their giant shiny mahogany bed as one on weekends and they try to grab at my circumcised penis to see how it has turned out and if it has grown in accordance with the *All-Soviet Guide to Boys' Development*. *"Dai posmotret'!"* they shout. *Let us see it! What are you ashamed of?* I'm twisting away from them, clutching at my goods, filled to the brim with that stupid new American word: *privacy*. But, also, I have to say, I am excited and happy that they take such an interest in me, even though I know from SSSQ that nobody should touch my *zain*. This much has been explained to us somewhere between Leviticus and Prophets.

And so, privacy. Because there are three bedrooms, and my parents are very pleased with having even one, I am handed over the remaining two. This is also a statement on their part: They love me so much that everything that is in excess to their meager possessions is automatically mine. I would estimate their own entertainment budget during the fiscal years 1979–1985 at about twenty dollars a year, mostly hooks for my father's fishing stick.

My first bedroom, formerly the apartment's dining room, covered entirely in cheap wood paneling, is given over to my folding couch, which is itself draped in velvety green-and-yellow stripes, oh-so-soft to the touch. When erect, the couch feels like it could belong in a corporate office of the famous International Business Machines, and when folded open, it feels luxurious beyond belief. Only now do I realize that, minus the polka dots, the couch has the same striped color scheme as the singular shirt I brought with me from Leningrad. Next to the couch is a typewriter stand, and on the stand is an IBM Selectric typewriter that my mother has liberated from her place of work. At first I am not sure what to do with it, but I know that holding the font ball labeled COURIER 72 is somehow important, and I hold it in both of my hands for quite a while. Between my Courier ball and the *All-Soviet Guide to Boys' Development* there is a terrible chasm that will take half a lifetime to fill.

On the other side of the couch is the glass-and-mahogany bookcase that is the focal point of every Russian household. This kind of unit usually goes in the living room where visitors can appraise their hosts and take notes on their intellectual deficiencies. My parents aren't telling me to become a writer—everyone knows that immigrant children have to go into law, medicine, or maybe that strange new category known only as "computer"—but placing the bookcase in my room sends the unmistakable message that I am our family's future and that I have to be the best of the best. *Which I will be, Mama and Papa, I swear.*

The bookcase contains the collected works of Anton Chekhov in eight dark blue volumes with the author's seagull-like signature across every volume's cover, and most of the collected works of Tolstoy, Dostoyevsky, and Pushkin. In front of the Russian greats stands a siddur (the Jewish daily prayer book), enclosed in a plastic case and coated with fake silver and fake emeralds. It is written in a language none of us understands, but it is so *holy* that it blocks out the Pushkin that my parents have all but committed to memory. Beneath the siddur, on the inferior shelves, is the small but growing collection of American children's books that I am now capable of reading. There is the book on how Harriet "Moses" Tubman freed the black people from Maryland, there is a short history of George Washington (how handsome he looks astride his white mare, a real *amerikanets*!), and a book called *The Boy from the UFO*. An unhappy white boy, Barney, who lives with his foster parents meets an alien boy in his backyard and agrees to go back to his home planet. When he finds out he'll never see his foster parents again, he learns to love them. On the cover is Barney, also very handsome and American in his pretty pajamas on a rooftop that is the personal property of his foster parents (just like we own our roof now!), and a spherical metal container, the UFO, floats promisingly in front of him. I don't know why, but reading this book makes me cry at night.

Opposite the bed is the closet in which the Lightman with only the white sclera for eyes shares his quarters with my shirt, a V-neck sweater, and a pair of yellowish corduroy pants, part of my Stinky Russian Bear ensemble at SSSQ, wide waled in a style that will make a confusing comeback when I enroll at Oberlin College less than a decade later.

Lest the reader get the wrong impression, let me say now that I am *agog* with Bedroom Number 1. There is so much happiness here. This is my first stab at keeping and maintaining my own space, even if my father will saunter in without knocking to pick up Dostoyevsky's *The Insulted and Humiliated* from the bookshelves, and my mother will come over regularly to pet me and make sure I am still alive.

And then, as if that's not enough, my kingdom extends to Bedroom Number 2. We do not have enough money to furnish this bedroom, but this is when the amazing American curb—the land of miracles—will provide us with another couch, of coarse plaid, upon which we will stick an even coarser red carpet, the kind that used to hang on the wall above my Culture Couch in Leningrad. Eventually we will find a little black-and-white Zenith television in the trash can outside our building, and that will find its pride of place, and when I will grow even older and have access to a Sanyo AM/FM Stereo Cassette Player with Headphones and Anti-Rolling Mechanism I will sit on the coarse Russian carpet covering the coarse American couch and, while listening to Annie Lennox lamenting the weather in "Here Comes the Rain Again," brood in the singular odorous way of a boy sinking into his teenage years.

• • •

Outside our storm windows there is also a new world. Deepdale Gardens must have once been a pretty redbrick maze of two-story buildings and interlocking parking garages, but by 1981 it has all faded to a brownish color. This red-fading-into-brown defines Queens for me; it is quiet and melancholy and postsuccessful, vaguely British in its disposition. But at the time all I know is that there are pathways and roundabouts on which I can ride my shitty used bike, and all of this territory belongs to the cooperative and, hence, partly, to me. In fact, there are signs everywhere attesting to the private-property nature of Deepdale Gardens—meaning *It is our complex, so you keep out, mister.*

THIS AREA UNDER SURVEILLANCE OF UNIFORMED PATROLS AND CAMERAS should definitely deter the people who don't look like us from stealing our fake-jewel-encrusted siddur.

As the evening settles over Deepdale Gardens, my father and I stroll through the courtyards—alive with pansies and hydrangeas and lilies and daisies—like two newly minted lords of the realm. Father is very nice to me on these walks, although sometimes as a joke he likes to sneak up to me and give me a *podzhopnik,* a little side kick in the ass. *Ow, stop it!* I say, but it's okay because it's a love kick and he's not angry, just playful. When he *is* angry, he'll shake his head and murmur, "*Ne v soldaty, ne v matrosy, ne podmazivat' kolyosa*"—roughly, You won't make it as a soldier nor a sailor nor a polisher of car tires—which is what Stepfather Ilya, Goebbels to his friends, used to say to him when Papa was growing up in a little village outside Leningrad. I guess I know that what my father means is that I am not good at physical activities such as carrying more than one grocery bag at a time from the Grand Union to his waiting Chevrolet Malibu Classic, but the Russian phrase is so archaic and convoluted that it easily misses its mark. Well of course I won't be a soldier or a sailor or a gas station attendant. At the very least, I'll be a corporate lawyer, Papa.

But then there are the good times, when my father will open up the vast larder of his imagination and tell me a story from a long-running series he calls *The Planet of the Yids* (*Planeta Zhidov*). "Please, Papa!" I chant. "*Planet of the Yids! Planet of the Yids!* Tell me!"

In Papa's telling, the Planet of the Yids is a clever Hebraic corner of the Andromeda Galaxy, constantly besieged by gentile spacemen who attack it with space torpedoes filled with highly unkosher but oh-so-delicious Russian *salo,* which is salted raw pig fat, lard, a lumpy cousin of the French suet. The planet is run by Natan Sharansky, the famous Jewish dissident. But the KGB can't leave him alone, even though he's light-years away, and keeps trying to sabotage the planet. And always, just as it seems it's curtains for the Yids—"the goys have burst through the Shputnik Shield and into the ionosphere!"—the circumcised ones, led by the fearless Captain Igor, manage to outsmart their enemies, à la the Bible, à la Leon Uris's *Exodus,* à la us. For this is, of course, our story, and I crave it almost as much as I crave that forbidden *salo,* which you can't really buy at the Grand Union anyway, almost as much as I crave my father's love.

We have walked the lengths and breadths of Deepdale Gardens, past the FAA Air Traffic Control Facility down the street with its five skyscraper-sized antennas, past the playground where Papa has let me sink in one basketball more than him to win yet another "close" game, past the hydrangeas of our cooperative Eden, and up the carpeted stairs of 252-67 Sixty-Third Avenue. Since we have tasted the forbidden fruit of the Publishers Clearing House, our mailbox is filled to overflowing with offers from around the country for one S. SHITGART and his family, not to mention the latest issue of *Isaac Asimov's Science Fiction Magazine.* We won't bite again, but those bright fat envelopes tell our story, too.

We are living on the Planet of the Yids.

We have already won.

11.

GARY GNU III

*The author in his favorite (and only) shirt pens the masterpiece
"Bionic Friends" on an IBM Selectric typewriter. The chair is
from Hungary, the couch from Manhattan.*

J UST BEFORE PUBERTY BEGINS in earnest, I come down with
Dissociative Identity Disorder, evidenced by "The presence of
two or more distinct identities or personality states, [with] at
least two of these identities or personality states recurrently [taking]
control of the person's behavior" (DSM-5).

At least two? I've got four! To my parents and Grandma Polya I am
Igor Semyonovich Shteyngart, disobedient son and beloved grandson, respectfully. Very respectfully. To the American teachers at
SSSQ, I am Gary Shteyngart, strange salami-smelling boy with some
aptitude at math. To the Hebrew teachers at SSSQ I am Yitzhak Ben
Shimon or some shit like that. And to the children, to my fellow pupils in their Macy's regalia, I am Gary Gnu the Third.

If a psychiatrist had been present (and why the hell wasn't she present?) to ask me who I was, undoubtedly I would have answered with my slightly manicured but still thick Russian accent, *Doctor, I am Gary Gnu the Third, ruler of the Holy Gnuish Empire, author of the Holy Gnorah and commander of the Mighty Gnuish Imperial Army.*

How do things come to such a pass?

• • •

In 1982, I decide that I can no longer be me. The name "Gary" is a fig leaf, and what I really am is a fucking Red Gerbil, a Commie. A year later the Soviets will shoot down Korean Air Lines flight 007, and the topical New York pop-radio station 95.5 WPLJ will play a parody of the hit song "Eye of the Tiger" by the important American rock band Survivor, only instead of "Eye of the Tiger" the song will be renamed "The Russians Are Liars." ("As those Communist killers / try to sleep late at night . . .")

And as awful as those lyrics are, I can't stop singing them. In the shower beneath our amazing frosted window opening out on the Deepdale Gardens parking garage, in my father's car on the way to SSSQ, both of us morning-moody and unfriendly, even beneath the slurs and swipes of my classmates. *The Russians are liars, The Russians are liars, The Russians are liars.*

The Soviet leadership are liars; that much I now understand. Latin Lenin in Moscow Square was not always on the up and up. Fine. But am I a liar? No, I am truthful most of the time. Except when one day after one Commie comment too many, I tell my fellow pupils that I wasn't born in Russia at all. Yes, I just remembered it! It had all been a big misunderstanding! I was actually born in Berlin, right next to Flughafen Berlin-Schönefeld, surely you've heard of it.

So here I am, trying to convince *Jewish* children in a *Hebrew* school that I am actually *a German*.

And can't these little bastards see that I love America more than anyone loves America? I am a ten-year-old Republican. I believe that taxes should only be levied on the poor, and the rest of Americans should be left alone. But how do I bridge that gap between being a Russian and being loved?

I start to write.

· · ·

Papa's space opera, *The Planet of the Yids,* is high on my mind when I open up a Square Deal Composition Notebook, 120 pages, Wide Ruled with Margin, and begin my first unpublished novel in English. It is called *The Chalenge* [*sic*]. On the first page "I give aknowlegments [*sic*] to the book Manseed [probably *sic*] in this issue of Isac [*sic*] Isimov [*sic*] Siance [*sic*] Fiction magazine. I also give thanks to the makers of Start [*sic*] Treck [*sic*]."

The book, much like this one, is dedicated "To Mom and Dad."

The novel—well, at fifty-nine pages let's call it a novella—concerns a "mistirious* race" which "began to search for a planet like Earth and they found one and called it Atlanta."

Yes, Atlanta. We have recently heard from some fellow immigrants that the cost of living in Georgia's largest city is much lower than New York's, and one can even own a house and a swimming pool in the suburbs of that fast-growing metropolis for about the price of our garden apartment in Queens.

Opposite the celestial body that is Atlanta with its conservative politics and strong retail base shimmers an alien planet named Lopes, sometimes more correctly spelled as Lopez. "Lopes was a hot world. It was a wonder it didn't explode . . . It also contained many parrots." Somehow I have restrained myself from giving the steamy proto-Latinos of Planet Lopez a set of transistor radios to play at full blast, but I did endow them with three legs each.

There is also an evil, wisecracking scientist named, of course, Dr. Omar. "Hello," Omar says, "I'm Dr. Omar it's no pleasure meeting you, now if you mind zipping up that big whole in the middle of your face I can show you my discovery."

---

* From this point the "*sic*" will be omitted for the sake of brevity.

Dr. Omar's discovery is the "Chalenge Machine" that "perhaps will prove *which race is the right one*": the Atlantans with their corporate tax breaks or the Lopezians with their parrots and weak academic records?

As I reread *The Chalenge,* I want to cry out to its ten-year-old author, *Jesus Christ, why can't you just doodle in the corner of your notebook, dream of* Star Wars *action figures, and play pick-up sticks with your friends?* (Therein, I suppose, lies the answer: *what* friends?) *Why at this young age does it have to already be a race war in outer space and one without the self-deprecating humor of Papa's* Planet of the Yids? *What the hell are you talking about, you who have never met a Lopez or an Omar on the wild streets of Little Neck?*

The hero of *The Chalenge* is a space fighter pilot named Flyboy, modeled after a kid who has just transferred into SSSQ, a kid so blond and handsome and retroussé-nosed it's hard for some of us to believe he's fully Jewish. Flyboy's best friend is fellow pilot Saturn, and the love of his life is a fly girl named Iarda. Even at this early stage of my writing career, I realize the importance of a love triangle: "Flyboy smiled his best smile which the other two were jelous off. It of course was clear [Iarda] liked him best."

"Oh no," Iarda says. "Fourteen more ships from the other side."

"Look," says Saturn. "Twenty more ships in Atlanta battle formachions. Our kind."

"It hit the electronic scanner shaft and all the scanners and other equipment apart."

"Well how stupit can people get?" Flyboy wonders.

And then, once the space battle is complete, and *our kind* has won: "The fourth ship was bound to come. On Atlanta things were going wild."

I write dutifully, excitedly, asthmatically. I get up every weekend morning even if the Lightman has kept me awake all night, the little pinpricks of light that form his hand spilling out of the cracks between closet door and jamb, reaching out for me, scared breathless on my foldout couch. Five years earlier I had written the novel *Lenin and*

His Magical Goose for my grandmother Galya, who is now six years away from a horrible death back in Leningrad. But now I know to avoid *anything* even remotely Russian. My Flyboy is as Atlantan as apple pie. And his Iarda, while vaguely Israeli sounding (a reference to the *Yordan,* the River Jordan?), is also a hot, principled taxpayer who can blow a Lopez or a Rodriguez out of the sky as surely as Ronald Reagan will soon joke, "We begin bombing [the Soviet Union] in five minutes." Bombing Grandma Galya back in Leningrad, he means, and the rest of us Russian liars.

I write because there is nothing as joyful as writing, even when the writing is twisted and full of hate, the self-hate that makes writing not only possible but necessary. I hate myself, I hate the people around me, but what I crave is the fulfillment of some ideal. Lenin didn't work out; joining the Komsomol youth league didn't work out; my family— Papa hits me; my religion—children hit me; but America/Atlanta is still full of power and force and rage, a power and force and rage I can fuel myself with until I feel myself zooming for the stars with Flyboy and Saturn and Iarda and Secretary of Defense Caspar Weinberger.

• • •

There is a teacher at school, a Ms. S, who has just transferred in to substitute for some Mrs. A–Z, and who herself won't last long within the unique educational environment of SSSQ. Ms. S is as nice to me as the liberals' son. She has, like almost all the women at the school, an enormous weight of spectacular Jewish hair and a small pretty mouth. On one of her first days on the job, Ms. S asks us all to bring in our favorite items in the world and to explain why they make us who we are. I bring in my latest toy, a dysfunctional Apollo rocket whose capsule pops off with the press of a lever (but only under certain atmospheric conditions, humidity must be below 54 percent), and explain that who I am is a combination of my father's *Planet of the Yids* tales and the complicated stories in *Isaac Asimov's Science Fiction Magazine* by the likes of Harlan Ellison and Dr. Asimov himself, and that I have even written my own novel. This passes largely unremarked as the latest batch of *Star Wars* X-Wing fighters and My Little Ponies are paraded around.

Finally, Ms. S holds up a sneaker and explains that her favorite activity is jogging.

"Pee-yooh!" a boy cries out, pointing at the sneaker and holding his nose, and everyone except me laughs a wicked child laugh. Jerry Himmelstein *agoof*s.

I am shocked. Here is a young, kind, pretty teacher, and the children are intimating that her feet smell. Only me and my two-hundred-pound Leningrad fur are allowed to smell around here! I look to Ms. S, so worried that she will cry, but instead she laughs and then goes on about how running makes her feel good.

She has laughed at herself and emerged unscathed!

After we have all finished explaining who we are, Ms. S calls me over to her desk. "You really wrote a novel?" she asks.

"Yes," I say. "It is called *The Chalenge*."

"May I read it?"

"You may read it. I will brink it."

And *brink* it I do, with the worried admonition "Please don't lose, Meez S."

And then it happens.

• • •

At the end of the English period, when a book about a mouse who has learned to fly in an airplane has been thoroughly dissected, Ms. S announces, "And now Gary will read from his novel."

His *what*? Oh, but it doesn't matter, because I'm standing there holding my composition notebook straight from the Square Deal Notebook people of Dayton, OH, Zip Code 45463, and looking out at me are the boys beneath their little flying-saucer yarmulkes, and the girls with their sweet aromatic bangs, their blouses studded with stars. And there's Ms. S, whom I'm already terribly in love with but who I've recently learned has a fiancé (not sure what that means, can't be good), but whose bright American face is not just encouraging me but *priding* me on.

Am I scared? No. I am eager. Eager to begin my life. "Introduction," I say. "The Mistirious Race. Before the age of dinousaurs There was Human life on Earth. They looked just like the man of today. But they were a lot more inteligent than the men of today."

"Slowly," Ms. S says. "Read slowly, Gary. Let us enjoy the words."

I breathe that in. *Ms. S wants to enjoy the words.* And then slower: "They built all kinds of spaceships and other wonders. But at that time the Earth circled the moon because the moon was bigger than the Earth. One day a gigantic comet came and blew up the moon to the size it is today. The pieces of the moon began to Fall on Earth. The race of people got on their spaceships and took off. They began to search for a planet like Earth and they found one and called it Atlanta. But there was another planet named Lopez with a race of three legged Humanoids. War started soon." Big breath. "Book One: Before the First Chalenge."

As I'm reading it, I am hearing a different language come out of my mouth. I do full justice to the many misspellings ("the Earth cir-*culed* the moon"), and the Russian accent is still thick, but I am speaking in what is more or less comprehensible English. And as I am speaking, along with my strange new English voice, I am also hearing something entirely foreign to the squealing and shouting and *sheket bevakasha!* that constitute the background noise of SSSQ: *silence.* The children are silent. They are listening to my every word, following the battles of the Atlantans and Lopezians as far as the ten minutes of allotted time will go. And they will listen to the story for the next five weeks as well, because Ms. S will designate the end of every English period as *Chalenge* Time, and they will shout out throughout the English period, "When will Gary read already?" and I will sit there in my chair, oblivious to all but Ms. S's smile, excused from following the discussion of the mouse who learned how to fly, so that I may go over the words I will soon read to my adoring audience.

And God bless these kids for giving me a chance. May their G-d bless them, every one.

Don't get me wrong. I'm still a hated freak. But here's what I'm doing: I am redefining the terms under which I am a hated freak. I am moving the children away from my *Russianness* and toward storytelling. And toward the ideology of strength and Republicanism, which is life around the Shteyngart dinner table. "Did you write anything new?" shouts a kid in the morning, a merchant's son, renowned for his lack of basic literacy. "Will the Lopezians attack? What's Dr. Omar gonna do next?"

What indeed? I am now so far beyond Jerry Himmelstein that I don't even bother studying him and trying to avoid his social miscues. With my newfound lesser brand of hate comes the responsibility that will haunt me for the rest of my life. The responsibility of writing something *every day,* lest I fall out of favor again and be restored to Red Gerbil status.

What I need is to expand my repertoire. And that means more access to popular culture. When I've run out of *The Chalenge* to read I follow up with another fifty-pager called *Invasion from Outer Space,* featuring the evildoings of the Academy of Moors (Yasser Arafat has been back in the news), and that one goes over reasonably well. But what I really need is access to a television set.

Enter Grandmother Polya.

• • •

Behind every great Russian child, there is a Russian grandmother who acts as chef de cuisine, bodyguard, personal shopper, and PR agent. You can see her in action in the quiet, leafy neighborhood of Rego Park, Queens, running after her thick-limbed grandson with a dish of buckwheat, fruit, or farmer's cheese—"Sasha, come back, my treasure! I have plums for you!"—or flipping through rows of slacks at the Alexander's (now Marshalls) on Queens Boulevard, getting Sasha ready for the new school year.

Rego Park, Queens. This is where I go after school while my parents work. Close enough to Little Neck for my father to strike with his Chevy Malibu Classic, but far enough away that I may develop my own personality. The homey, low-rise redbrick neighborhood is over-shadowed by the three modernist Birchwood Towers, each nearly thirty stories in height and featuring the tackiest themed lobbies on the Eastern Seaboard—the Bel Air, the Toledo, and the Kyoto, with its marble Japanese statuette and hanging scrolls. I spot my first limousine parked in the Bel Air's circular driveway and promise to myself that one day I will own one. Other less gargantuan co-op buildings have pretty gardens and names like the Lexington and New Hampshire House. In one of these, my grandmother, over sixty but still full of country strength, cleans toilets for an American woman.

• • •

Grandma lives at 102–17 Sixty-Fourth Avenue, a cheap six-story redbrick facing a public school that contains black children and that we circle with care. She holds court on a wooden bench outside, presenting me to fellow Russian retirees, demanding that attention be paid as she explains how I am the best, most successful grandson that ever walked the streets of Queens.

My grandmother loves me more than the Madonna del Granduca loved her Son, and when I come to stay at her house after school this love is expressed through a three-hour gorging process.

Back at my parents' house, we feast on Russian or, I should say, Soviet cuisine. Breakfast is a plate of roasted buckwheat groats with a puddle of butter soaking up the middle. Supper is a plate of thick, salty farmer's cheese with a can of frozen peaches dumped on it. ("Just like they serve in the restaurants!" my mother cries, as if she's ever been to a restaurant.) Around 3:00 P.M. a piece of boiled meat and some kind of wan vegetable are beaten into submission. "Please," I beg my mother. "If you let me eat only half a plate of buckwheat groats, I'll vacuum the whole apartment tomorrow. If we skip the farmer's cheese, I'll give you back part of my allowance. Please, Mama, don't feed me." When my mother isn't looking, I run to the bathroom and spit out the inedible bricks of farmer's cheese, watching the toilet water turn cloudy white with my misery.

At Grandmother's life is different. Whilst I recline on a divan like a pasha, three hamburgers topped with coleslaw and mustard and a fart of ketchup are quickly brought to me. I eat them up with trembling hands as my grandmother peers turtle-like from behind the kitchen door, eyes wide with anxiety. "Are you still hungry, my favorite one?" she whispers. "Do you want more? I'll run to Queens Boulevard. I'll run to 108th Street. I'll run anywhere!"

"Run, Grandma, run!" And Grandma raises dust through central Queens, her arms straining under the weight of pepperoni pizza pies, greenish pickle slices, cervelat smoked sausages from Misha and Monya's Russian *gastronom,* ridged potato chips covered in some kind of orange crud, mayonnaise-heavy tuna-fish salad from the kosher store, thick pretzels that I pretend to smoke like cigars, ranch dips that bring to mind a hint of the garlic that's all but absent in our Little Neck garden apartment, packets of creamy chocolaty Ding Dongs, cartons of Sara Lee layer cake. I eat and eat, trans fats clogging my little body, pockets of fat popping up in unlikely places. Sometimes I find Grandma in the kitchen sucking on a chicken bone amid an orange landscape of government cheese while she leafs through a fresh packet of food stamps, each graced with a beautiful drawing of Philadelphia's Liberty Bell. Grandma survived the wartime evacuation of Leningrad with her three-year-old son, my father, to suck poultry marrow in a Queens kitchen. But she looks happy with her meager meal, philosophical. Anything to keep Little Igor (or Gary, as the Americans are now calling him) in Ding Dongs.

. . .

Grandma's one-bedroom apartment is a thing of wonder. Besides the hamburger-producing kitchen there is my mean step-grandfather Ilya glowering at the dining table, who will die soon anyway, partly of cancer and partly because he's never really found anyone in Rego Park with whom to hoist 150 grams of the good stuff (alcoholic heartbreak should be a classifiable Russian disease). Then there are the bright medals Ilya won "for bravery" while serving with the Soviet navy in the Arctic Circle, which I love to pin across my chest, because, yes, the Russians are liars, but we still fought and won the Great Patriotic War against the Germans, so . . . And most important, there is the television set.

Grandma has a television set.

• • •

The television came with the apartment, along with the crumbling divan and the scary children's clown drawings, probably because moving it would require all the men of the Twenty-Third Soviet Arctic Division. The screen is not big, but it is encased within a kind of gigantic wooden armoire (not too different from the three-ton Hungarian specimen Grandma has brought with her from Leningrad), and the whole contraption stands on two sturdy legs splayed at a decisive angle. The Zenith is probably from the latter portion of the 1950s or the very early 1960s, and the problem with it is that, like a dog too old to run after the ball, it's no longer interested in catching the electromagnetic signals that transmit picture and sound. Or rather it catches *either* picture *or* sound.

The only way to get the sound is if I hold on to the tip of the antenna and then point one of my arms outside the window. Then it is possible to follow the plot but not to see the action. In reverse, if I don't become a part of the antenna, if I lie opposite the Zenith on Grandma's divan, it is possible to see the action but not to hear anything but cold static. Soon I catch on to the fact that episodes of the most popular series are frequently rebroadcast on American television. I turn myself into the antenna to hear the storyline and, upon commercial break, jot down as much of the dialogue as I can. When the show is reaired a few months later, I watch it with my notes, so that I am able to put the dialogue and action together.

Given this method, it is still hard to understand why Buck Rogers is trapped in the twenty-fifth century or why the Incredible Hulk is sometimes green and sometimes not. Buck Rogers, a favorite of the schoolchildren—all the boys have a crush on Colonel Wilma Deering, played by shapely model Erin Gray in a sexy one-piece jumpsuit, but none's crush is greater than my own—requires special adjustment because it comes on at 4:00 P.M. on WWOR, channel 9. The thing about channel 9 is that to receive transmission between 4:00 and 6:00 P.M. necessitates more than just my leaning out the window while holding the antenna. Exactly every seven seconds I have to make a "come over here" motion with my hand, as if inviting the electromagnetic signals into Grandma's living room, so that I may hear Colonel Wilma Deering cry, "Buck Rogers, I'm ordering you back to the base! This is against all principles of modern aerial combat!" as her blue eyes open up in hot, simulated panic and, if I may extrapolate, desire.

Later I have Grandma petition my parents to buy her a Hitachi nineteen-inch television with limited remote-control capacity. They don't realize that the three hours I spend at Grandma's before Papa rolls in on his car-boat are spent exclusively on being fed like some pre-foie-gras goose and watching her Zenith. I lie and tell them that I am doing my homework for those three hours, and Grandma keeps mum; she's just happy to see me eating Doritos while the Germans are not advancing past the border set down by the Molotov-Ribbentrop pact. Homework at SSSQ takes about three minutes of my time. You add up how many hot-air balloons there are floating in a photograph of New Mexico, and then you identify some prophet and miserably scratch יְחֶזְקֵאל into the *machberet,* the blue Israeli notebook. (My father has already called the Hebrew school and demanded that they give me more difficult math problems. They have categorically refused.) And then when you're done with the Prophet Ezekiel you're free to watch *Diff'rent Strokes.* The problem is that even with my growing English vocabulary and the excellent visibility on Grandma's new Hitachi, *Diff'rent Strokes,* ostensibly the story of a rich white man who adopts many black children, makes no sense on cultural grounds. In fact, none of it does.

The more I watch, the more the questions keep mounting. *Just what exactly is going on in this country of mine? And why won't President Reagan do something about it?* For instance:

The Brady Bunch: Why are Mr. and Mrs. Brady always so happy even though Mrs. Brady has clearly already had a *razvod* with her previous husband and now they are both raising children who are not theirs? Also, what is the origin of their white slave Alice?

Three's Company: What does it mean, "gay"? Why does everyone think the blond girl is so pretty, when it is clearly the brunette who is beautiful?

Gilligan's Island: Is it really possible that a country as powerful as the United States would not be able to locate two of its best citizens lost at sea, to wit, the millionaire and his wife? Also, Gilligan is comical and bumbling like an immigrant, but people seem to like him. Make notes for further study? Emulate?

Planet of the Apes: If Charlton Heston is a Republican, are the monkeys Soviet?

• • •

After three hours of watching television and eating government cheese on Grandma's food-stamp-bought Ritz crackers I am ostensibly as American as anyone else. In the kitchen Grandma is preparing still more food for the next day's feedings, and I now wonder how it is possible to love someone so much just because she gave me what I wanted when no one else would.

Although I am afraid of heights I climb out on the fire escape some six floors above the patchy grass of central Queens and watch the TWA jets descend sharply into LaGuardia Airport. Soon Papa will come and take me home to Little Neck, to my real home, where my parents will fight about the wolfish relatives until 10:30 P.M., until it is time for all of us to get enough sleep to face another difficult day in America.

Outside Grandma's apartment, the car honks stretch way out to the Grand Central Parkway, and people in the apartment house next door are playing English and Spanish radios and just being alive and free, and the air is city-scented with gasoline and grilled meat, which is in its own way delicious. When I shut my eyes I hear the addictively cloying *Three's Company* theme song ("Come and knock on our door / We've been waiting for you") and the commercial for Juicy Fruit gum sung with such intense abandon it makes me scared (*"Jew-seh froooot is gonna moooove ya / it gotta taaaaste that cut raaaaght throoo ya-ugh"*).

Even a few years back I was angrier than I am now, and when I'd watch the TWA jets descend I wanted some of them to fall out of the sky and explode against the little houses beyond the jumble of red-brick apartment buildings. But now I just think, *Vow*, how lucky are people that they can take a flight somewhere. And will that be me someday up in the air again? Where will I land this time? Will it be at Flughafen Berlin-Schönefeld? At Israel's Ben Gurion Airport, so I can fight Omar and the other Arabs? Will someone other than Grandma ever love me?

• • •

"You're Gary Gnu." It's some kid on a public, non-Jewish playground.

Me: "Vat?"

"Your name's Gary. So you're Gary Gnu. From the Great Space Coaster."

"Vat coaster?"

"Don't be a dick. You're Gary Gnu."

"I am Gnu?"

But before I am Gnu, let me discourse on one more television show I have caught on Grandma's Zenith. It is called *The Six Million Dollar Man*. First, let's be honest here: This man is expensive. Not ten-million-dollar expensive per the Publishers Clearing House sweepstakes we almost won, but nearly two-thirds as expensive. Steve Austin is his name, and he was an astronaut until a terrible accident deprived him of many body parts and he was resurrected at taxpayers' expense to have all kinds of adventures. (Famous opening sequence: "Gentlemen, we can rebuild him . . . We have the technology.") As in love as I am with Colonel Wilma Deering of *Buck Rogers*, I am even more fascinated with bionic Steve Austin. Because when I think about it, the man is a cripple. He is missing one arm, two legs, and one eye. Imagine if I showed up at SSSQ without those things, and with my toy Monkey missing an arm as well. The Israeli kids would mop the floor with me, or the parts of the floor Jimmy and George, the two black custodians, have missed. And yet, Steve Austin is not deficient. Although parts of him aren't real, Steve takes advantage of his new powers. He is, in the words of the show, "Better than he was before. Better, stronger, faster." After all, this is America, and you can swap out the parts of yourself that don't work. You can rebuild yourself piece by piece.

In my "novel" *Invasion from Outer Space,* I include a chapter called "Bionic Friends," about, well, two bionic friends. The pretty Ms. S, now sadly a Mrs., likes that chapter in particular, and I remember the incident with her sneaker at the Show and Tell, when one of the kids pointed at her sneaker and said "Pee-yooh":

She laughed at herself and emerged unscathed!

Me, back on the playground: "Who is Gary Gnu?"

"It's you, dick. Your name is Gary, right? So you're Gary Gnu, ass-hole."

It is hard to argue with this Christian boy's logic.

Gary Gnu is a comical furry green muppet in a mauve turtleneck on the children's television show *The Great Space Coaster.* All the other kids at SSSQ are familiar with him, but I do not watch *The Great Space Coaster* because it comes on in the morning when I am without Grandma's Zenith. A gnu is one of the "stocky, oxlike antelopes of the genus Connochaetes," resident of Africa. Gnu is pronounced *nu.* Gary Gnu clearly has a problem with the silent *g* in his name because he adds it to every word that starts with the letter *n* in annoying fashion: "Absolutely *gnot.* You're a *gnuisance* who's sure to bring *gnothing* but bad *gnews.*" His motto on *The Great Space Coaster* is "No *gnews* is good *gnews* with Gary Gnu." I do not know any of this, but as the goy-boy on the playground pointed out, the antelope's name is Gary just like mine. So I try it out on the kids. "I'm Gary Gnu!"

"Gary Gnu! Gary Gnu! No gnews is good gnews!"

Well, that went over pretty well. No "Commie" or "Red" there. And then I am reminded of Thurston Howell III, the millionaire on *Gilligan's Island* who is so inspiring to a young Republican immigrant. "I'm Gary Gnu the Third."

"Gary Gnu the Third! Gary Gnu the Third! No gnews," etc.

And then it hits me. I'm not a Russian. Never was. I'm an antelope. I've always been an antelope. It is time to commit this discovery to paper.

• • •

I write my own Torah. It's called the Gnorah, an allusion to my new Gnu-ness. The Gnorah is written on an actual scroll of paper to give it the feel of a Torah. I type it on a new kind of device that my father has brought over from work, which is a computer keyboard that receives signals via a telephone line and translates such signals into dot-matrix-like characters that it then spits out on paper. To make the whole thing even more Torah-like I have my father carve two sticks to simulate the rollers used for scrolling the Torah.

The Gnorah is a hatchet job directed at the entirety of the SSSQ religious experience, the rote memorization of ancient texts, the aggressive shouting of blessings and counterblessings before and after lunch, the ornery rabbi who claims the Jews brought on the Holocaust by their overconsumption of delicious pork products. In Hebrew, the words of the Old Testament are pure gibberish to our ears. *Bereishit bara Elohim* . . . (In the beginning God created . . .). In English, the words are not much better, the start of a long lesson in overzealous genealogy meant, I suppose, to convey to us youngsters the permanence and uniqueness of our race. Only take one look at the redheaded merchant's son unable to form two coherent sentences in English, incurious about any and all aspects of life save the ongoing excavation of his own nose, and *bereishit,* indeed. The Gnorah merely, humbly, takes the Old Testament to its own logical conclusion circa 1984.

1. First There was nothing, just a piece of Hubba Bubba. 2. And then it popped and the earth formed. 3. And the sugar of it turned into dust. 4. Just one piece of Nutra Sweet turned into a man.

God creates Adam (or, rather, Madman) and gives him a garden called Cleaveland, referring, I'm guessing, both to the unsuccessful city in Ohio and Genesis 2:24 ("Therefore shall a man leave his father and his mother, and shall cleave unto his wife").

In subsequent chapters there are references to Wendy's famous Where's the Beef? campaign, Mister Rogers, Howard Cosell, *Playboy* magazine, and the Waldbaum's supermarket chain. Every pop reference I have learned from the Zenith and elsewhere is crammed into use, alongside poor Jerry Himmelstein. The Twelve Gnuish Tribes multiply—"Princess Leia gave him Shlomo, Shlemazel, Shmuck, Nudnik, Dino, Gloria, Dror, Virginia, Jolly and Jim"—and somehow end up in Australia instead of Egypt.

Exodus becomes Sexodus. Henry Miller would have been proud. Moses is renamed Mishugana, and instead of a Burning Bush there is the Burning Television. God sends the Australians twelve plagues, the last one of which is Rabbi Sofer, SSSQ's potbellied Hebrew principal and strongman, "and the Australians couldn't take it anymore and they said go, go and take Rabbi Sofer with you." The Gnuish tribes make their way from Australia to Hawaii, "the land of silk and money." The fifth commandment handed down by the Gnuish God is simple: "Abuse your teachers."

And G-d spoke: Don't worry about ethics, this does not however mean you can act like John Macaenroe. Do not pray to statues of Michael Jackson or Tom Sellek: I am your G-d. If you see a blind man do not cheat him: for example do not sell him cocaine when it is really angel dust. Don't swear in the name of Brook Shields, by doing so you are insulting my name.

And G-d continued: Whatever form of government you have tax the people highly and unfairly. You are not to become emotionally

involved with Boy George or his mother. Allow abortion because
what if someone like Jerry Himmelstein is born in such cases it is
wise to say the two parents *agoofed*. And what if a natural disaster
like Eedo Kaplan [an Israeli boy who harasses the two Russian girls
in school] is born? Think about it. Here are things you should not
crossbreed . . .

A long list that includes "Ronald Reagan and Geraldine Ferraro" and
ends, sadly, with "Gary Gnu and any Female Gnu" and then the same
words with which my father would end all of his *Planet of the Yids*
tales: "To be continued."

Once it is finished I read it over and over again. I cannot sleep. I
want to be loved so badly, it verges on mild insanity. The next day in
school I wait impatiently until recess, and then unfurl my Gnorah for
a few kids, mindful of Rabbi Sofer's thick presence. More children
gather around me. With each new adherent I am crossing the line
from unclubbable fruitcake to tolerated eccentric. By the final period,
the Gnorah has been passed around the entire school. By the next day,
it is being quoted in the boys' bathroom, the center of power. Even
Jerry Himmelstein seems pleased by my disgustingly cruel remarks
about him. Not that I care. And as, in class, we recite mindlessly about
the prophets and the women who loved them, as we chant things that
mean nothing to us, as Rabbi Sofer waddles around with his bullhorn
telling us what bad children we are, me and my small band of—wait,
are they really *my friends*?—we laugh and rejoice in the Gnuish tribes
and their hard, horny Sexodus from Australia and their worship of
the much-loved Brooke Shields, who, rumor has it, really might be
Jewish, or Gnuish, or whatever.

· · ·

The Gnorah marks the end of Russian as my primary tongue and the
beginning of my true assimilation into American English. Back in my
stuffy bedroom in Little Neck, I eagerly jot down the Constitution of
the Holy Gnuish Empire (the HGE), which is built on solidly Repub-

lican principles. The love of two countries, America and Israel, the love of the smooth, always laughing, unconcerned-seeming Reagan, the love of unfettered capitalism (even though my father works for the government and my mother for a nonprofit), the love of the mighty Republican Party is a way for me to share something with my father. To my well-thumbed *Isaac Asimov's Science Fiction Magazine* I have added a subscription to the *National Review*. William F. Buckley Jr.'s conservative magazine ostensibly has fewer space monsters between its covers than Isaac Asimov's, but even though I can understand maybe 50 percent of the words Buckley and his friends use, I can already discern the angry, unhappy rhetoric about certain kinds of people that so neatly mirrors our own. On the cover of the Holy Gnuish Constitution I draw a set of scales marked "Welfare" and "Military Spending," tipping resolutely toward the latter. Take that, you welfare queens with your Cadillacs. And then another unbidden delight. Having established my Republican bona fides by subscribing to the *National Review,* I am sent a thick card featuring an American eagle sitting upon two rifles. Even though I am too young to own a gun and to be able to shoot a black person on the subway who might rob me (I've actually taken the subway maybe thrice thus far), I am being welcomed, with great Second Amendment fanfare, into the National Rifle Association.

At SSSQ, another overly imaginative boy named David creates the Imperial Lands of David (the ILD), mirroring the Democratic politics to which most Queens Jewish kids' parents subscribe. He calls himself the Mighty Khan Caesar. As a matter of course, the Holy Gnuish Empire and the Imperial Lands of David go to war. David and I talk peace treaties and how we will divide the known universe between us in the same way Spain and Portugal once split the globe according to the Treaty of Zaragoza. As we settle our foreign affairs, our followers run around the SSSQ gym stacked with prayer books, where in the morning we sing the "Star-Spangled Banner," and, with a feeling that almost brings us to tears, the "Hatikvah," the Israeli national anthem. But today the kids are not crying out about *Nefesh*

Yehudi ("the Jewish soul"). They are chanting my anthem ("*Nefesh Gnushi . . .*") and hoisting my flag, the drawing of a gnu standing resplendent in the African veldt, photocopied from Merriam-Webster's dictionary.

Until high school, I will never be called Gary again. I am Gary Gnu or just Gnu. Even the teachers refer to me as such. One of them, in a bid to forgo teaching for a day, decides to devote the class periods to the Constitution of the Holy Gnuish Empire. This development makes me so excited I have an asthma attack that lasts an entire week. The children, my Gnuish representatives, carry on while in his sickbed the Gnuish leader, mesmerized by the Lightman reconstituting himself in his closet, wheezes his way into some future world, some future personality.

Three years from now we will graduate, and a yearbook will be issued. There will be humorous quotes about each of the students—for example, the song titles that best personify us. The three other Russian children will get quotes solely about their Russianness (e.g., favorite song: "Back in the U.S.S.R."), but mine will be about my Republicanism or my strangeness ("They're Coming to Take Me Away, Ha-Haaa!").

Better, stronger, faster.

• • •

But not really, of course. As every so-called creative spirit soon learns, the rest of the world doesn't particularly give a damn. And as the hoopla around my Gnuish Empire dies down, a beefy kid whose last name means both "Oak" and "Dullard" in Russian waddles over to me and says, "Hey, Gnu. What do you listen to? *The classical music station?*" And I begin to protest, because I've learned *never* to talk about high culture in public nor mention the fact that both my parents have musical training. "I don't know about classical music!" I say, loudly, too loudly. "I have the Duran Duran *Seven and the Ragged Tiger* cassette tape *and* the Cyndi Lauper!"

But the "Oak" and a small, pretty Mesopotamian-eyed girl in the seat next to him are already laughing at my terrible affliction. If only they knew what a wide berth I have given to my father's Tchaikovsky and my mother's Chopin. How in my father's car, on the way home from my grandmother's, I turn on the Duran Duran tape as loudly as he will let me, and, with my face turned to my window, as if I'm watching the fascinating cement scenery of Grand Central Parkway go by, I *mouth* the British words I cannot even begin to comprehend ("The re-flex, flex-flex") under my tuna-fish breath. I *mouth* them with every last little bit of hope inside me.

12.

IMMORTALITY

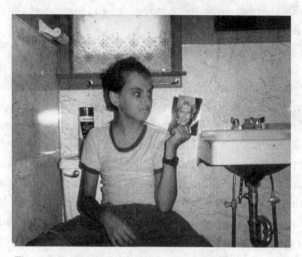

The author poses as the popular music singer Billy Idol on the toilet of his family's upstate bungalow. Puberty is coming, and the author is about to get chubby.

THE SUMMER OF 1985. I am about to become a man according to Jewish tradition. As in the past few summers, my family is staying in a Russian bungalow colony in the Catskill Mountains. The colony consists of a dozen sunburned wooden cottages squeezed in between some unimpressive hills and a daunting forest-and-brook combination that to kids from Queens might as well be the Amazon. During the workweek it is just our grandmas and their charges (a few grandpas have survived World War II to play competitive chess beneath the easygoing American sun), our lives revolving around the intermittent delivery of stale baked goods from the back of a station wagon. "Bread! Cakes!" an unhappy middle-aged local woman yells at us, and the grandmothers and kids jostle for a week-old raspberry Danish on sale for a quarter that tastes as good as anything we have ever known. (I clutch my change so tight it makes treads in my palms.) Otherwise, we children play The Fool, a Russian card game requiring little skill, and launch shuttlecocks into the air with our defective badminton rackets, not really caring whether they come down or not, because we are relaxed and happy and among our own kind.

My grandmother is always in the background, chewing an apricot down to its pit, her eyes firmly affixed on my once-skinny and now-somewhat-flabby body. She is making sure nothing and no one will cause me harm. The other kids have similar minders, women who grew up under Stalin whose entire lives in the USSR were devoted to crisis management, to making sure the arbitrary world around them would treat their children better than it had treated them. These days my grandmother is talking about going to "the next world," and that Bar Mitzvah summer, having passed a milestone of my own, I begin to see her as an older woman in decline, the shaking hands clutching the apricot pit, the trembling voice as she begs me to swallow another forkful of sausage. She is a figure as anxious and helpless before eternity as any other. Maybe this is what America does to you. With the daily fight for survival abated, one can either reminisce about the past or face the singular destiny of the future. For all her talk of the paradise to come, my grandmother does not want to die.

On weekends our parents come up to visit from the city, and on Friday nights we kids sit at a picnic table by the quiet country road running past our bungalows, alert as terriers for the difficult sounds our fathers' secondhand cars make. I remember my first love of that year—not a girl, but the gleaming new Mitsubishi Tredia-S sedan that my parents have bought, a boxy little number known mostly for its fuel efficiency. The beige front-wheel-drive Tredia-S is proof positive that we are ascending to the middle class, and whenever my father and I are out on the road I rejoice upon seeing the more basic Tredia model (the one without the S).

My father is at the apex of middle age, a deeply physical man who feasts with great emphasis upon entire garlic cloves on hunks of black bread and, with his small, tough physique, best resembles a cherry tomato. He lives for fishing. Each year he plucks hundreds, if not thousands, of fish out of streams, lakes, and oceans with his fishing stick and a chilling competence. He single-handedly empties out a lake near Middletown, New York, leaving behind just a small school of dazed, orphaned crappies. Compared with my father I am nothing. The Bar Mitzvah may soon make me a man, but when we enter the forbidding grasshopper-ridden forest by the bungalow colony, and he reaches into the ground with his bare hands to sift for the juiciest worms, I feel coursing through me the Russian word for "weak"— *slabyi,* an adjective that from my father's mouth reduces me to near zero.

"*Akh, ty, slabyi.*" Eh, you, weakling.

• • •

When we aren't fishing, we entertain ourselves at humble cinemas in towns with names like Liberty and Ellenville. The movie of the summer is *Cocoon.* Its premise: Aliens, Antareans to be exact, descend upon southern Florida to offer eternal life to a group of nursing-home residents, played by the likes of Wilford Brimley and Don Ameche. At this point in my life, Hollywood can sell me anything—from Daryl Hannah as a mermaid to Shelley Duvall as Olive Oyl and Al Pacino as a rather violent Cuban émigré. Watching movies in the air-conditioned chill I find myself wholly immersed and in love with everything that passes the camera lens. I feel close to my father, removed from the difficulties of worm gathering while being attacked by aggressive grasshoppers, free of my constant fear of getting my thumb impaled by one of the gigantic rusty hooks with which he terrorizes the local trout. At the movie theater my father and I are essentially two immigrant men—one smaller than the other and yet to be swaddled by a thick carpet of body hair—sitting before the canned spectacle of our new homeland, silent, attentive, enthralled.

Cocoon has everything I want from a movie. Here is the geriatric Don Ameche break-dancing after being energized by the aliens' fountain of youth, while back at our bungalow colony my grandmother and her fellow senior citizens mull over the price of farmer's cheese. Here are Floridian palm trees, ocean breezes, and Tahnee Welch—daughter of Raquel—taking off her clothes while Steve Guttenberg, playing essentially himself, peeks through a peephole. I have never seen a woman as easily beautiful, as effortlessly tanned and New World lovely, as Ms. Welch the Younger. The fact that my sexual awakening peripherally involves Steve Guttenberg I have gradually accepted.

The theme of the movie is immortality. "We'll never be sick," the Wilford Brimley character tells his grandson before the aliens beam him up. "We won't get any older. And we'll never die." As he speaks, Mr. Brimley's character is casting a fishing line into the Atlantic Ocean while his worried grandson looks on, a sliver of a boy next to a fully formed, famously mustached mastodon of a man. As my father guides the Mitsubishi Tredia-S beneath the bright rural canopy of stars on our way home, our sedan redolent of dead fish, live worms, and male sweat, I wonder why Wilford Brimley doesn't take his grandson with him to Antarea. Wouldn't that mean that he would eventually outlive his grandson? Are some of us destined for a flicker of physical existence while others explode like supernovas across the cold mountain sky? If so, where is the American fairness in that? That night, as my father's healthy snores rumble in the bed next to mine and my grandmother wanders in and out of the bathroom, sighing to the depth of her ample, peasant bosom, I consider in great detail both the nothingness to which we will all eventually succumb and its very opposite, the backside of Tahnee Welch partly shrouded in a pair of white summer shorts. I want Wilford Brimley to be my grandpa, and I want him to die. I keep thinking of what he tells his *slabyi* obsessive little grandson at the start of the film: "The trouble with you is you think too much and that's when a guy gets scared."

• • •

Ann Mason's Bungalow Colony lies near the village of Ellenville, not far from the old Jewish Borscht Belt hotels. It sits on the slope of a hill, beneath which there is a circular hayfield that belongs to a rabidly anti-Semitic Polish man who will hunt us down with his German shepherd if we go near, or so our grandmothers tell us. We share our meandering country road with a fading hotel named the Tamarack Lodge and a settlement of free-range Hasids who descend on our bungalows with their prayer books and forelocks, trying to induct us Russians into their hirsute ways. My mother and I sneak into the nearby Tamarack Lodge, where Eddie Fisher and Buddy Hackett once shared a stage, to witness giant, tanned American Jews lying belly up next to an Olympic-sized outdoor pool or sleepwalking to the auditorium in bedroom slippers to watch Neil Diamond in *The Jazz Singer*. After one showing we are herded into a dining room where the American Jews are served their meals—grilled chicken breasts and ice-cold Cokes!—and when the waiter comes up to ask for our room number my mother blurts out "Room 431." Mama and I wolf down our purloined chicken breasts and make a run for it.

Back at Ann Mason's Bungalow Colony, we survive without Neil Diamond, and the pool can fit maybe a half-dozen small Russian children at a time. Ann Mason, the proprietor, is an old Yiddish-spouting behemoth with three muumuus to her wardrobe. The children (there are about ten of us, from Leningrad, Kiev, Kishinev, and Vilnius) adore Ann Mason's husband, a ridiculous, potbellied, red-bearded runt named Marvin, an avid reader of the Sunday funny papers whose fly is always open and whose favorite phrase is "Everybody in the pool!" When Ann Mason cuts enough coupons, she and Marvin take some of us to the Ponderosa Steakhouse for T-bones and mashed potatoes. The all-you-can-eat salad bar is the nexus of capitalism and gluttony we've all been waiting for.

These Russian children are as close as I have come to compatriots.

I look forward to being with them all year. There is no doubt that several of the girls are maturing into incomparable beauties, their tiny faces acquiring a round Eurasian cast, slim-hipped tomboyish bodies growing soft here and sometimes there. But what I love most are the sounds of our hoarse, excited voices. The Russian nouns lacing the barrage of English verbs, or vice versa ("*Babushka, oni poshli* shopping *vmeste v ellenvilli*"—"Grandma, they went shopping together in Ellenville").

Fresh from my success with the Gnorah, I decide to write the lyrics for a music album, popular American songs with a Russian inflection. Madonna's "Like a Virgin" becomes "Like a Sturgeon." There are paeans to babushkas, to farmer's cheese, to budding sexuality. We record these songs on a tape recorder I buy at a drugstore. For the album-cover photograph I pose as Bruce Springsteen on his *Born in the U.S.A.* album, dressed in jeans and a T-shirt, a red baseball cap sticking out of my back pocket. Several of the girls pose around my "Bruce" dressed like the singers Cyndi Lauper and Madonna with hopeful applications of mascara and lipstick. *Born in the USSR* is what we call the album. (*I was bo-ho-rn down in-uh Le-nin-grad . . . wore a big fur* shapka *on my head, yeah . . .*)

As soon as our parents roll in from their jobs in the city, the men take off their shirts and point their hairy chests at the sky; the women gather in the little bungalow kitchens to talk in low tones about their husbands. We kids cram into a tiny station wagon and head for one of the nearest towns where, along with a growing Hasidic population, there is a theater that shows last summer's movies for two dollars (giant bag of popcorn with fake butter—fifty cents). On the return trip to Ann Mason's Bungalow Colony, sitting on each other's laps, we discuss the finer points of *E.T.: The Extra-Terrestrial*. I wonder aloud why the film never ventured into outer space, never revealed to us the wrinkled fellow's planet, his birthplace and true home.

We continue our discussion into the night, the stars lighting up the bull's-eye of the anti-Semitic hayfield. Tomorrow, a long stretch of noncompetitive badminton. The day after that, Marvin will bring out the funny papers, and we will laugh at *Beetle Bailey* and *Garfield,* not always knowing why we're laughing. It's something like happiness, the not knowing why.

• • •

The girl I love is named Natasha. I understand there is a cartoon show with characters Boris and Natasha, which makes fun of Russians, and at SSSQ I would never be seen with a person so named. The only girl to go out with me for the school dance is a former Muscovite named Irina,* and although a part of me understands that she is a slim, attractive girl, far prettier than most of the native-born or the Israelis, most of me is upset that she is not the former or at least the latter. Up in the bungalow colony, such considerations are not valid. We are all the same, and we treat one another with surprising gentleness.

On the other hand, I am not pretty. My body and face are changing, and not for the better. Grandma's feedings combined with puberty have given me what steroid-using bodybuilders call "bitch tits," and these tits are straining at the already tight T-shirts donated by the SSSQ secretarial staff. Along my right shoulder there is the result of a Soviet inoculation gone terribly wrong: a giant, flesh-colored keloid scar over which I wear a king's ransom of Band-Aids. My face, once boyish and pleasant, is acquiring adult features that make little sense. Hair everywhere, my nose beginning to hook; my father has started calling me *gubastyi,* or "big lips," and some days he grabs me by the chin and says, *"Akh, ty, zhidovskaya morda."* Eh, you, Yid-face. In his *Planet of the Yids* stories, being a clever Jew is good, but here I sense that he is referring to the less pleasant attributes of our race. It is very confusing.

---

* Curiously enough, she will become the novelist and essayist Irina Reyn. A graduating class of fewer than thirty Hebrew school children produced two writers, both of them from the USSR.

Here's what isn't confusing: Natasha is beautiful. Kind of like Tahnee Welch is beautiful in *Cocoon*. She even has the same short hairstyle that wonderfully exposes the slim architecture of her neck and eyes of blue that burn with pleasure as she gets ready to swing her badminton racket. She is boyish and athletic and is usually seen gliding through the Ann Mason's Bungalow Colony grounds with her brown boxer by her side. It is sad that I can no longer remember the boxer's name, because once I knew it as surely as I know my own.

Natasha is sweet and kind and in full control of herself. She does not whine, she does not complain, and if there are insecurities about her place in the world, she deals with them elsewhere. When she somersaults or does a headstand in front of me, it is not to show off but because she is . . . happy? And when she's standing on her hands, and her T-shirt succumbs to gravity, and I am looking at her tanned, brown, flat stomach, I am happy, too. She will never be my "girlfriend," obviously, but she exists somewhere in the world, and that will be good enough until college.

By this stage everyone simply calls me Gnu (to my grandma: "*Mozhet Gnu s nami poigraet?*" May Gnu come out and play with us?), but Natasha always calls me Gary. I try to time my encounters with Natasha so that I am only playing every *second* game of badminton or Little Fool or Spit with her, but the children, especially since most of them are girls and hence smart, take notice. I am sitting at a green picnic table with Natasha, our calves touching for thirty-seven seconds (my mind: "thirty-four, thirty-five, thirty-six, thirty-seven, ah, she moved"), when one of the girls says, "Gnu likes Natasha."

I start getting up, because killing myself will take some preparation, when Natasha says: "I like Gary, too. He's my friend." She then maneuvers one playing card on top of her pile and says to her slower adversary: "Spit!"

The cards fall on the table at great speed. And I am left with this duality. She likes me. Hence, I am likable. And not for this Gnu shit either. To her, I am Gary. But I am also her *friend,* and that statement is irrevocable as well.

. . .

What does it mean to love someone? At SSSQ, I am not allowed to be near the native-born girls, because I am of the *dalit* caste, untouchable, and my presence may pollute them. But at Ann Mason's, as you have seen, I can touch my skinned knee to Natasha's glowing one for thirty-seven seconds, and she will be my friend, if not more. One early summer day I am shielding myself from the sun beneath an oak tree, reading *Isaac Asimov's Science Fiction Magazine,* sneezing from the rich American pollen and dreaming of distant allergen-free planets, when I encounter these lines in a story: "I stood up and hugged her to me in that humid darkness, running my hand along her thin back and then around to cup one little breast. 'I love you, Jane,' I said." I close my eyes and picture a little bag of weight in my hand. *Cup.* You *cup* the little breast of a *Jane.* So this is love.

At home, there is love between my parents, and sometimes I can hear them loving each other. But love mostly means fighting. My mother has perfected the silent treatment to such an extent that she will not speak to my father for many days, sometimes weeks, even as they continue to share their mahogany full-sized bed together. When this happens, I serve as the emissary between them. My parents schedule meetings with me to air their grievances and to discuss the prospects for a *razvod.* And so I shuttle between them, sometimes allowing tears to strengthen my bid for them to stay together. "He apologizes, Mama. He will not fall under the influence of his wolfish relatives any longer." "Papa, she knows she should not have been an hour late when you were picking her up, but suddenly there was extra typing at work and she wanted to earn overtime."

Indeed, the most dangerous part of my day is when my father has to pick my mother up after work, after he has collected me from my grandma's, so that we may all go back to distant Little Neck together in the Tredia. We wait for Mother near a subway station at the corner of Union Turnpike and Queens Boulevard, not far from the Queens Criminal Court. There is a 1920s statue on that corner called *Triumph of Civic Virtue:* a naked, well-muscled man with a drawn sword is step-ping on two bare-chested mermaids who symbolize corruption and vice. "Where is she? *Suka tvoya mat'!*" my father cries, because my *bitch-mother* is late, ten minutes, twenty, thirty, forty, an hour late. And with each gradation of lateness I know the fight will ratchet right up the *razvod* scale.

To pass the time, and stem his anger and my worry, Papa and I play a nervous version of hide-and-seek around the well-endowed, tight-assed Civic Virtue God and his vanquished mermaids, absorbing the sickening lessons in gender relations the statue so clearly presents. (In 2012, after much outcry, the *Triumph of Civic Virtue* was removed to a Brooklyn cemetery.)

Finally, my mother puffs out of the subway in her rabbit-fur coat, the one indulgence no Russian woman can do without, and we pack into the car, and the fighting begins.

Suka! Suka! Suka!

Go to the khui*!*

In front of the child she is cursing like this. How much did you send to your relatives?

Ne-tvoyo sobache delo. *It is not your dog-business.*

Then where were you, bitch?

My mother is sick! My mother is dying! Ah, you wolfish breed!

And then my father to me, quietly, but loud enough for her to hear in the backseat, *Other men hit their wives. But I never hit her. And look what good it did.*

And I am turning in to my window, leaning my head against the cold pane, as Murray Head's "One Night in Bangkok" from the nerd-musical *Chess* plays as loudly as it may on the car's stereo. I picture an Asian girl beneath an enormous Thai *stupa* in some kind of silky na-tive dress. I'm not sure what it means other than the urge to go some-where else right now, to leap out of the car and run toward Kennedy Airport, which is not very far away.

One thing I know for certain is that my parents can *never* get a *razvod.* Why? Because we are the Family Shteyngart, population three, and with already such low numbers we are not supposed to be apart. Not to mention that maintaining two households will mean our living standards will erode, we will no longer be middle-middle class, and we might have to give up the Mitsubishi, which I have already pointed out to my unimpressed SSSQ classmates: "Behold! The Tredia-*S*." And finally, if either of my parents was to remarry (unthinkable), their American spouses would look down on my keloid scar and borrowed Batman T-shirt, and I might end up with no family at all.

. . .

Sometimes I get angry. On the school bus back at SSSQ, I find an Israeli girl—some Shlomit or Osnat—whose star shines even less brightly than my own, and I make fun of her mercilessly. She has a mustache like my grandmother's and a training bra. I slide into the seat next to her and make jokes about her need to wax her mustache with something called "turtle wax," an insult that I've overheard from another bus mate and that seems like just the right kind of topical cruelty to use on this small, dark, friendly creature. I tease her about her training bra and what I can only imagine lies beneath it. What I can't quite understand is that I have a crush on this girl precisely because she has a mustache just like my grandmother's, which makes me want to hug her and tell her all of my troubles. The girl informs on me to Mrs. R, the kindly educator who helped me with my shoelaces and sang *Troo-loo-loo-loo* when I was in first grade. Mrs. R takes me aside on the bus line and tells me to stop bothering the girl. Mrs. R's gentle opprobrium, much worse than her anger, makes me so ashamed I consider skipping the school bus and walking across Queens to my grandmother's house. The truth is I don't even understand what turtle wax is. The truth is that if those furry lips were to graze my own, I would not turn away.

I get angry even among the peaceable kingdom of Ann Mason's Bungalow Colony. There is a new kid no one likes exactly. Straight out of Minsk or somewhere, scrawny, undernourished, weak, Belorussian. He is with his grandmother, and we don't know the where-abouts of his parents. He looks like a younger version of my step-grandfather Ilya—the unhappy eyes, the Leninist forehead—and that makes me hate him even more. My favorite book of the summer of 1984 and the two subsequent summers is *Nineteen Eighty-Four*. I commit the passages in which O'Brien tortures Winston to memory. When the kid is alone staring sullenly at a comic book over a picnic table, I approach him. I sit down and begin to speak in measured tones. "Power is not a means, *Vinston;* it is an end. One does not establish a dictatorship in order to safeguard a revolution; one makes the revolution in order to establish the dictatorship. The object of persecution is persecution. The object of torture is torture. The object of power is power."

I slide over to the kid. He cowers before me, which I both love and hate. He is more *slabyi* than I am, which is good. But I am about to sing from my Bar Mitzvah Torah portion at the Congregation Ezrath Israel in Ellenville, which makes me—what? A man. What would a man do?

Before he can stop me, before I can stop me, I grab his hand. I hold up my left hand, thumb hidden, four fingers extended, just like in Orwell's book. "How many fingers am I holding up, *Vinston?*"

He doesn't understand me. Doesn't understand my English. Doesn't understand who is *Vinston*. I repeat in Russian. "Four," he says finally, his whole little sardine body trembling.

"And if the Republican Party says that it is not four but five—then how many?"

"Four."

I begin twisting his fingers. He cries out in pain. I am bearing down on him, hating this, hating this. *"Pyat'!"* he cries in Russian. "Five!"

Trying to keep back the welling tears in my own eyes: "No, Vinston, that is no use. You are lying. You still think there are four. How many fingers, please?"

He breaks free and runs down the vast green lawn separating our bungalows. "*Baaaaa-buuuuuu-shkaaaa!*"

· · ·

Later, out my bedroom window, I see his old babushka talking to mine, a stooped, tired, emaciated figure confiding to a thick, voracious, quasi-American one. Now I will be punished! Now I will be punished! I savor it. I did this terrible thing, and now I will be punished. I rush out to meet Grandma. She sighs and looks at me. She loves me so much. Why does she love me so much?

"That boy's babushka says you hit him," Grandma says.

"I didn't hit him," I say. "I read to him from a book."

"Did he do something to you?"

"No."

"My shining sun," Grandmother says. "Whatever you did to him, I'm certain he deserved it."

When Grandma leaves I go to the bedroom and weep over the monster I now am, but the next day I do the same thing. And then again. And again. *How many fingers, Vinston?* After a few weeks the boy leaves the bungalow colony for good.

The summer sun is down around eight-thirty. Grandma is already in bed and snoring with all her might. The country folk in the Russian novel *Oblomov* by Ivan Goncharov greet each nightfall with the phrase "Well, that's another day over, praise God!" and something similar can be said of Grandma's worldview. I quietly pour myself out past her bed and into the new night. The stars are constellating above, and the bungalow colony is quiet, but somewhere I hear girlish giggles and the scratchy warble of Culture Club's "Karma Chameleon" on a no-brand radio. The children are out bathed in moonlight and they are so happy to see me. "Gnu! Gnu!"

"Shhh, Eva . . . You'll wake Babushka."

"You shhh."

Natasha is sitting on an Adirondack chair, wearing her favorite green hooded sweatshirt, her boxer faithfully at her feet. "Come here, Gary," she gestures at her lap. It is not manly to sit on top of a girl, I know, but we are roughly the same height, and I do want to feel her warmth so. The boxer looks up protectively as I sit on her lap, then lowers his frothy muzzle with disregard. Oh, it's just him. Boy George is crooning: "I'm a man (a man) without conviction / I'm a man (a man) who doesn't know." Natasha leans forward, and I feel her cheek, still heated by the day's sun, against my ear. "Gnu, tell a joke," someone says. I want to lower my eyelids and be in this moment forever, but I understand what these children want of me. I tell the joke.

13.

SIXTY-NINE CENTS

*Disney World, 1986. Father and son out for a spin. Mothers up and down
Florida are locking up their daughters.*

WHEN I TURN FOURTEEN, I lose my Russian accent. I can,
in theory, walk up to a girl and the words "Oh, hi there"
would not sound like *Okht Hyzer,* possibly the name of a
Turkish politician. There are three things I want to do in my new incarnation: go to Florida, where I understand that our nation's best
and brightest had built themselves a sandy, vice-filled paradise; have a
girl tell me that she likes me in some way; and eat all my meals at Mc-
Donald's. I did not have the pleasure of eating at McDonald's often.
Mama and Papa think that going to restaurants and buying clothes
not sold by weight on Orchard Street are things done only by the very
wealthy or the very profligate. Even my parents, however, as uncriti-
cally in love with America as only immigrants can be, cannot resist
the iconic pull of Florida, the call of the beach and the Mouse.

And so, in the midst of my Hebrew-school winter vacation, two Russian families cram into a large used sedan and take I-95 down to the Sunshine State. The other family—three members in all—mirror our own, except that their single offspring is a girl and they are, on the whole, more ample; by contrast, my entire family weighs three hundred pounds. There's a picture of us beneath the monorail at EPCOT Center, each of us trying out a different smile to express the déjà-vu feeling of standing squarely in our new country's greatest attraction, my own megawatt grin that of a turn-of-the-last-century Jewish peddler scampering after a potential sidewalk sale. The Disney tickets are a freebie, for which we had had to sit through a sales pitch for an Orlando time-share. "You're from Moscow?" the time-share salesman asks, appraising the polyester cut of my father's jib.

"Leningrad."

"Let me guess: mechanical engineer?"

"Yes, mechanical engineer . . . Eh, please Disney tickets now."

The ride over the MacArthur Causeway to Miami Beach is my real naturalization ceremony. I want all of it—the palm trees, the yachts bobbing beside the hard-currency mansions, the concrete-and-glass condominiums preening at their own reflections in the azure pool water below, the implicit availability of relations with amoral women. I can see myself on a balcony eating a Big Mac, casually throwing fries over my shoulder into the sea-salted air. But I will have to wait. The hotel reserved by my parents' friends features army cots instead of beds and a half-foot-long cockroach evolved enough to wave what looks like a fist at us. Scared out of Miami Beach, we decamp for Fort Lauderdale, where a Yugoslav woman shelters us in a faded motel, beach adjacent and featuring free UHF reception. We always seem to be at the margins of places: the driveway of the Fontainebleau Hilton or the glassed-in elevator leading to a rooftop restaurant where we can momentarily peek over the PLEASE WAIT TO BE SEATED sign at the endless ocean below, the Old World we have left behind so far and yet deceptively near.

To my parents and their friends, the Yugoslav motel is an unquestioned paradise, a lucky coda to a set of difficult lives. My father lies magnificently beneath the sun in his red-and-black-striped imitation Speedo while I stalk down the beach, past baking midwestern girls, my keloid scar, my secret sharer, radiating beneath an extra-large Band-Aid. *Oh, hi there.* The words, perfectly American, not a birthright but an acquisition, perch between my lips, but to walk up to one of these girls and say something so casual requires a deep rootedness to the hot sand beneath me, a historical presence thicker than the green card embossed with my thumbprint and freckled face. Back at the motel, the *Star Trek* reruns loop endlessly on channel 73 or 31 or some other prime number, the washed-out Technicolor planets more familiar to me than our own.

On the drive back to New York, I plug myself firmly into my Sanyo AM/FM Stereo Cassette Player with Headphones and Anti-Rolling Mechanism, hoping to forget our vacation. Sometime after the palm trees run out, somewhere in southern Georgia, we stop at a McDonald's. I can already taste it: The sixty-nine-cent hamburger. The ketchup, red and decadent, embedded with little flecks of grated onion. The uplift of the pickle slices; the obliterating rush of fresh Coca-Cola; the soda tingle at the back of the throat signifying that the act is complete. I run into the meat-fumigated coldness of the magical place, the larger Russians following behind me, lugging something big and red. It is a cooler, packed, before we left the motel, by the other mother, the kindly, round-faced equivalent of my own mother. She has prepared a full Russian lunch for us. Soft-boiled eggs wrapped in tinfoil; *vinegret,* the Russian beet salad, overflowing a re-used container of sour cream; cold chicken served between crisp white furrows of a *bulka.* "But it's not allowed," I plead. "We have to buy the food here."

I feel coldness, not the air-conditioned chill of southern Georgia, but the coldness of a body understanding the ramifications of its own demise, the pointlessness of it all. I sit down at a table as far away from my parents and their friends as possible. I watch the spectacle of the newly tanned resident aliens eating their ethnic meal—jowls working, jowls working—the soft-boiled eggs that quiver lightly as they are brought to the mouth; the girl, my coeval, sullen like me but with a hint of pliant equanimity; her parents, dishing out the chunks of beet with plastic spoons; my parents, getting up to use free McDonald's napkins and straws while American motorists with their noisy tow-headed children buy themselves the happiest of meals.

My parents laugh at my haughtiness. Sitting there hungry and all alone—what a strange man I am becoming! So unlike them. My pockets are filled with several quarters and dimes, enough for a hamburger and a small Coke. I consider the possibility of redeeming my own dignity, of leaving behind our beet-salad heritage. My parents don't spend money, because they live with the idea that disaster is close at hand, that a liver-function test will come back marked with a doctor's urgent scrawl, that they will be fired from their jobs because their English does not suffice. Seven years in America, and we are still representatives of a shadow society, cowering under a cloud of bad tidings that will never come. The silver coins stay in my pocket, the anger burrows and expands into some future ulcer. I am my parents' son.

· · ·

But not entirely. The next summer, my mother announces that we will be going to Cape Cod. Aware of the beet-salad connotations of any journey with my mother, I ask her if we will be staying at a fine hotel like the Days Inn or maybe even the storied Holiday Inn. If not, if it's some kind of Russian hut with a do-it-yourself cottage-cheese station, then I do not wish to go. I can just picture walking down to the beach where all the young ladies are from decent resorts with ice machines, and me, already with my unattractiveness trailing some kind of sad buckwheat odor in from breakfast. I do not want to be both poor *and* Russian in front of people my age for ten entire days. I want a vacation from Hebrew School, not an immersion into Gentile School. This summer I am ready to say, *Oh, hi there.*

"Better than Holiday Inn," my mother says. "I think it's called Hilton."

I sit down hard on a copy of the *National Review*. But how could it be, Hilton? What about baby steps? First the Motel 6, then the Motel 7, then a few years down the road, Hilton.

We arrive on the balmy Massachusetts cape in late June. Our accommodation is a ramshackle Russian dacha, several stories of grime and peeling wallpaper, a toilet that should not really be indoors, a dinner setting of aging Odessa somnambulists shuffling down for *shchi*, cold summer sauerkraut soup. Am I forgetting something? Beet salad? You bet.

"What?" my mother says. "It's almost like the Hilton."

And then it occurs to me: If to my father I am an object of love-hate, both a best friend and an adversary, to my mother I am not even a person.

It's more than a realization on my part; it's a realignment. My mother is from a country of lies, and I am still one of its citizens. She can lie to me at will. She can lie to me without even using her imagination. And whatever comes out of her mouth I am supposed to accept as truth, as Doubleplusgood. No, I can never trust her again. As I fume alongside the beach, and tanned kids my age gather beneath the magnificent steps of some middle-class hotel that lets out directly onto the shore—ours is up a highway—I formulate my first act of rebellion.

The next day I pack two gigantic garbage bags with my summer clothes and my *Isaac Asimov*s. I tell my father to drive me to the Peter Pan bus station. I cannot remember most of the fight that takes place between me and my mother as I announce my leave-taking, except for the fact that she does not retreat one centimeter, does not even acknowledge that the Sauerkraut Arms is not the Hilton. "What's the difference between the two?" she shouts. "Show me *one* difference!" It is a frightening fight, with my mother's harshest words and her silent treatment somehow woven into one. But it's an important fight, too. I stand my ground. I will not be lied to.

"I'd like to see you live alone at home!" my mother says. "I'd like to see you starve."

"I have fifty-three dollars," I say.

And so my father, my partner in this particular crime, wheels me over to the bus station with my two garbage bags full of clothes and books. He kisses me on both cheeks. He looks me in the eye. *"Bud' zdorov, synok,"* he says. *Be well, little son.* And then a sly but respectful wink. He knows I have triumphed over her.

• • •

Only what have I done? The scenery is scrolling past me, the bridges and woods of New England giving way to the grilled-cheese patty-melt of a New York City summer. I am alone in the Peter Pan, sur-rounded by American adults and their Walkmans. All alone, but what else? Emancipated, liberated, giddy, with fifty-three dollars in allow-ance money to last me one and a half weeks.

At the Port Authority, I scramble past the subway turnstile with my two garbage bags. By the time I reach eastern Queens, two hours and many subway trains later, one of them breaks. (Our family is not the kind to use Hefty and other premier-class bags.) I try to tie off the hole in the bag with my hands, but you have to be very handy to do this successfully, and I am, no point denying it, a mama's boy, unable to perform basic tasks. I take some of the clothes out of the distressed garbage bag and wear them in layers around me, tying several T-shirts around my neck. Not wanting to spend an extra token, I trudge the last segment to our garden apartment on foot, sweating for about five miles in the early summer heat beneath many layers of clothing as I drag my one and a half garbage bags behind me.

I run down to the Waldbaum's supermarket and invest in forty dol-lars' worth of Swanson Hungry-Man TV dinners, a half-dozen full-sized bags of Doritos, which my family *never* eats (my parents call them *rvota,* or "vomit"), and several fun-sized bottles of Coke. There isn't a McDonald's within striking distance, and I do not wish to try my luck with the Burger King, where I believe the basic hamburger is costlier and inauthentic.

Back home, I take my clothes off down to my underwear and turn on the television for 240 hours. *Mama, what have I done to you?* I cry as the morning news turns into the nightly news and a comic show about an inventive orphaned child named Punky Brewster takes up some of the time in between. *How could I have run away from you like that? Am I really any better now than this motherless Punky?*

My father calls from Cape Cod to check up on me.

"Could you put Mama on?" I ask.

"She doesn't want to speak to you."

And I know what will happen when she returns, at least a month of silence, of doing a little whinny with her head whenever I so much as come into her line of vision, and sometimes even pushing away the air in front of her with her palm as if to signify that I am no longer welcome to share the earth's atmosphere with her.

But one day, deep within my ten-day escape, all alone with my science fiction and my forbidden Doritos, my ass sore from sitting on the scruffy couch for so long, my eyes television red, my mind television numb, my fifty-three-dollar capitalization reduced to a pocketful of quarters, I think to myself: This is not so bad.

It's actually kind of good.

It's actually kind of perfect.

Maybe this is who I really am.

Not a loner, exactly.

But someone who can be alone.

14.

JONATHAN

*Prisoners of Zion: Gary and Jonathan face
another day of Hebrew school.*

ACK AT SSSQ, the bodies have been piling up for years. Ausch-
witz, Birkenau, Treblinka. We have special presentations in the
gym, a protective fortress of prayer books around us, the American flag on one side of the stage, the Israeli flag on the other, and
between them the slaughter of our innocents. As I watch the ovens
open and the skeletons crumble, I become angry at the Germans and
also at the Arabs, who are the same thing as the Nazis, Jew-killers,
fucking murderers, they took our land or something, I hate them.

Then the other images that disturb us: Kids, *white kids like us,* are
putting marijuana needles into their arms. They are smoking the heroin cigarettes. First Lady Nancy Reagan, standing next to the actor
Clint Eastwood, a somber black background behind them, tells us,
"The thrill *can* kill. Drug dealers need to know that we want them out
of our schools, neighborhoods and our lives. Say no to drugs. And say
yes to life."

The children of the Solomon Schechter School of Queens are scared of Nazis and we are scared of drugs. If the *Jewish Week* had published an article revealing that Goebbels had been dealing dope to Hitler up at the Eagle's Nest the world would finally click into place. But for now, the sad fact is that some of us will not go on to Jewish educations. We will go to public high schools where there will be gentiles, and gentiles love to "do" drugs. And how will we be able to resist the peer pressure when those thrilling drugs come our way? Clint Eastwood, sneering: "What would I do if someone offered me *these drugs*? I'd tell them to take a hike."

I picture myself walking past the lockers of Cardozo High School in Bayside, Queens, the mild-mannered public school I'm zoned for. A kid walks up to me. He seems all-American, but there's something not quite right in his eyes. "Hey, Gnu," he says, "you want *these drugs*?"

And then I punch him in his face and scream, "Take a hike! Take a hike, you Nazi PLO scum!" And there's a Jewish girl they're trying to stick with their needles, and I run over to her, fists swinging, and scream, "Take a hike! Take a hike from her!" And she falls into my arms and I kiss her needle marks, and I say, "It's going to be okay, Rivka. I love you. Maybe they didn't give you the AIDS."

· · ·

The other holocaust we're scared of is the nuclear one. The 1983 ABC-TV movie *The Day After* showed us what could happen to the good people of Kansas City, MO, and Lawrence, KS, if the Soviets were to vaporize them with thermonuclear devices. Then there is the BBC version, *Threads,* shown on PBS, which is widely acknowledged to be more realistic: babies and milk bottles are instantly turned to cinders, cats asphyxiate, survivors are left to eat raw radioactive sheep. ("Is it safe to eat?" "It's got a thick coat, that should have protected it.") I memorize the final moments before the bomb hits Yorkshire, an exchange between two ill-prepared bureaucrats, and I chant it to myself in the middle of the sclerotic hum that is Talmud class:

"Attack warning red!"

"Attack warning? Is it for real?"

"Attack warning is for bloody real!"

And then in the matter-of-fact tones of a BBC announcer: "The first dust settles on Sheffield. It's an hour and twenty-five minutes after the attack. This level of attack has broken most of the windows in Britain. Many roofs are open to the sky. Some of the lethal dust gets in. In these early stages the symptoms of radiation sickness and the symptoms of panic are identical."

Yes, they are quite identical. I am nearly shitting my pants. The problem with *Threads,* shot in the washed-out industrialized colors of its locale, is that it's often hard to distinguish the city of Sheffield before the bomb hits from Sheffield after the devastation. The raw radioactive sheep actually looks like a step up from the shelled peas they're serving at a family dinner in the opening shots; at least the mutton hasn't been boiled to death.

The Day After, on the other hand, soft-pedals the devastation. The world falls apart far more brightly; how could it not with Steve Guttenberg (God, there he is again) playing one of the irradiated leads? But what I love about *The Day After* are the scenes of hardworking Missourians and Kansans reveling in their station-wagon lifestyles before the attack. Kids are riding their bikes through many-acred lawns, adults play horseshoes without worrying about mortgage payments, at the Kansas City Board of Trade soybean prices are up, and at Memorial General Hospital Dr. Jason Robards arranges for a patient to get his favorite flavor of ice cream. Vanilla. Whatever we've heard about the cost of living in Atlanta, Georgia, seems *doubly* true of this place. Here, my parents' income if they don't get a *razvod*—roughly $42,459.34 in 1983 dollars, give or take a cent—would make our family upper middle class. And then, fifty minutes into the film, when the enormous pines are uprooted by the nuclear blast, and the atomic flash reduces a wedding ceremony to so many skeletons, you really feel that these people have lost something special.

For its faults, *The Day After is* growing up in the early 1980s. This is our vocabulary. Pershing II. SAC Airborne Command. Launch on warning. "This is the Emergency Broadcast System." "Sir, we need access to the keys and authentication documents." "Confidence is high. I repeat, confidence is high." "I want to confirm, is this an exercise? Roger. Copy. This is *not* an exercise." "We have a massive attack against the U.S. at this time. Multiple ICBMs. Over three hundred missiles inbound now." "Message follows. Alpha. Seven. Eight. November. Foxtrot. One. Five. Two. Two." "We have execution from the President." "Stand by. Unlock code inserted." "Honey, we're going to have to get used to things being a lot different. What matters is, we're alive. And we're together." "The catastrophic events you have just witnessed are, in all likelihood, less severe than the destruction that would actually occur in the event of a full nuclear strike against the United States." When I close my eyes I can almost *feel* the eerie still as Steve Guttenberg walks down a Kansas country road minutes before the Soviet missiles reach their targets. The children's swings are empty. A crow buzzes over the state's ample wheat.

My parents will buy a twenty-seven-inch salmon-colored Sony Trinitron, with a sleek remote control that would decimate the Zenith Space Command, just in time for Peter Jennings to tell us that the space shuttle *Challenger* has fallen into the ocean, but when *The Day After* comes out we have just a little nine-incher from a local dump, which we unveil for special occasions. So I start a subscription to *TV Guide* magazine to get a better grip on the important shows. I am not allowed to watch TV, but I am allowed the *TV Guide,* which we take to be America's version of literature. *The Day After,* of course, is accompanied by many articles in the *Guide,* and I save that copy for many years to come, sometimes looking at the picture on the cover: a man shielding a boy from a mushroom cloud, the Lightman in my closet peering over my shoulder, so caught up in the horror he's actually stroking my wounded ear. The boy will suffer flash blindness from the blast, and the thought of being alive in the post-nuclear-holocaust world without eyesight is devastating to me. The first order of business for when the Soviets attack—and I know those lying bastards, they *will* attack—is to get a good pair of sunglasses from the Stern's department store in the Douglaston Mall.

• • •

"When the bombs fall, I will take my children outside so that we can die together instantly." This is Mrs. A, a teacher of social studies and affiliated subjects. When she says that, I feel the true horror of nuclear war because Mrs. A is terribly attractive with her slim figure and bushel of kinky Ashkenazi hair, and her daughters, who attend SSSQ's lower grades, are both similarly situated. All the cool kids and their mothers at SSSQ seem to know Mrs. A intimately, and she will often interrupt a monologue on the Suez Canal Crisis to say to her all-time favorite student, "Chava, remember when . . ."

Also, she is very keen to tell us that her daughter is an amazing ballerina and how she played Lincoln Center when she was eight months old or something of the sort. This love of child makes me tear up. My father once showed up to a parent-teacher conference where one of the teachers informed him that "Gary is very smart. We hear he reads Dostoyevsky in the original."

"*Phh,*" Papa said. "Only Chekhov."

So, after *The Day After* I keep replaying the bit about Mrs. A taking her kids out to meet the mushroom cloud. How could the Soviets possibly kill Mrs. A and her ballerina daughter? What would Jewish television personality Abba Eban have to say about this? Before she made that announcement, I had not been entirely anti–nuclear war. My research indicated that two of the Soviet missiles would target JFK and LaGuardia airports in Queens. SSSQ is geographically equidistant from the two airports, and the school's glass-heavy modernist structure would probably buckle and split into shards from the initial blasts, burning up the siddur prayer books like so many blue pancakes, and certainly the subsequent radiation exposure would kill everyone with the exception of the rotund, self-insulated Rabbi Sofer.

So far so good.

Meanwhile, Little Neck does not lie next to any obvious targets, the nearest one would be the Brookhaven National Laboratory in far-away Suffolk County, where my father will soon be toiling on a component of Ronald Reagan's new "Star Wars" missile defense program, and the Deepdale Gardens cooperative is made out of millennial bricks that can withstand a heat blast up to 1,125 degrees Fahrenheit, by my sober calculations. All I need is to have my sunglasses handy and to shelter from the radiation for a few weeks. Then I will emerge into a world without Hebrew school. In this world, with my Russian accent scrubbed away, and with the superior mathematical skills I have picked up from my father's Soviet textbooks, I will help start a new Republican civilization along with my new American best friend, Jonathan.

That is right. I have a best friend.

• • •

Mrs. A runs something called "Pilot Program," which is for the smartest kids in SSSQ, a number that can fit around a small dining table. For an entire school period, we geniuses are separated from the usual debility of the rest of the school and are sent to a teachers' lounge, where there is a refrigerator stocked with sad teacher sandwiches and a pall of cigarette smoke to make us feel quite adult. It is very hard to figure out what Mrs. A's "Pilot Program" is about. It is safe to say that my father's dream for a heavy workload in theoretical physics and higher mathematics will not come true. Activities include making caramel candies in the mold of *E.T.: The Extra-Terrestrial* and discussing the TV special *Something About Amelia,* in which Ted Danson has sex with his own daughter. Mrs. A is a born conversationalist, and Pilot Program gives her a chance to free-associate while making baked goods. When someone mentions the Steven Spielberg movie *Jaws,* Mrs. A tells a fascinating story about an Israeli soldier caught in an explosion during the Yom Kippur War, who was left with nothing but three holes where his face should have been. We cautiously eat our *E.T.* caramels.

. . .

There are five boys who are marginalized at SSSQ. There is Jerry Himmelstein, whose victimization deserves its own after-school special and who will transfer out of our moronic inferno by grade 6. There's Sammy (not his real name), a slim, sad, hyperactive boy who likes to jump on us while screaming "*URSH! UUUUURSH!*"—some deep-seated primal scream that can be translated into neither Hebrew nor English. There's David the Mighty Khan Caesar, ruler of the Imperial Lands of David, the main enemy and sometimes ally of my mythical Holy Gnuish Empire. David's a smart son of a rabbi who takes out a little spaceship in the middle of class and floats it before his freckled face while humming, "*Noooooo . . . Mmm . . . Woooo . . .* ," rather similar to the aviation pursuits I enjoy with my pen. There is me. And then there is Jonathan.

Jonathan's personality has not been reduced to the level where he has to call himself Gary Gnu III or the Mighty Khan Caesar, but he is clearly not cut out for SSSQ either. He has kind and attractive parents, an adorable sister, the collie of my dreams; and this perfect-to-my-eyes family lives in a spacious, castle-like Tudor in Jamaica Estates, the kind of Tudor Dr. Jason Robards and his beautiful elderly wife enjoyed before it was vaporized in *The Day After.* Jonathan is short like me, and his good looks are partially hidden by a layer of baby fat. When an Israeli throws a dodgeball at him with all of his compressed Canaanite fury, Jonathan will get hit and fall to the ground clutching his elbow, just like me. Another strike against him is that his mom and dad are too shy to participate in the shtetl network of SSSQ parents, a network that's mirrored in the friendships of the kids themselves. My own parents ("*Ver* is man toilet?"), of course, are completely unclubbable.

Finally, Jonathan is smart. Brilliant. And, as the old stereotype of Jews as the People of the Book dies a quiet daily death around us, Jonathan and I are also so very fucking bored. And now that my accent has faded and my English is strong and I can converse at a kilometer a minute, we become friends to the exclusion of everything else.

Saturday is his house; Sunday is mine. Or the other way around. The Jamaica Estates Tudor with its dedicated computer room or my Deepdale Gardens apartment with its treacherous red shag carpet. His Apple //e computer or my new Commodore 64 with Datasette drive (forty-three minutes to load a game). And when our playdates are over and we are shuttled back to our respective homes in Papa's Tredia-S, or his dad's AMC wagon, we rush to our push-button phones to call each other, work out further clues to Infocom Software's Hitchhiker's Guide to the Galaxy or Zork II, the nerdacious new "interactive fiction" computer games that don't just take over our lives but *are* our lives, our brains buzzing with the idea that there are problems in the world that can actually be solved.

When Jonathan's father drives me home I feel safer than ever. One day I want to have a son or daughter I can drive home in a sturdy car like this AMC wagon. My father has only recently taken to the road, and his car has been known to flip over a median and fall into a ditch, but Jonathan's father is clearly to the wheel born. He asks me questions about school, and we laugh about some of the wackier aspects of SSSQ: Pilot Program and how easy the homework is, and whether Jonathan and I should go to Harvard or Yale when we grow up (Jonathan will eventually go to Yale, me not so much). When he delivers me to my own parents, their very expressions change; they become softer, as if the Americanness is transferrable somehow. In another decade I will find out that even as my parents are slowly clawing up the ladder, Jonathan's father's business—he owns a company that installs doors throughout the city—is in great difficulty, to the point that some of his SSSQ tuition is paid for in repair work. Later, cancer will take his life. The thought that this kind man, this perfect family, was going through something more painful than my own never occurs to me. On most days, I have my head so far up my family's ass I can taste yesterday's borscht. And that doesn't leave much room for empathy for others, especially for Americans who the new Sony Trinitron says "have it all." Sometimes, drunk off of three consecutive hours of Zork, I close the door to Jonathan's cavernous bathroom, lie down on the soft mat riddled with collie hairs, and breathe in the floral air-freshener scent that even to this day I associate with home. What makes me want to cry is that Jamaica Estates is very close to JFK airport, and when the Soviets strike, my new family will be gone in a flash.

My father is also like a second father to Jonathan. Here is this strong man, manly to a fault, who takes us fishing on a pier off the wealthy suburb of Great Neck. The docks are clearly meant for Great Neck residents only, but my father has found a hole in a chain-link fence, and the three of us scamper through illegally to fish off the rich man's pier. "*Prokhod dlya oslov!*" Papa proudly declares. "Gary, translate."

"It's the passage for donkeys," I say to Jonathan.

Sometimes we invade the pier of the U.S. Merchant Marine Academy in Kings Point and haul in a catch between the hulls of the military training ships. I love my father's gentleness with Jonathan, though I am a little jealous, too. Proud that I have a father who can sneak into enemy territory and steal striped bass with just a few jerks of his fishing stick, but wishing that my father could be like that all the time—his English wrong but patient, tender, instructive. "Over *zer* is mostly *flyook* and *zer* is *flaunder* . . . Guys, don't pull *feesh* so fast! Give him time to get on hook, okay?" Guys. We are guys together in front of my papa. It occurs to me that if we had spoken English instead of Russian at home, my father would have lost some of the natural cruelty that comes with our mother tongue. *Eh, you, Snotty. Eh, you, weakling.* Because all I want to do now is to speak to Papa and Mama in Jonathan's English. Which also happens to be my own.

But it's too late for that.

· · ·

Sexuality is ripening around us in a way that makes us scared. I can never tell Jonathan about Natasha, my Russian summertime crush, because talk of girls will remind us of our *dalit* status and shatter the pixilated world we've created around ourselves. One beautiful fall day, the parents of one of the wealthiest SSSQ kids rent out the top of the World Trade Center for his Bar Mitzvah, complete with a harpsichordist strumming a classical version of "Hava Nagila" in the sky lobby, sevruga caviar by the spoonful, men in uniform bearing the boy's name on their lapels at the toilet stations, and a series of buses to ferry us from Queens to the monstrous twin skyscrapers.

On the way home to Queens in the rented buses, two of the more advanced boys crowd around the girl who has developed the most breasts and jerk themselves off to her loud laughter. The news reaches our front row, and Jonathan and I are duly shocked. This never happens in our computer games. We have seen Brooke Shields in a swimsuit in *People* magazine, and we tried to put two Panasonic VHS recorders together to dub the R-rated version of the John Boorman film *Excalibur*, rife with both frontal and dorsal nudity (it never quite worked out for us). But the idea that two boys, one not even an Israeli, would take out their *zains* in the back of a plush rented bus and cream themselves over a girl is beyond our sense of reality. As I fold myself into my safe red Soviet comforter at bedtime, Papa sometimes makes an appearance in my bedroom with the encouraging words "Are you tugging yourself? Well, don't tug too hard. It'll fall off." And then deep in the night Dr. Ruth Westheimer will whisper into my headphones the difference between clitoral and vaginal orgasms, but these are just words for me to put away for another lifetime, maybe for after law school. Am I supposed to tug at myself like those boys? Will that make my parents and my teachers happy? It's too much to think about. I'd rather just play Zork with my best friend, Jonathan.

```
ZORK I: The Great Underground Empire
Copyright (c) 1981, 1982, 1983 Infocom, Inc. All rights reserved.
ZORK is a registered trademark of Infocom, Inc.
Revision 88 / Serial number 840726

West of House
You are standing in an open field west of a white house, with a
```

```
boarded front door.
There is a small mailbox here.


>
```

In the dim light of Jonathan's computer room his two five-and-one-quarter-inch Apple disk drives are twirling with anticipation. The > represents the so-called status line, upon which the player would give directions. For example:

```
>W
```

would mean the player wanted to go west. Or

```
>Open mailbox
```

would be another self-evident command. And so, without the intrusion of the graphics or sounds found in other video games, Jonathan and I journey into the Great Underground Empire, land of dungeons and treasure, trolls and grues and Elvish swords, and the dreaded Flood Control Dam #3. After hours of > we pause play and stagger onto the brightly lit world of Union Turnpike, to the Hapisgah (the Peak) kosher kebab restaurant, where Israeli waitresses ignore us as blithely as our own damsels at SSSQ while heaping up some of the juiciest kebabs in Queens for pocket change. These are the rhythms of my new Life with American Friend: Union Turnpike, kebab platter with hummus and Israeli salad, video rental store, Mel Brooks's *History of the World, Part 1,* Mark Russell's safe political comedy on PBS ("Read my lips, no new taxes, read my lips, they're going to raise the old ones!"), and the wielding of our collective `Elvish sword of great antiquity` against enemies great and small.

In school, we mostly wield our Elvish sword, too. We are inseparable. Of course, there's my outsize Gary Gnu III personality, and sometimes I have to act out in public, have to make the class laugh.

When I am cast as Julius Caesar in a school play I go around performing the Roman salute, which is, unfortunately, identical to the Nazi salute. "*Heil* Caesar!" I cry as I run around Hebrew school with my arm outstretched. Mrs. A looks at me with disgust. "That's not funny," she says. "You think everything is funny, but it's not. Not everything is a joke." And I feel like she's punched right through my Gnu persona, this woman who I so wish would love me. I can barely breathe as I say, "It's the Roman salute, Mrs. A. I lived in Italy once." But Mrs. A has already brushed me aside and is talking once more of her daughter's ballet excellence and how she and her favorite student's family should get together soon in the "Berkshires," whatever those are.

There is one history teacher Jonathan and I love, and his name is Mr. Korn. Mr. Korn has three disabilities: (1) he stutters terribly ("T-t-t-tea-p-p-pot D-d-d-dome S-s-s-scandal . . ."); (2) his teeth are yellow and pebbly; and (3) he owns a total of three plaid shirts, each nearly as Soviet as my own. Mr. Korn actually *wants* us to learn something other than the birth order of Jacob's sons. His signature line, the one he doesn't stutter through, is "Stop and think about it." Which is a weighty thing to ask of a class of troglodytes screaming at fever pitch about their *zains* and their father's import-export business. I behave like a jackass in Mr. Korn's class, but I do stop and think about what he has to say. About the fact that America is not merely a place for the extraction of capital but a landmass built partly on the miseries of others, that my future doesn't have to be a mere triumphalist immigrant march from the streets of Queens to the Best Little Tudor in Scarsdale.

To reward Mr. Korn for giving me an education, I torment him all the more. Robert is his name, so I scream out, "Hey, Bob!" whenever I burst into class. Or "Yessiree, Bobert!"

Last year I learned that Mr. Korn recently died of a terribly well-known disease, because, in local parlance, "He liked theater," and that knowledge merely affirms everything I know about the way the universe is held in place, the way the scales tip away from the good and the weak and toward the angry and the strong. Stop and think about it.

As my outbursts grow worse, Mr. Korn sends me to the principal of general studies (the non-Hebrew half of the curriculum), another relatively humane man, with the unfortunate name of Mr. Dicker, whom we will soon reward with a heart attack. "How do you think you can work on your behavior?" Mr. Dicker asks. I stretch out my arm. "Now that's a Roman salute, not a Nazi salute, right?"

"Yes," I say. "I'm Julius Caesar. *Heil* Caesar!"

Back in the classroom Mr. Korn is going over our nonsensical essays on the ups and further ups of American history. I lean over the desk and feel his cigarette breath clouding the Fruit-Roll-Ups-and-Carvel-Flying-Saucer-ice-cream scent of an SSSQ classroom. Children are screaming around us. Jonathan is deep in sketching out our next rampage through the Great Underground Empire of Zork. "Hey, Bob," I say.

"Hey, G-g-gnu."

"I really think we paid too much for the Louisiana Purchase. Fifteen million bucks for Arkansas?"

"I know, Gnu." And we smile at each other, so many broken, stunted teeth between us.

• • •

By eighth grade, Jonathan and I give up on a Solomon Schechter education entirely. We create our own game called Snork II: A Snork Forever Voyaging. We sit next to each other in class, and we play it all day long using pen and paper instead of the computer screen, coming up for air only when Mr. Korn stutters into class to complain about the Tet Offensive. I am the writer, and Jonathan is the player. His absurdist quest involves the rescue of a shipment of SSSQ's Spanish textbooks, the *Español al Días*, which have been mistakenly kidnapped by Soviet intelligence and buried deep in a toilet in Leningrad. Jonathan is the main adventurer, but at times he is also joined by Gnu, Sammy "the Ursher," and the Mighty Khan Caesar, in other words, our whole sorry gang. The adventure begins in Queens, continues on to Honk [*sic*] Kong, then mainland China ("Welcome to Communist China, the home of the whopper!"), the *Orient Express,* Venice, Germany, Sverdlovsk (where Lenin, who somehow never died, has been reduced to a third-rank poultry interrogator), and on to Leningrad. A series of self-destructing recorded messages, à la *Mission: Impossible,* drives Jonathan forward as I supply the horribly misspelled narrative and he writes commands into the status line (>).

```
page 120
Embankment (Leningrad)
P.S. This message will self-destruct in thirty hours.
> Drop recorder.
You wanna leave the recorder behind?
> Yes
Ya shure?
> Yes
Absoludly?
> Yes
Todally?
> Yes
I can't hear ya!
> Yes
OK, you leave it behind it explodes 30 seconds later, and kills 60
people. Happy?
> Yes
I'm not.
> Go to party.
Gnu takes you to Tipanovskaya Street . . . Coincidentally Gnu lived
there. You see a party going on indoors, a guard is guarding the
entrance.
```

And on like that for hundreds of densely scribbled pages, with one-liners in the mode of Mel Brooks or maybe the Marx Brothers. "You are enemies of the state. We're not shure which state but probably a sparsely populated one like Wyoming." Riffs on "condems," "vibrators" and "other exotic devices," and occasional hints of romance, influenced, I suppose, by our recent dorkish reading of *A Tale of Two Cities:* "She's beautiful, petite, and Victorian, what more do you want?"

But there is something I want more than Dickens's divine Lucie Manette, which is to take Jonathan on an adventure into my childhood, which is why A Snork Forever Voyaging can only go back to one place, back to Leningrad, back to Tipanov Street. At home, my parents and I are watching the reformist new Soviet leader Gorbachev on television with great suspicion. Is the smiling round-faced man with the giant wine splotch on his forehead really going to bring all that Soviet nonsense to an end? "Trust but verify," as our hero Ronald Reagan likes to intone. And I rarely bring up Grandmother Galya, whom we've left behind, because I know that anything *rodstvenniki*-related can only bring trouble. I am forgetting what she looked like, I am forgetting the taste of the cheese sandwiches that paid for my first novel, and I am forgetting that I should love her even though she's not here.

Maybe that's why I'm taking Jonathan back to Leningrad. I am telling Jonathan something I can never say to the boys and girls of SSSQ. That I am not some kind of Gary Gnu antelope whatever-the-fuck who is there to act crazy for their amusement. That I am a Russian boy, of Jewish lineage, sure, but a Russian boy from Russia, with half his life spent in that country.

And Jonathan, because he is a true friend, will go there with me. *Coincidentally Gnu lived there.*

• • •

My father stops hitting me. Perhaps it's because I'm a little taller now, my jumble of sweaty dark black hair hanging just a few inches below his thick lips. Perhaps it's American life, Jonathan's family, slowly seeping into him. The last time he gives me "one across the neck," I've allegedly been a *grubiyan* (a "boor") to my grandma Polya. I suppose I have been rude to her, refusing to let her hold my hand as we cross the violent streets of Forest Hills (I am almost fifteen) and not being as appreciative of her eight-course meals now that each bite of a Klondike bar goes right to my tits. But also I can sense my grandmother's decline. Every year her mental faculties are withering, and the American drugs aren't helping. A series of strokes are about to commence, reducing her to a wheelchair, one side of her body inoperable. Even before that happens, I want to withdraw from her. I *cannot* allow the woman who loves me so much to die slowly before me. I have to look away.

And so my father gives me one across the neck. Fine. Good. I simmer quietly in my room. Every penny I earn doing chores has been spent decorating my bedroom to resemble the office of J. R. Ewing, the villain of the television show *Dallas*. Luckily, it already has the right wood paneling, and to further the vibe I've installed a desktop computer, a fancy-looking Panasonic telephone with an LCD, and a luxurious chair from the dump. All I need is the model golden oil derrick to make the look complete. But even without the derrick, whenever I feel blue I stride into my so-called office, grab the expensive phone, and, with what I think is a Texan accent, shout into the receiver, "Hi darlin'! You just hang tight, y'hear?"

After giving me one across the neck, my father comes into my bedroom, and I brace my neck for another one. "Let's go for a walk," my father says. He seems sad. I sigh and shuffle the pile of carefully typed stories I am about to submit for rejection to *Isaac Asimov's Science Fiction Magazine*.

We walk through the blooming Deepdale Gardens, past all the places where my father has entertained me with his *Planet of the Yids* tales and where he has given me the *podzhopniks,* the little side kicks in the ass. But those kicks symbolize gaiety and our funny father-son bond. Today, Papa is serious, and my neck is tense. He is taking his time with what he wants to say, and usually words just roll off him in thick bursts of anger or glee or philosophy. We are passing the five skyscraper-high, insect-like air traffic antennas down the street from us with their fearsome signage: WARNING THIS FACILITY IS USED IN FAA TRAFFIC CONTROL. LOSS OF HUMAN LIFE MAY RESULT FROM SERVICE INTERRUPTION. ANY PERSON WHO INTERFERES WITH AIR TRAFFIC CONTROL . . . WILL BE PROSECUTED UNDER FEDERAL LAW.

I do not want to be prosecuted under federal or familial law. Or maybe I do. "Listen," Papa says. "I shouldn't have hit you. You were rude to your grandmother, but I shouldn't have hit you. I behaved badly."

I rub my neck and shrug. "It's okay," I say. But what I want to say is: *Don't you want this? Don't you want to keep hitting me? Don't you love me anymore? Or am I so bad that I am beyond the redemption of getting one across the neck?*

You have not behaved badly, Papa. Only *I* can behave badly. I am the child. You are the father. How can you say such an awful thing?

We pass by the basketball court where I've hit so many backboards and missed so many hoops with my imprecise aim, my fingers, my arms, my lungs straining to make good for him. We talk about fishing, cars, the odds of my getting into Stuyvesant, the specialized science high school in Manhattan where the tuition is free. My father will yell at me again. And threaten me. And be disappointed in me. But without his hands upon me, the family romance is over. Just like my asthma is over. Now I am supposed to be the man. To learn to hit and earn and make others fear me. *How many fingers am I holding up, Vinston?*

• • •

The children of the Solomon Schechter School of Queens have gathered at the Forest Hills Jewish Center to hear my best friend, Jonathan, still a sweet little boy in his purple nylon graduation robe, recite a prayer for peace and against nuclear annihilation. We will then sing the Israeli national anthem and graduate. My family is also about to graduate, from our garden apartment to a real house with a forty-by-sixty-foot backyard in a different, slightly more affluent, part of Little Neck.

A yearbook of essays and photographs has been prepared. On one page, two young Jewish girls have submitted essays entitled "DEATH," "FEAR," and "THE TERRIBLE PAIN" next to a drawing of the Grim Reaper. Male children are supposed to shroud their inner life with so much active horseshit, but these girls are honestly scared of death, scared of the void, scared of the terrible pain that precedes death for a good 80.3 years in the United States. Who would have known the general sadness and anxiety—beyond the sadness of adolescence, beyond the anxiety of being Jewish—have infected the tiny hallways and tidy *Bionic Woman* lunch boxes of Solomon Schechter?

On another page, there is a photograph of a smiling Israeli kid mock punching me in the face, his hand choking my neck, as I mock cringe in fear. Next to that is a photograph of bearded Mr. Korn in a yellow plaid doozy of a shirt about to hit me over the head with a rolled-up copy of the *Times*. The look on my face says: *I love this man.*

Twenty-five years later, Jonathan and I will become friends again, after drifting apart as good childhood friends with traumatic schooling often need to do. We will return to our alma mater, a diminished place where more than a third of the kids are now from the former Soviet Union, mostly Bukharan Jews from Uzbekistan who have settled this stretch of Queens. Mrs. A is still there, looking remarkably young and vital. She remembers Jonathan and, in particular, his pretty mother, but not me. "You're an author?" she asks me. "Do you do anything else?" She'll send us on our way with the mission of spreading the good word about Solomon Schechter education. "Prove to them our graduates aren't ax murderers!"

I attend the twenty-fifth SSSQ reunion at the Forest Hills Jewish Center. The scene has changed only slightly. There are a lot of bald *machers* and their gleaming wives, entire tables speaking in Hebrew, teachers shushing us, a "Chinese auction" of vaguely Chagallesque paintings, a hired comedian making jokes about Hispanics and Iranians. "We taught you *Chumash*,"* a new but familiar-sounding female authority figure is screaming at us, "but we didn't teach you manners. Stop talking! I have a hostile audience here!"

And as I glance around at my former classmates, a thought occurs to me. *This is a community.* These people know one another, understand one another, came of age with one another. They were tied by kin and outlook, as were their parents. As were their parents before them. Moms making rugelach in advanced baking ovens, dads talking mileage on their new Lincolns, the drowsy, hypnotic hum of cantors and rabbis on Saturday mornings. What happened here, this was nobody's fault. We Soviet Jews were simply invited to the wrong party. And then we were too frightened to leave. Because we didn't know who we were. In this book, I'm trying to say who we were.

> "Dear Gnu, You are a funny republican who will be a democrat in
> a few years. Fuck Reagan! Bring on Jesse [Jackson]! Enjoy the
> Chinese whiz kids.† Love . . . Rachel W."—from a classmate in
> the SSSQ autograph book, 1987

> "Dear Gary, Just one question: Do you ever cry?"—another
> classmate

> "P.S. For every fortune made—a <u>crime</u> has been
> committed."—Mr. Korn.

> "*Genug* ["enough," Yiddish], Gnu. Begin anew."—a concerned art
> teacher

• • •

In our computer games, there's a series of commands the player types on the status line when he finds himself in an entirely new environment.

---

* The Torah in printed form.
† At Stuyvesant High School, where I will soon enroll.

>Look. Hear. Taste. Smell. Feel.

All my books are packed for our move to the new house with the backyard. The wood-paneled closet is empty. I open it with the same trepidation as always, but the Lightman is sitting in the corner, shaking, little pinpricks of light falling off his body. Now that my asthma is gone, I can breathe in fully as I watch him disappear. But this is no catharsis for me, I'm afraid. No metamorphosis. Even as my tormentor drowns in the darkness around him, my fists are clenched. "You motherfucker," I say in my now-perfect English. *You motherfucker.*

15.

TAKE THE K TRAIN

*The author's grandmother never passed judgment on the amazing
shirt he is sporting here. He saved his best smiles for her.*

FOR THE FIRST FEW YEARS of my life in Queens, America, I
have no idea where Manhattan is. There are two or three skyscrapers of maybe twenty stories apiece rearing up where Union
Turnpike smashes into Queens Boulevard. I am under the impression
that *that* is Manhattan.

Eventually, I am taken to the bargain emporiums of Orchard Street
on the Lower East Side, where I spend most of the day rooting around
the clothing bins like a curious piglet, pulling out underwear and
belts, socks and slacks, a winter jacket with a hood designed to cover
the head of an urban Goliath, not a little milksop like myself. There's
something *visually* unclean about this whole place; in contrast to the
park-like spreads of eastern Queens, Manhattan's colors are reminis-
cent of a Soviet newscast—tractor browns, beet reds, cabbage greens.
Mama and I turn off Orchard Street onto Delancey, where the steel

cauldron of the Williamsburg Bridge overwhelms the cityscape, leaving me worried for the cars disappearing between its vast girders. And then—a loud pop. Gunfire! I grab my mother's hand and pull myself into her coat. The violent, unhappy Manhattanites are shooting at us! We hear a few yelps from passersby, but soon the halfhearted terror gives way to laughter and Spanish. What happened? A car backfired, that's what.

As a Hebrew school boy, I dream of someday moving to the most suburban of suburbs, where I will never have to look into another unfamiliar face, or indeed any faces at all. I see myself as a prosperous Republican left to his own devices in a backyard that stretches over a hill, swallows up a formerly public lake, and ends in a fierce bramble of barbed wire festooned with a PRIVATE PROPERTY sign. It's an appropriate way to spend the 1980s. Young immigrant to city: *Drop dead*.

And then I am accepted to the Stuyvesant High School for the maths *and* the sciences on Fifteenth Street, between First and Second Avenues and between the dangerous districts of East Village, Greenwich Village, Union Square, Times Square, and the Ladies' Mile.

• • •

September 1987. Manhattan Island. The car of visiting relatives makes its way down Second Avenue, with me and my knapsack in tow. The relatives, from some second-tier American or Canadian city, glance out apprehensively at the busy, dirty city. "Leave him here," my mother says. "*Igoryochek*"—Little Igor—"can you walk across the street by yourself?"

"Yes, Mama." We are worried that just like at Hebrew school the nonmagnificent car of our relatives will create problems for me with the student body. We don't seem to understand that more than half the students at Stuyvesant are lower- to middle-class immigrant strivers much like ourselves, that China's Fujian Province, the Indian state of Kerala, and Russia's Leningrad Oblast lie at different corners of the same body of land. (The notoriously hard-to-get-into school requires top marks on a math test that students from the dweebiest countries can easily achieve.)

I also do not understand that I am about to walk into the rest of my life.

In the weeks before the start of Stuyvesant, I sit down with my mother and I tell her that I need to wear better clothes than I did at Solomon Schechter. I don't tell my mother about the eight years of being subhuman at Hebrew school, because that would be tantamount to saying something bad about the Jews, which is treason, a capital offense. My parents sacrificed everything to bring me here to be free and Jewish, and I have taken that lesson to heart. I may have written my blasphemous Gnorah, yes, but only a year ago I led my parents on an insane hunt against crumbs of chametz, the leavened bread that is forbidden during the Passover holiday, castigating them for their lack of vigilance, nearly tearing off the shag carpet in search of month-old chunks of Lithuanian rye. When I pee I know that I am not allowed to think of any of the names of G-d or He will punish me, will lop off whatever's left, although these days I mostly can't help letting loose a stream of *YahwehYahwehYahweh,* followed by hours of deep existential grief.

"Mama, I have to dress better."

In my quest for sartorial funding, I may have also mentioned to my mother that dressing better is a prerequisite for acceptance to an Ivy League college. This (sort of) lie may have loosened the clasp of her wallet, because getting into a top college has been the first, second, third, and last concern of all Stuyvesant students and their mamas from the day the high school was founded in 1904 and will be until the day its new waterfront campus finally sinks beneath the climate-stoked waves in 2104.

And so my first Stuyvesant memory actually takes place at Macy's. My mother and I are roaming that midtown maze for the new hot brands, Generra, Union Bay, Aéropostale. I want to dress like the rich girls in Hebrew school did, so I am trying on loose, baggy shirts and sweaters, which will also hide my tits and settle softly over the pink keloid scar taking up the real estate of my right shoulder. No one shops like my mother. A small budget is stretched out into a shirt for every day of the week and pants and sweaters for every other day. I come out of the dressing room, and Mama presses the shirts against my body, holds them tight, to make sure I don't bulge out upstairs, and, if I'm trying on jeans, to certify there is at least the suggestion of an ass. Until I make the acquaintance of a series of girlfriends in my thirties who will accompany me to dressing rooms all over Manhattan and Williamsburg, this is the closest I come to the ministrations of a woman.

When we walk out of Macy's with two tightly packed bags under each arm, I feel my mother's sacrifice far more than when she talks about what she's left behind in Russia. I love my mother truly, but I am a teenager. The fact that my mother has just visited my dying grandma Galya in Leningrad and found her unable to speak or even recognize her, while the rest of her family, cold and hungry, waited in line for hours to score a desiccated, inedible eggplant, means much too little to me.

All I can hear are the electronic zaps—*tttrick*—of the $39.99 Generra shirts being scanned at the counter, the green dollar figures adding up on the register, the final indignity, the New York sales tax, soaring the numbers into an unexpected new realm. *I am so sorry, Mama, to spend our money like this.*

At Solomon Schechter boys had to wear shirts with collars because that's how Yahweh wanted it, but secular Stuyvesant has no dress code, and so we invest in a colorful collection of OP T-shirts. "OP" stands for "Ocean Pacific," and it is a California surfers' brand. I am, of course, the world's most consummate Californian surfer. ("Dude, that breaker was boss! I am like so amped!") Still, despite my lack of surfer credentials, these T-shirts are wonderful: They stretch out over the uncertainty of my teenage frame, and their bright visages of wave-riding surfers distract a little from the bobbing Adam's apple above the neckline. One of the shirts features three grannies in polka-dot dresses next to a long-haired surfer carrying his boogie board, and I'm guessing this is some kind of easygoing California humor, but it is also a reminder that in the center of Queens, so far from the scary world of Manhattan, there still lives my grandmother, who is proud of me for getting into the prestigious math and science academy.

Wearing my OP grandmother shirt, I walk through parklike Stuyvesant Square, sweaty-palmed and scared. I know I cannot be Gary Gnu any longer, but then what will I be? A serious, hardworking Republican boy bound for Harvard, Yale, or, in the worst scenario, Princeton. That's me. I'll be funny only when it's called for. *No more clowning around.* I'll keep my mouth shut. I have just seen Oliver Stone's *Wall Street* with my family, and the lessons were clear. Don't trust outsiders. Don't get caught. Focus only on wealth creation. Greed is good. I also think I have a trump card: the $280,000 colonial my family has just bought in Little Neck. Packed in my school bag, just in case, I carry an engineer's report testifying to our new house's value, including a photograph of the house in the morning sun, its southern exposure swaddled by a row of hyacinths. Every step of the process, from picking out the actual house among a casting call of colonial look-alikes to calculating the mortgage payments, was done with my obsessive participation. I even created a Commodore 64 computer program called Family Real Estate Transaction Calculator to help us make sense of our descent into institutional debt. I wonder what children whose parents have money think about in their spare time.

And the other thing I want to do is to make a friend. Jonathan has gone off to the Ramaz School, a Hebrew school on the Upper East Side, many of whose children enjoy the kind of prosperity that would make my old Solomon Schechter comrades blanch. The difference between Stuy and Ramaz is too severe, the memory of our common suffering still too recent, and our friendship quickly fades away. Now there is no one to play Zork or eat juicy kosher kebabs with, no daily phone calls, no car rides with a kind native-born father, and I realize, after having a real American friend, that friendship is almost as important to me as the acquisition of prime outer-borough real estate. Since I can't use humor to advance myself at Stuyvesant, I must learn a different way to make people like me and spend time with me.

And so here I am standing in front of Stuyvesant High School in my Ocean Pacific granny T-shirt. The building is a muscular Beaux-Arts monster, five stories of brick academic excellence that scare the boy from Little Neck to no end. But my fellow first-year students look no better than I do. Most of the boys are my height, or maybe a little taller, thin, and pallid, smelling of something stale and ethnic, the world around them reflected in spectacles so thick they could generate solar energy. Our natural enemies are the truly urban kids from low-performing Washington Irving High School, a few blocks away, who will supposedly beat the shit out of us at will (in four years at Stuyvesant, I encounter exactly zero of them). A special "Safe Train" is arranged by the board of education at the First Avenue L stop. This subway train departs under full police protection to make sure our Einsteins are not attacked by ruffians as they connect to, say, the number 7 train to Flushing, Queens. Apparently, I've gone from a Judaic Benetton showroom to a holding pen for multinational nerds.

Which brings me to the next thing I notice.

About half of these kids are "Chinese." I've been told to expect this interesting twist and to develop all kinds of formal strategies for relating to children of the Far East, because one day they might employ me. While it is an accepted fact that the black and Hispanic kids will be violent, the Chinese kids are supposed to be smart and polite, if maybe a little otherworldly, because their culture is just so different from normal culture. An important tidbit I pick up somewhere on the streets of Queens: You must never refer to these Chinese kids as "Chinese," because some of them are actually Korean.

Inside, bedlam. The halls of the old Stuyvesant—the school presently occupies a deluxe mini-skyscraper in Battery Park City—were meant for a handful of boys at the turn of the previous century. By 1987, the school somehow crams in nearly three thousand geeks of both genders. Freshman orientation involves reams of printouts, sequences of precalculus and full-on calculus and postcalculus and meta-calculus, along with lethal doses of biology, physics, and chemistry. A thick white-and-blue handbook gives us the first taste of what we're to expect in the next four years: the College Highest Average Rejected, Lowest Average Accepted Chart (CHARLAAC),* which we will soon know by heart. The numbers are numbing. Without at least a 91 percent average, even the lowliest Ivy League school is out of bounds.

At the end of the day, my mother and I have worked out a plan. Because Manhattan is so dangerous, Mama will hide behind a tree outside of the main entrance of Stuyvesant, and when I come out she will shadow me to the subway and, from there on, back to the safety of Little Neck. When I ran away from the Sauerkraut Arms on Cape Cod, I had managed this long subway journey by myself. But back then I had the two garbage bags full of books and clothes that made me look so destitute even potential muggers averted their eyes out of sympathy.

And so it is resolved: I need a subway companion. But our plan goes awry in the most awful way for Mama. Because by the end of the first day of Stuy with its great scholarly disquisitions on the different schools of Cornell (the School of Industrial and Labor Relations is a good option if you can't get into Arts and Sciences and if you can convince the admissions people that you like labor), I have made something of a friend, and he is . . . black. With just a tiny dribble of finely cut hair on his head and an urban uniform of no-brand sweatpants and no-brand sweatshirt, black. And this new friend has asked me to go to the Central Park and play something called Ultimate Frisbee with him and some other Stuyvesant kids, black.

A terrible choice is upon me. Do I betray Mama, who is hiding behind a tree, anxiously scanning the horizon for me as waves of Chinese kids run past her to the Safe Train? Or do I go with this black to the Central Park? I choose friend making. And it hurts me so much,

* Acronym mine.

because my mother has just bought all these nice clothes for me and our shopping has made us close. Mama is a friend, my best confidante now that Jonathan has gone to Ramaz, and she is waiting for me under the tree. Just three years ago at Ann Mason's Bungalow Colony I had taken her aside and informed her of the most important development of my life to date: "Mama, we played Spin the Bottle and Natasha had to kiss me."

What to do?

The young man and I leave by the back exit as I try on different excuses for my mother: We've already discussed peer pressure and come to the conclusion that sometimes one must strategically succumb to it. And my new companion isn't black, he's Chinese. We went to the park to do some athletics and to discuss the College Highest Average Rejected, Lowest Average Accepted Chart. This boy, Wong, will steadfastly see me through Wharton, and with luck we will crunch numbers at the same brokerage house in time for Dan Quayle's first presidential term in 1996.

• • •

My new friend is walking through the subway cars, and I mean *through* them. The signs on the car doors caution you not to do so, to stay safely inside, but this city boy just slides right through from one end of the train to the other, with me in tow, and him dancing ahead. Just one misstep and you will fall into the void between the half-moon platforms—but the boy doesn't care! He actually *whistles* as he goes through the cars and holds the doors open for me with a smile and a nod. (Me, scared, through my teeth: "Thank you, *dude*.") Our train is an ancient silvery beast belonging to a subway line I've never heard of, not the relatively clean and modern F, which hoofs it to somewhere near Jonathan's house and the Hapisgah kosher kebab restaurant, but the B or T or P train, which shoots arrow-like up skinny Manhattan Island and doesn't go to Queens at all.

Am I being bad? Am I setting myself up for a mugging? I forgot to pack a "mugger's wallet," which should have only one five-dollar bill for the mugger, with the rest of the money secreted away in one of my socks or in my tighty whities (even my underwear has a statement to make about race).

But whatever *this* is, it doesn't feel wrong.

We climb out of the underground at Seventy-Second Street and breathe in the sunshine. I wonder what my new chum sees in me, why he asked me to come to the park with him. It must be my Ocean Pacific T-shirt and friendly surfer manner. The boy confidently walks through the Central Park and toward a green space laid out, carpet-like, amid the skyscrapers. Two hundred days later, by next spring, I will know it quite well as the Sheep Meadow. Right now, I look at it askance. How did this happen, this clean bit of beauty smack in the middle of the world's second most dangerous city after Beirut? All this greenery, all these got-off-from-work-early, quietly content people lying on their stomachs, the late summer wind billowing the backs of their cotton tees.

"Shit," my new amigo says, appreciatively.

My father is no stranger to cursing in English. Every encounter with a household appliance or a motor vehicle will bring on a torrent of "Sheeets" and "Faaaks" sometimes leading to an operatic "Faaak Sheeet Faaak, Faaak Faaak Sheeet," which, before he stopped hitting me, would put my upper torso on high alert. But at Hebrew school the curses were mostly in that language and the province of the Israeli boys. Which brings me to my next question: How does one talk to a gentile?

"Shit," I say. All casual and loose.

My new colleague puts a brown hand to his brow as a visor and scans the horizon. "Fuck," he says.

"Yeah," I say. "Fuck." And it feels good, it feels right and strong, and I'm not entirely familiar with the word yet, but I've caught on to something of the concept: It feels *cool*. My buddy spots the kids we're to play Frisbee with and wow—they're goys big-time. Goys from China and India and Haiti and the Bronx and the Brooklyn and the

Staten Island, too. But even though they're not Jews, it's pretty clear from the get-go that they're not going to mug me or heroin me. They just want to toss around a fucking Frisbee.

And while I'm not good at the urbane sport of Ultimate, which combines disk throwing with American football (but without the oc-casional paraplegia), I do well enough that no one laughs at me. And as I run through the Sheep Meadow with my hands in the air trying to capture the disk and speed it to the "end zone," I long for the mo-ment when we will stop running, just so I can take this in.

Where am I? I am in Manhattan, the chief borough of New York City, the biggest city in America. Where am I not? I'm not in Little Neck; I'm not with my mother and father.

The park is a respite from the urban grid. Beyond it I am sur-rounded by buildings of heroic proportions, buildings that dwarf me, buildings that tell me I'm not all that special, but I am not scared of them. What if . . . It occurs to me right away. What if one day I were to live in one of them?

I am surrounded by women who are beautiful. Not the way I was taught was beautiful, the idyllic proportions of sword-and-sorcery maidens, the chesty reproductive heights of yeshiva, but beautiful with their slender bodies lying on blankets, just a little bit of chest staring out over their bras, a strip of white, a strip of brown, don't look too hard, look away.

In Henry Roth's novel of turn-of-the-last-century immigration *Call It Sleep,* the young Jewish protagonist, David Schearl, leaves the familiar contours of his Brownsville ghetto with a Polish boy, and he thinks of his new friend, *Not afraid! Leo wasn't afraid!* And here I am, just a few hours out of my mother's loving grasp in the big terrible city, not afraid.

"Time out, time out," I say, and manage to do the American per-pendicular thing with my hands that signals to my playmates that I need to take a breather. I sit down on the grass, my blue Guess? jeans collecting the grass stains I know I should protect them from because, even on sale at Macy's, they cost Mama forty-five dollars. I breathe in with great lust. Late-summer grass. Tanning lotion off the backs of females. Seventy-five-cent hot dogs boiling in dirty water.

I take stock.

Ultimately speaking, the disk throwers around me will not be my friends. Stuyvesant does not have a cool elite, because everyone's a nerd at heart, but these kids I see on the Sheep Meadow today will be our most athletic and most "popular," if that word even applies. Some of them will even wear ski jackets with the lift tickets still attached. As I watch them race around the park in pursuit of their prized disk, I do not begrudge what I already know will happen, that they will not be close to me.

. . .

There will be so many awful tests to come, in mathematics and the sciences, of course, but I passed the most important one of them on my very first day. I blended in. I ran around. I yelled and was yelled at. I caught a disk. I let the disk tumble out of my hand at the last minute and screamed "*FUCK!*" I fell on a boy, and then another boy fell on me, and I smelled the sweat that coated all of us and found none of special distinction. I was not Russian today. I was just a boy of fifteen for a late afternoon, an early evening; I was just a boy of fifteen until some of the Asian kids had to knock off for Flushing and we called "Game!" And then I went back into the subway, back into the belly of the B or P or T train, and I walked its length; I walked in letting the doors slam behind me, as the people, the *New Yorkers,* watched me pass, and they watched me without love, without hatred, without criticism. This is my new happiness. Their complete indifference.

16.

LITTLE FAILURE

No caption needed.

M Y FIRST YEAR AT STUYVESANT I discover something new about me, something my family never suspected.

I am a terrible student.

In grade school, my father taught me from advanced Soviet textbooks. I would try to solve the math problems in the back of the composition books in which I wrote *The Chalenge, Invasion from Outer Space,* and my other sci-fi novellas. The algebraic scrawl looks impressive enough for a third grader, but above the math problems I have written for my father to see: *YA NICHEVO* [*sic*] *NEZNAYU,* I don't know anything. On another page, in English, "All wrong."

Schoolwork has always come easy for me. In Hebrew school, my competition was Best Friend Jonathan, David the Mighty Khan Caesar, and maybe three girls. At Stuyvesant there are two thousand and eight hundred children far more gifted than I am, half of them hailing from points east of Leningrad. In class they are bent over their desks like so many human architect lamps, humming softly, insanely, to themselves the way Glenn Gould would hum over his piano, little pockets of drool shining on their chins, the corners of their eyes covered with the only sleep they'll ever know, their pencils assuredly making magic against their notebooks as equations are swiftly put to bed. What accounts for their commitment? Who is tending their home fires? What awaits them if they fail? I always thought Papa beat me too much, but what if he didn't beat me enough?

I am scared. At Hebrew school, I thought I would outgrow my subhumanity by sheer force of will, by clawing my way into the Ivy League and then into the graces of the upper class. I would out-Jaguar my classmates with my *sechel,* my thick Jewish brain. That was my way out. By the end of the first two weeks of Stuyvesant I conclude that this path will be closed to me forever. At Stuyvesant, that's how quickly you know whether or not you will succeed in life.

The teacher—an African American woman in a bright designer blouse, an impeccably coiffed bun at the back of her neck—questioningly clicks her brilliant chalk against the board as the immigrant students call out the right and proper answers. She calls, they respond. Except for one student in his Ocean Pacific T-shirt covered with waves of flop sweat under the armpits who is staring blankly at the board as the new language of Sine, Cosine, Tangent is called out around him, as students who got the answer only *partially* right smack themselves violently across the forehead. "Nice going," one of them keeps saying to himself, sarcastically. "Nice going."

Won't someone please take me back to Hebrew school? I'll do anything, I'll believe anything! I'll memorize the Passover Haggadah. I'll chant all the gibberish at the top of my lungs. *Baruch atah Adonai, Eloheinu melech ha parabola.* Just get me out of here. Just let me be a good student again, so at least my parents will have *that.*

In biology class, I am paired with a Vietnamese girl of some ninety pounds, most of them brain matter, who swiftly dismembers a frog and labels all of its organs in English and Latin. "Aren't you going to do *anything*?" she says as I stand there with my scalpel as impotent as it is erect. "Are you, like, retarded?"

I was once the Red Gerbil; I was once Gary Gnu. You could spit at me or bean me with your spit-covered Carvel ice-cream stick or not invite me to your Great Neck roller rink Bat Mitzvah. But you could never say I was stupid. And now I am. Stupid enough to almost fail out of Spanish class. Stupid enough to stare at a page of geometry for half a day and come away with nothing but the conclusion that triangles have three sides. And if I could understand what a negative feedback loop is in biology class, I could maybe understand that the more I feel stupid, the stupider I become. The anxiety grows and reinforces itself. The tests—and they are daily—grow more difficult, not less. And with each week, with each test, I am getting closer to *it*.

It is the report card. *It* tells you what your station in life will be. Because the immigrant children of Stuyvesant do not have backup plans. We will not be filling in at our daddy's firm or taking a gap year in Laos. Some of us are *from* Laos.

The report card, printed on flimsy dot-matrix toilet paper, is handed out in morning homeroom, our eyes instantly skirting past the individual grades to the bottom number, the average.

I am crying even before I see the four digits.

82.33.

Essentially, a B.

Harvard, Yale, Princeton?

Lehigh, Lafayette, *maybe* Bucknell.

What does it mean for an immigrant child of the top rank to go to Bucknell University?

It means I have failed my parents. I have failed myself. I have failed my future. We may as well have never come here.

• • •

Stuyvesant in 1987 resembles a Lower East Side tenement at the turn of the last century: The school's snot-colored passages are filled to bursting; central hallways form their own crowded Broadways; smaller hallways are the equivalent of major crosstown streets. The first-year students latch on to others who look like them; they travel in packs. Here is Tiny Taiwan, Mini Macao, Petite Port-au-Prince, and Lesser Leningrad. Despite my first-day success playing Ultimate Frisbee with some future jocks, I am still much too shy and unsure of myself to fully make friends, and I spend half my lunch breaks hiding out in the bathroom, where a triad of Chinese "toughs" smoke at one another.

On Tuesdays and Thursdays, a Filipino-or-maybe-Mexican kid accompanies me to a sandwich shop called Blimpie, where I buy a breaded chicken sandwich that is too big, but that I eat anyway because it costs 499 cents. My parents give me six dollars a day for food, which makes me comparatively rich, but the guilt of eating an expensive breaded chicken while getting a Lehigh average is too much to bear.

"Yo."

"'Sup."

"What's your average?"

"82.33."

"Shit."

"I know."

"What are you thinking?"

"Lehigh."

"Fuck."

"Maybe Bucknell."

"You might as well go to SUNY-Albany, save some money, do really well, and then transfer someplace better."

"Haverford accepted an Albany transfer with just a 3.78 in 1984."

"Dude, that was 1983. Their selectivity ranking's gone up since then."

"I thought they dropped to ninth place on *U.S. News & World Report.*"

"Medicine or law after?"

"Law."

"Hastings in California. They're a sleeper school, but they take a lot of SUNY kids."

"I just got the latest *Essays That Worked for Law School*."

"My mother just left one under my pillow with Duke, like, high-lighted three times."

Just two fifteen-year-old kids with ghastly new mustaches talking, one a relatively spoiled son of a Russian engineer, the other trying to work his way out of his parents' grocery store.

Just two boys shooting the shit.

• • •

The weather has turned cold. My first Manhattan winter. Snowdrifts form around Beth Israel's psychiatric ward, where, soon enough, two of my classmates will find a home, one after retiring to Central Park to build his own igloo in the middle of the frozen night. On the 1.5-floor landing of our new Little Neck colonial, I stare out the window as the snow makes pretty the future site of my father's productive raspberry patch. (Between my father's weekly fishing and his growing fruits and vegetables, we will soon be entirely self-sustaining!) The next house over is already in Great Neck. Little Neck is middle class; Great Neck is *rich*. That next house over had been the plan for me. Until now.

"Son of a bitch!" my father cries from the first floor. "He promised to vacuum the stairs! Look at that *debil*. He's just going to stand there with his mouth open."

"I'm thinking about homework," I lie. And then with some of the attitude I've been working on in high school, "*Otstan' ot menya.*" Leave me alone.

"I'll give you *otstan' ot menya*!" my father shouts. "I'll beat your ass!"

But he doesn't.

I flop down on my bed with my biology text. How Does the Structure of a Paramecium Enable It to Function in Its Environment? How

Is the Heart Adapted for Its Function? I've covered one of my walls' with a poster of the troop uniforms of the different NATO nations, which I ordered out of an anti-Communist survivalist magazine. Above my new color TV I've hung a CIA recruiting poster. On a third wall: an ivy-covered quadrangle of the University of Michigan, my new reach school. My parents have started subscribing to *Playboy,* and once they're through with the issues in their bedroom I stack them openly next to my bed. *Essays That Worked for Law School* will soon lie beneath a *Playboy* issue featuring topless La Toya Jackson, sister of Michael, wearing a snake around her glistening neck. Meanwhile, old friend Chekhov is yellowing away on a bookshelf across the landing.

My Ocean Pacific T-shirts have given way to a black-and-beige Union Bay sweater that, unbeknownst to me, marks me as the ultimate in Bridge and Tunnel. In warmer weather, the children of Stuyvesant High School used to cluster around the front and back entrances of the school, waiting for their next pop quiz the way astronauts wait for the mission countdown clock. Now they seek refuge inside the school's vast auditorium. Some of them, depleted by study, are asleep on their backpacks as if they had just survived a terrible natural calamity and are now huddled in a FEMA shelter. Some of the Asian kids, with touching familiarity, are asleep on each other's laps. Nearly all of us have headphones on, gigantic fuzzy headphones plugged into a tiny reward for all our hard work, a late-model Aiwa Cassette Boy with the new equalizer function that makes one feel just a little bit like a DJ.

Back home in our sweaty bedrooms, our outsiders' angst finds itself in the "Eurotrash" new-wave tunes of a Long Island radio station called WLIR (later renamed WDRE), broadcasting from deep in the suburban interior of Garden City. We—and by "we" I mean young, pimply Russians, Koreans, Chinese, Indians—are lost between two worlds. We go to school in Manhattan, but our immigrant enclaves of Flushing, Jackson Heights, Midwood, Bayside, and Little Neck are too close to Long Island for us to resist WLIR, that clarion call of squeaky synthesizer music, narcoleptic goth outfits, and spiky, in-clined hair. The usual British suspects rule the airwaves: Depeche Mode, Erasure (their ecstatic hit "Oh l'Amour" is an inspiration to the loveless), and, of course, the princes of the gelled-hair set, the Smiths.

Who will rescue us from ourselves? Who will teach us about the right drugs and the proper music? Who will integrate us into Man-hattan? For this we will need the native-born.

They occupy the far-southern edge of the auditorium, just a few rows hanging over the precipice beneath which the string section is perpetually tuning away. They hail from Manhattan and brownstone Brooklyn. The boys are hippies, stoners, and punks or just kids who have extensive personalities and interests but lack the work ethic to compete with the fierce academic warriors of Stuyvesant. The girls wear long, flowing skirts, tie-dyes with pictures of horses and manda-las on them, slashed jeans, flannels, green army jackets, and peasant kerchiefs and seem to have struck a reasonable balance between self-expression and academic achievement. That is to say, they will one day attend college. The vibe is densely unmaterialistic. When I present evidence of my family's $280,000 Little Neck colonial, the girls are too kind to tell me that their parents' classic sixes on the Upper West Side are worth four times as much.

Unlike Haverford and the UC Hastings College of the Law, these kids have flexible admissions standards.

Maybe they will be my friends.

17.

STUY HIGH, 1990

Prom for one?

O N ELECTION DAY 1988, I come to the Marriott Marquis ballroom thinking, This is the day. The day I will finally get laid.

I have volunteered for George Bush Sr.'s scorched-earth presidential campaign against the hapless Michael Dukakis, laughing along with Bush's racist, hysterical Willie Horton commercials and all they imply about the liberal Massachusetts Greek. Compassion, after all, is a virtue only rich Americans can afford, tolerance the purview of slick Manhattanites who already have everything I want.

I plug away at Bush's New York headquarters, manning the phone banks with two older women in fur-trimmed coats. Our duties are to call the Republican faithful and solicit their support. My colleagues, who despite their garb never seem to shed a drop of sweat in the lingering summer heat, have a grand old time on the phone, laughing and flirting with old classmates and lost loves while I clutch the receiver with shaking hands, whispering to suburban housewives about the twin evils of taxes and Soviets. "Let me tell you something, Mrs. Sacciatelli, I grew up in the USSR, and you just cannot *trust* these people."

"But what about Gorbachev? What about glasnost?" Mrs. Sacciatelli of Howard Beach wants to know. "Didn't Ronald Reagan say, 'Trust but verify'?"

"I would never second-guess the Gipper, Mrs. Sacciatelli. But when it comes to Russians, *believe me,* they're animals. I should know."

Come Election Day, I am invited to attend what is sure to be a Republican victory party at the Marriott Marquis, the ugly slab of a building near Times Square, whose revolving restaurant will one day host my mother's birthdays. The invitation to the party features a scornful cartoon of the big-eared Dukakis sticking his head out of an M1 Abrams tank (the most unfortunate photo op of his campaign), and I expect an evening of arrogant crowing, of being pressed to the bosom of my fellow conservatives while dancing a Protestant hora over the grave of American liberalism.

Yes, tonight is a special night. It is the night I am to meet a Republican girl from a clean, white home. Her name will be Jane. Jane Coruthers, let's say. *Hi, Jane, I'm Gary Shteyngart from Little Neck. My family owns a colonial worth two hundred eighty thousand dollars. I'm the brains behind the Family Real Estate Transaction Calculator. I go to Stuyvesant High School, where my grades aren't so great, but I hope to get into the honors college at the University of Michigan. I guess tonight it's going to be curtains for the governor of Taxachusetts, hee-hee.*

I enter the ballroom, a dark, gap-toothed immigrant wearing sweat socks and brown penny loafers and my special and only suit, a highly flammable polyester number. I navigate the room filled with sparkling Anglos clutching single malts without a word said in my direction, without a pair of happy blue eyes reflecting the gray sheen of the crisp nylon tie I had picked up for two dollars from a Broadway vendor. As George Herbert Walker Bush racks up state after state on the big screen above us, as cheers and laughter circulate around the massively hideous ballroom, I stand alone in a corner biting down on my plastic cup filled with ginger ale and swatting the colorful balloons that seem to have an affinity for my static-inducing polyester, until a pair of teenage blond lovelies, the girls I had been waiting for all my life, finally approach with needy smiles on their faces, one of them beckoning me to come hither with her hand. I'm so excited I somehow fail to see myself for what I am—a short teenage boy, born to a failing country, trapped inside a shiny gunmetal jacket, carrying about a mop of the blackest hair in the room, blacker even than Michael Dukakis's Hellenic do.

Which one will be my Jane? Which one will trace the W of my weak chin with her pewter fingers? Which one will take me on her boat and introduce me to the millionaire and his wife? *You know something, Daddy? Gary survived Communist Russia just so he could join the GOP. I think that's very courageous, son. Would you like to throw the old pigskin around with me and Jack Kemp after cocktails? Just leave your Top-Siders in the mudroom.*

"Hey," one of the lovelies says.

Me, debonair, unconcerned: "Hey."

"So, I'll have a rum and Coke, just a splash of ice and a lime. Mandy, you said no ice, right? She'll have a Diet Coke, lime, no ice."

I have been mistaken for the waiter.

· · ·

The racism inside me is dying. A difficult, smelly death. Looking down at others is one of the few things that has kept me afloat through the years, the comfort in thinking that entire races are lower than my family, lower than me. But New York City is making it hard. Stuyvesant is making it hard. What's there to say when the smartest boy in school is of Palestinian descent by way of South Africa? His name happens to be Omar, the name of the evil scientist in my adolescent novel *The Chalenge.* And how can I not notice that the prettiest girl in all of Stuyvesant, a brief glimpse of her strong, miniskirt-clad legs in physics enough to lower my average by 1.54 points for the semester, is Puerto Rican? And that the masses around me, blazing their sleepless paths toward the Albert Einstein College of Medicine, are, simply, not white?

When the racism goes away, it leaves an empty, lonely place. For so long I have not wanted to be a Russian, but now, without the anger-fueled right-wing fanaticism, I'm *really* not a Russian. At dining tables across the Eastern Seaboard, among little *ryumochki* of vodka and slicks of oily sturgeon, I could lean back and join in the hate and be a part of something bigger than myself. Two decades after Bush Senior's campaign against Dukakis, from the mouth of a relation expressing herself in English for the benefit of the few non-Russians at the Thanksgiving table: "I think Obama *should* be president. But of African country. This is *white* country."

Only suddenly it's not a white country. Or, for me, a white city. A white school. The awful words still come out of me, but now they're just meant to be antagonistic and contrarian, or maybe just funny. Welfare this. Trickle-down that. When the toxic and outré American right-wing pundit Glenn Beck declared himself a "rodeo clown" a few years back, I understood his recipe well: part clown, part bully. *How many fingers, Vinston?*

After the debacle at the Bush victory party, I write a fifty-page novella for a social studies class, set in the independent Republic of Palestine in the then-distant year of 1999. The novella, pretentiously titled *Shooting Rubberbands* [*sic*] *at the Stars,* features my horniest line to date, something about "the smooth expanse of thigh, breast and shoulder." But *Rubberbands* is also, for me, surprisingly evenhanded. Six years after the intergalactic racial insanity of *The Chalenge,* the Palestinians are, like my fellow student Omar, human. "Your materialist exterior hides a sensitive aesthetic soul," my teacher, a white-bearded leftie, has written, along with a grade of A++. I focus on the grade, my average now inching slightly past Michigan on the College

Highest Average Rejected, Lowest Average Accepted Chart, and I put away the description of my sensitive, aesthetic soul for college. Specifically, for a woman named Jennifer.

• • •

But back to that "smooth expanse of thigh, breast and shoulder." My dying Republicanism and provincialism aren't the only things keeping me from getting some. I don't know how to talk to a girl without either going into pathetic overdrive (*Hey, baby, want to listen to my new Aiwa Cassette Boy?*) or swallowing my tongue. Sophomore year, somehow the tongue finds its way into the mouth of another, a blond, tie-dye-wearing girl from one grade junior, on a park bench in the western, more manicured half of nearby Stuyvesant Square, or the Park, as we call it. I am too scared to enjoy the moment for its actual value: the fact that someone I just met wants to share a mouth with me. At the time I'm more attuned to the fact that some of my new stoner friends over on a neighboring bench are shouting "Wooo!" and "Go, Shteyngart!"

If only I could have slowed myself down that night, enjoyed being alive with someone equally young and, I assume, happy to be there with me. Those soft skinny legs, the awkward overhang of her arms around my neck, the seriousness with which we go at it: my first real kiss, maybe hers as well. In any case, when I see the young lady the next day at school, there's just the exchange of awkward looks, and nothing more happens. Forget it, Jake, it's Stuyvesant. She goes back to her studies and friends; I go back to tallboys and gold-stamped hash.

• • •

It's one o'clock at the Park. Do you know where your child is?

Me, I'm drunk and stoned. I've been drunk and stoned for three years now.

I've rigged my senior-year schedule so that I take meteorology, one of the amazing horseshit classes taught by one Mr. Orna, a middle-aged hero for us burnouts who revels in nonsensical, self-invented, quasi-Yiddish phrases such as "Ooooh, *macha kacha!*" and "Oh, *schrotzel!*," conducts cloud-watching field trips to the Park, does not take attendance all through the semester, but then takes your final exam *for you,* guaranteeing my one perfect grade at Stuy. Between Mr. Orna's meteorology and his other Jacques Cousteau–like undersea adventure, oceanography, I've slotted in two lunch periods. Now I have four periods to get high and crush twenty-four-ounce tallboys or to roam around the city with my friends. Around 2:00 P.M. I will check into the one class I still have an interest in attending, metaphysics. The class is run by Dr. Bindman, a psychoanalyst-guru whom we all adore but whose grading practices are far tougher than Mr. Orna's, and far more metaphysical—a coin flip determines your grade. I stop into Dr. Bindman's class because he lets me lead a tantric-sex demonstration, whereupon we lower the shades, light scented candles, and I get to lock my forehead with one of the many girls I'm in love with.

Her name's Sara, and she's a half Filipina with terrifyingly true hazel eyes and lungs that can hold in a bowl of pot smoke for an entire lunch period. The closest I will get to her seagull lips is the rim of a paper cup. We buy diner coffee cups in bulk, the ones with the Greek-styled legend WE ARE HAPPY TO SERVE YOU, and fill them with Kahlúa and milk so that the school guards think we're sipping coffee with a drop of cream. Back in Dr. Bindman's metaphysics, with the shades drawn, with four cups of Kahlúa and milk inside me, I touch Sara's warm forehead with mine, concentrating on not sweating all over her, as our classmates *om* pleasurably around us. Par for the course, Sara's in love not with me but with Dr. Bindman, his kind American face, his calming voice and luxuriant mustache.

· · ·

Back at the Park, I'm still wearing that idiotic Union Bay sweater down to my knees, a kind of homage to the girls of Solomon Schechter, but I've accessorized it with a studded leather cuff around my left wrist, and my feet are shod in Reebok Pump sneakers, a new kind of high-tops that inflate when you press a stylized orange basketball hanging off the tongue. One of my inane catchphrases: "Hey, baby, you want to pump me up?"

Or in reference to some contemporary rap song and the latest news on television: "Peace in the Middle East, Gary out of the ghetto, no sellout!"

Or brandishing my new Discover card, the one that has found a snug place in my wallet where my NRA membership card used to be: "Dinner's on me. Jew Money Power!"

I am a kind of joke, but the question is: which kind? My job is to keep everyone guessing. Because what I do is part performance art, part ineloquent plea for help, part unprocessed outer-borough aggression, part just me being a jackass. None of it will lead me where I want to go, which is simply, pathetically, into the arms of a girl. But every Valentine's Day, I go to the corner florist on First Avenue and buy three dozen roses, and I give one to each of the thirty-six girls I have a crush on, my silent tribute to the fact that somewhere deep inside the beige-and-black Union Bay sweater there is a person who wants what everyone else wants but is too scared to say it.

On my drunk, stoned lips I am wearing a smile I would describe as depressed but optimistic. If I had to guess, that smile comes from my matrilineal line, somewhere before Stalin but after the pogroms, when the apples hung plumply from the branches of Belorussian trees, and my grandmother's family's kosher butchery was in its prime. I will soon find myself absolutely stunned when looking into the white space of my Stuy yearbook. I find one of the girls of our crew has penned: "I always thought you were a sweetheart underneath that ridiculous grin."

The Park girls sit around us in a semicircle talking about Grinnell and Wesleyan, dear ones all, but, in contravention of all teenage rules, or perhaps in full support of them, it's the boys I'm interested in. Getting in with the boys, getting in with this crowd of stoners and freaks, that is what my teenage years have become.

To my left, cleaning the resin out of his chrome Proto Pipe, is Ben, half Vietnamese, half Finnish, tall and square shouldered, with rock-star hair and an easy laugh, dressed in a dramatic German army coat with a paperback sticking out of one pocket, usually *Siddhartha* or *Zen and the Art of Motorcycle Maintenance,* which neither of us will ever finish—which, as far as I know, no one will ever finish. Girls like to do tarot card readings with Ben or lean against his broad back in times of need.

Ben doesn't like me at first. I'm a tough sell: a supposed Republican who talks up a storm about Ayn Rand and supply-side economics. When we first meet, Ben takes out a large water gun that he carries in his backpack for just such emergencies and sprays me well and good, my sweater stinking like a wet sheep all through chemistry. But at a party held inside a rambling Park Slope brownstone, at the behest of his free-floating and lovely girlfriend, Ben apologizes for being mean to me. "You try too hard," he says, passing me his Proto Pipe in a gesture of goodwill. "Everyone can tell."

More than twenty years later I find myself in an acting class taught by Louise Lasser of *Mary Hartman, Mary Hartman* fame (also Woody Allen's second wife). Ms. Lasser rakes the students with hell-fire for our cloying attempts at acting, reducing many young women to ninety minutes of sobbing. After my sad attempt at the Meisner technique (Actor 1: *You* are wearing a blue shirt; Actor 2: *I* am wearing a blue shirt), she screams at me: "You know what your problem is, Gary? You're fake and manipulative!"

And I want to say, *Yes, but this is New York. Who's* not *fake and manipulative?*

You try too hard. Everyone can tell.

Back on our bench in the Park, to my right, Brian is making out thoroughly with his girlfriend. Handsome and boyish, half Jewish, half black, with feminine lips so many of the girls around us have kissed, Brian is as preppy as we get, white tee tucked away beneath an oxford shirt, khakis, the whole package confusingly, antagonistically, wrapped in a leather jacket, its collar draped in soft brown fake fur. Brian's pretty-boy lips are locked fully with his stoned blond girlfriend's, and his hands are everywhere. It is understood that Ben and Brian are the best of our number, that they have access to the females and to the glory. If either were to speak down to me I would take it in stride, happy that I am spoken to, happy to take notes on how I can do better. *Do I try too hard? Gentlemen, I'll try harder.*

At the lateral level of Ben and Brian is another tall boy of stunning appearance, like them also of complex racial heritage. I cannot really talk about him at length because he seems so utterly outside of the galaxy in which I claim residency, and in the end I am a writer, not an astronomer. I'd like to similarly sigh at the stunning and cosmopolitan progression of their girlfriends. I see blue eyes, stoned smiles of unimpeachable placidity. I smell patchouli. I hear Deee-Lite's "Groove Is in the Heart." I feel the ease and happiness of these young women in the world.

Stretching away from Ben, Brian, and the Other Guy is a constellation of about a dozen boys emitting various degrees of funk. At one rung, close to Ben and Brian, but with only half membership in their caste, are me and John. As fellow eastern Queens sufferers, John and I are the barbarians trying to get through the gate with our laminated Long Island Rail Road monthly tickets and our willingness to do anything—John actually wears a lamp shade for the duration of a house party. My buddy is a beefy, hairy dyslexic in Hawaiian shirt and fedora and, like me, a budding writer and poseur. Although he usually addresses me as "You dolt," John is dear to my heart. I am not sure if he is completely insane or a genius. At times his writing is hilarious in a teenage gonzo way (random urban violence, German midget porn, exploding Saigon hookers, New York mutts out looking for love) and inching a little bit toward our mutual sadness—the sadness of being unable to communicate with others sans lamp shade.

In the end, John's deep desire to make me understand that "Western literature, post-Enlightenment, is centered around illusionism" is just too hard to take at 2:00 P.M. after the consumption of half a case of beer and the elementary particles of Ben's Proto Pipe. I'd rather touch foreheads with Sara in metaphysics class. Four years later, after John discovers something called humor studies, I have no choice but to place him smack in the middle of my first novel.

· · ·

And now let's zoom out a little. A bench on the eastern half of Stuyvesant Square, a then-shabby park divided by the screaming traffic of Second Avenue. A bunch of boys sitting on the bench, several stinking of Indonesian Djarum clove cigarettes and unwashed hair. Occasionally, for exercise, we will get up to play Jihad Ball with a rubber Koosh ball.

The rules are simple: You take the ball, point to someone, and shout, "I do declare jihad on *you*." Then you throw the ball at the jihadee and watch the rest of your friends pile on him. Ben and John are passing around the Proto Pipe, talking, as we all do, veryfast, veryfast, veryfast, Freud, Marx, Schubert, Foucault, Albert Einstein, Albert Hall, Fat Albert, Fats Domino, Domino Sugar refinery. Across the cement expanse of the Park, just a jihad ball's throw away, sit endless numbers of Asian girls picking away at stir-fry, steamed *mandoo* dumplings, and thick rounds of vegetable *kimbap* in white Styrofoam containers. In theory, at least, they are living the Stuyvesant dream of good grades and bright futures. A part of me wishes I could join them, but even more of me wishes I could understand who they are.* When the senior yearbook comes out I will be able to peek just a little bit inside their hearts:

"Children, obey your parents in the Lord, for this is right. Ephesians 6:1. I love you Mom, I love you Dad." —Kristin Chang

"I am crucified with Christ, therefore I no longer live. Jesus Christ now lives in me!—Embrace the Cross." —Julie Cheng

---

* Later, I will devote more than a decade to this task.

Meanwhile, Brian's lips are attached to his girlfriend's, a fact I jeal-ously espy, and mine are attached to a tallboy in a brown paper bag. Since I've started drinking, I've started *drinking*. Kahlúa and milk with Sara, Fifth Avenue rooftop screwdrivers with Alana, another girl I'm chastely in love with, vodka and tonic, vodka and grapefruit juice, vodka and vodka, pitchers of hard cider in the afternoon at the Life Café on the corner of Tenth and Avenue B. In true alcoholic fashion, I divide the day into quadrants of booze, the rise and fall of the sun regulated by clear and brown liquors. I'd tasted alcohol many years before Stuyvesant—I am from a Russian family, after all—but here with my outcast friends every twenty-four ounces' worth carries me a little bit away from the dreams I can no longer fulfill. Because even as I'm chugging away in the Park, my mother is deep in the bowels of the Beaux-Arts Stuyvesant building, standing at the head of a long line of similarly teary Asian mothers, begging the physics teacher to pass me in her sweet but not fully there English, telling him, "My son, he has trouble to adjust."

Booze. It sands away the edges. Or it makes me all edges. Take your pick. When I laugh now, I hear the laughter coming from far away, as if from another person. I hear that bright, crazy laughter of mine, and then I hear it submerged in the bright, crazy laughter of my colleagues, and I feel brotherhood. *Ben! Brian! John! Other Guy! I do declare jihad on you!*

Would it be outrageous to say that at this point in my life alcohol is the best thing to ever have happened to me?

Absolutely. It would be outrageous. Because there's also pot.

In an attempt to help me deal with peer pressure Mama and the newly arrived Aunt Tanya have shown me how to smoke a cigarette and stream it quickly out of the right side of my mouth without really inhaling. The three of us stand in the backyard of our Little Neck house, fall leaves scrunching underfoot, fake smoking, and acting nonchalant like in the movies. "*Vot tak, Igoryochek,*" Mama says as I let the smoke spill out of my mouth, my nose hungering after its sweet, forbidden smell. That's how it's done, Little Igor. Now I can pretend to smoke cigarettes or pot just like the cool kids. I apply this knowledge to my first fifty or so encounters with the evil weed, pretending to be even more stoned than the rest of my friends, screaming my nonsense: "Peace in the Middle East! Gary out of the ghetto! No sell-out!" But on the fifty-first time, somewhere at the beginning of junior year, I forget to exhale.

If alcohol obliterates me, the pot unpeels me. Down to the nub. The last 234 pages you have just read—they never happened. There was no Moscow Square, no *Lenin and His Magical Goose,* no *Buck Rogers in the 25th Century,* no "Gentlemen, we can rebuild him, we have the technology," no Gnorah, no Mama, no Papa, no Lightman, no Church and the Helicopter. Down to the nub, as I've said. But what if the nub's no good either?

And when the pot laughter comes out of me, it is slow and deliberate, starting from my toes and ending in my eyelashes. As it travels up my body, it tickles the nub, and it doesn't matter whether the nub is good or bad, just that it's there, stored away for future use.

How does one transition from Republican striver to absolute stoner? I will never be fully accepted into the crowd, much as I will never learn the words to Cream's "Sunshine of Your Love." If I'm lucky, I'm maybe invited to every *third* party, and the prettiest of the girls still keep their distance from me. But the "hippies," as they're called, are the closest I have to a group of friends. When I see carved into a rotting school desk the words "Fuck all Hippies, Gideon take a shower," I feel angry at the author of such words and also a strange wish that I myself could smell that bad. If only I could be the opposite of what I was raised to be. If only I could be a fully natural being like this Gideon, whose father happens to be some kind of American genius at something and whose family lives in a sprawling West Village penthouse.

• • •

I love the boys, but Manhattan is my best friend. Walking down Second Avenue on a Friday night, I pass a man and woman in cheap tight clothes, standing in the middle of the sidewalk crying in each other's arms. Crowds of teenagers gingerly walk around them, not exactly stunned by this display but respectful of the unabashed emotion. Everyone around me is silent for at least a block. I double back to take another look. The woman's face is barely visible, but as she leans back I notice her slightly Persian cast, the parabola of her long lashes, her coarse red lips. She is beautiful. But so is everyone else. It is hard to walk from the Safe Train on Fourteenth Street to the school on Fifteenth without falling desperately in love.

This is what I'm learning. Men and women, in various combinations of gender, are exchanging small bits of sexual information with their eyes, then rounding the next corner as if they had never met. *Yes,* my eyes say to nearly every woman who passes, but they only scowl and avert their eyes (*No*) or smile and look away (*No, but thanks for thinking of me*). Finally, on a soupy summer day, a young woman walking ahead of me lowers her shorts so that the curve of her posterior is visible. She turns around and flashes a brief, gap-toothed smile. She starts to walk faster. I can barely keep up. There are now several men on her trail, most of them young professionals in suits, all of us silent and needy. Every few blocks, she lowers her shorts a bit more, bringing out little bellows of disbelief from her followers. Suddenly she runs across the street and disappears into a doorway, laughing at us before slamming the door. We look around to discover we are on Avenue D, in the shadow of some fierce-looking projects. This is the farthest I have been from Little Neck, and I am never going back.

• • •

The greatest lies of our childhood are about who will keep us safe. And here an entire city is coming together with its fat, ugly arms around me. And here, for all the talk of muggers and blade swingers, no one will hit me. Because if there is a religion here, it is the one we've made. Parents, obey thy children in the Lord, for this is right.

18.

THE LONG ROAD TO OBERLIN

*The author has been rightfully crowned the
King of Medieval Times. To the left is his
blushing queen.*

BACK IN QUEENS, my parents sense that I'm going off the rails,
but they're actually quite nonviolent about it. My father pa-
tiently tries to diagram the workings of a combustion engine so
that I may survive physics. My mother begs forgiveness from teachers
on my behalf. Everything is being done to make sure I can recover
grade-wise in time for law school. And while my mother is unhappy
that I show up at three in the morning drunk—"Why, why didn't you

call us if you were going to be nine hours late?" "I ran out of quarters, Mama!"—my parents did both grow up in Russia and understand how young adult life works. On the few occasions when I return from a virginal night out with a girl, my father will take time out from slicing up one of his prized heirloom tomatoes at the kitchen table to query, "*Nu,* are you a man yet?" He'll lean in and smell the air around me. And I will sigh and say, "*Otstan' ot menya,*" Leave me alone, and stomp, stomp, stomp upstairs to my *Playboy*s and my *Essays That Worked for Law School.*

The elite among us, on the other hand, are waist-deep in *it*. There are parties all the time now. I am introduced to the best of Manhattan real estate. Lofts on Mercer Street, classic sixes along Amsterdam, a penthouse on West Tenth Street with wraparound views of that still-living, still-breathing animal Greenwich Village. A Battery Park City apartment so close to the towers of the World Trade Center that after a few joints I think I can spot my reflection within their steel-and-glass sheaths (not possible). There's teenage canoodling everywhere. And why not? The apartments all seem to be abandoned by their adult owners. The parents are gone. Building rocketry in distant lands, advising the Croatian constitutional court, growing coffee in the highlands of Kigali. All these brilliant progenitors of all these beautiful people are time zones away. It never occurs to me that having goofy immigrant parents in uncool Little Neck is somehow preferable to the wild state of affairs so many of my coevals now find themselves debauched in.

And so, in a dozen empty apartments, among several dozen hairy people, there is the happy exchange of sex to which I am not privy. Pleasantly stoned, headed to the bathroom, I hear light moans and giggles from one direction, bedsprings from another. I stand in front of the door, aroused, confused, trying to summon my Dr. Ruth knowledge. That sounded like a vaginal orgasm. That one, clitoral for sure. Out on the terrace, the sun is setting over the flaming fire-lookout tower of Jefferson Market and Fellow-Sufferer John is dismantling a turkey deli sandwich over a thing of beer. "Jew, *wakka-wakka*," he says. "Hermeneutics." And so on and so forth, for a good long while, until we take the Long Island Rail Road home.

• • •

Whom am I in love with? Let me count the girls. Ten? Fifteen? Twenty? I love indiscriminately and openly. A tall, classically pretty girl with circles under her eyes. I take her to the Central Park Zoo, my idea of romantic. She brings a friend. Then one of her long, alternative fingernails accidentally scratches my hand something terrible, a scar I still bear. There's a fluffy buxom blonde with clear blue eyes who lives in a Village townhouse with her divorced mother. Mama opens the door, appraises my harmlessness, and allows Fluffy out for a date to the Bronx Zoo, where I buy her an elephant we name Gandhi. I take her to a French restaurant in midtown. "Let's just be friends." There's Sara whom I have tantric sex with in metaphysics class. There's a tall Korean girl, Jen, who lets me massage her feet. "You have to be greedy, selfish, and immoral to survive in this lifetime" is Jen's yearbook quote. Mine: "'Virtue has never been as respectable as money'—Mark Twain." Soul mates. There's curly-haired, skinny Alana (not her real name), whose Fifth Avenue apartment and permissive parents I will soon appropriate for my first novel. I spend many nights, head spinning, on her spare couch, next to a bathroom smelling of kitty litter and two actual cats, Midnight and Cinnamon. Past midnight, love-sick, Alana comfortable in her big bed elsewhere, I once again stare out of the kitchen window next to my couch at the spire of a brown Gothic church. A mutual friend of ours has told me that Alana thinks my nose is too big, so that's not going to happen. Interesting about the nose: My father had always called me Yid-face, but he had said my lips were the problem. Now the nose, too. Anyway, I am in an apartment full of brilliant Manhattanites, next to a box of kitty litter, and outside a moon hovers over the church and the broad expanse of Fifth Avenue at the juncture where it leads up to the dramatically European flourish of the Washington Square Arch. The famous street is empty save for one beat-up old taxi. It is going to snow soon.

• • •

But someone does love me. His name is Paulie.* He's in his forties. I have an after-school job working for his _____† company in the meatpacking part of town, although it's hard to tell what exactly I'm supposed to be doing there. To bait me into his middle-aged clutches, Paulie puts up an advertisement on the Stuyvesant work board asking for a smart teenager and promising six dollars an hour. He first hires me and a Russian girl, but the Russian girl smells of meat and sweat, so she lasts only a few days. At my behest Paulie hires Alana, too, but it's not her he wants! It's me! Half of our days are spent tearing down city streets in his car as he leans out the window and shouts in his _____ accent‡ to passing women, "Hey, beau-tee-ful! Jew got a nice ass! Don't deny it!" Over the course of several years, we get lucky, let's say, never. "I'm no fag," Paulie says, brushing aside the curly remains of his dyed hair, but he does talk about how he would like to bend me over the desk and do _____ and _____ to my ass.

I am incredibly flattered by Paulie's attentions. Although he's much older, he also wants to become a writer someday, maybe chronicle his escape from _____§ on a raft with the help of the CIA. At work, I'm in charge of getting lunch for the whole crew, mainly burgers from Hector's Cafe or arroz con pollo from the Dominican place. He yells at me when I get it wrong, but when I get it right he calls me Prince Pineapple, along with some snatches of Spanish. "Nice going, Prince Pineapple, *puta maricón*." I can smile for an hour after he says that. One day Paulie takes me down to Florida for a little vacation, a jaunt that will inspire a long, scary chapter of my first novel. On the morning

---

* Oh no it's not.
† Let's just say it's a company that runs off the sweat of many brawny men with commercial driver's licenses.
‡ Let's just say it's a certain island nation.
§ Again, a certain island nation.

before I leave, my father sits next to me on the couch while my mother rifles through the bag I've packed for Florida to make sure I have my asthma inhaler and sunscreen. "Your boss . . . ," my father says. He sighs. I flex my white winter toes. *Does Papa suspect that my boss wants to pork me?* "Sometimes," my father says, "I'm jealous of Paulie because he seems like more of a father to you than I am."

"Oh, no," I say, "please. You're my father."

Several days later Paulie and I are sitting in a rented Buick in front of a deluxe Sarasota condo, his hand on my knee. Paulie points at the condo. He looks exhausted from pursuing me, as exhausted as I would be pursuing all those girls back at Stuy if I were his age. "Look," he says. "That condo up there can be yours. Your family can use it anytime. Think of how happy you'll make your parents. I just want . . ." And his hand creeps up my thigh.

I laugh the way girls laugh when I try to put the moves on them, and then I take his hand off my thigh, feeling its heat and heft. I'm a little scared and a little happy that my second father takes such an interest in me. If only I were at all turned on by him. This is just like one of those Tolstoy novels where X loves Y, but Y loves Z.

There's a picture from that trip with someone's arm over my shoulder. Not Paulie's, but the Queen's. I am standing there, curly haired, wearing some kind of Mexican blanket pullover along with the paper crown of Medieval Times, a dinner-and-jousting-tournament place near Orlando. The Queen looks like an advanced teenager in full medieval regalia. Off to the side, Paulie is laughing at me, making motions with his hand to show what I should do to Her Highness. My shoulders are slightly hunched, arms dangling beneath them, because it's unusual for a woman to touch me, but my off-white, Soviet-toothed smile tells me that I am loved. It is one of the happiest moments of my life to date.

• • •

Time is speeding up. College is almost upon us. Almost one-fucking-third of our graduating class has submitted research papers in the

Westinghouse Science Talent Search. I, on the other hand, still haven't been on top, beneath, or behind a woman. One of the few nights that I'm not out drinking and drugging with Ben, Brian, and John, or trying to get with Sara, Jen, Fluffy, et al., I'm lying in my bedroom with colorful American college brochures spread out around me. Downstairs, the *razvod* is looming. Aunt Tanya and her children have come to America. My lithe, pretty cousin Victoria, the ballerina, has been sharing a bed with my mother for more than a year, refugee style, while my father broods in his attic. Both her parents have died, including my mother's older sister Lyusya, and the twenty-year-old Victoria is stuck with us until she can find her own apartment. My father offers her valuable advice: With her looks, she should work in a strip club. I pass Victoria shyly on the stairs or look at her across the dinner table, scared and confused by her presence, wanting to talk to her but worried about taking sides between my mother and father. It's a little bit like when we were young and I stared at her across the glass of our French door in Leningrad, unable to touch her because of my mother's fear of *mikrobi* (microbes). But there's something else—for the past decade I've been working ridiculously hard at becoming an American, and now there's this Russian girl in our midst, a reminder of who I used to be. In the room she shares with my mother, Victoria listens to country radio because the words spill out slow and easy, and she can pick up some English. "Country music *sucks*," I tell her, rolling my eyes, ever the urbane, helpful cousin. Ever my father's emissary.

Because now it is total war. Now my father and his wolfish relatives are suddenly outmatched by the new arrivals. It is time for my parents to engage in a frank exchange of viewpoints. *"Zatkni svoi rot, suka!"* Shut your mouth, bitch.

But in my mind I'm already gone. I read about Cornell's "old boy, old girl network," and consider the marvels of a world in which I can be an Old Boy sitting around a fireplace at a university club with other Old Boys and maybe a sexy Old Girl, networking hard. Corneil, of course, is a difficult college to get into, but I have a chance at its School of Hotel Administration, because Paulie has gotten a bullshit note from one of his friends testifying to the fact that I am one of the finest bellhops at a prestigious Manhattan hotel. The brochure for kindly, progressive Grinnell College in Iowa literally makes me cry. All those morally strong boys and girls, all those international flags hanging amid the Gothic architecture. I curl up in my old Soviet comforter as Mama and Papa launch new fusillades downstairs. What kind of a person would I be if I went to a place like Grinnell? What if I jettisoned all of it, foreigner, Gnu, Gordon Gekko wannabe? What if I started from nothing? Am I crying because of the *razvod* downstairs? Am I crying because I can't wait to be loved for the little nub inside me, whatever it may contain? Or am I crying because, in a sense, I know I'm about to commit an act of suicide, an act that will take me fully through my twenties and thirties, fully through a decade of psychoanalysis, to complete?

• • •

I get into Michigan first. A red Jeep belonging to some rich friends of Ben's and Brian's is flying up the West Side Highway with me in the back screaming "Mee-shee-gun!" at the transvestites of the Meatpacking District. Then, my head filled with the lyrics of David Bowie's "Space Oddity" on endless loop, I am puking into a Penn Station wastebasket. Then, having drunkenly taken the Long Island Rail Road's Port Jefferson line some two hours into Long Island (Little Neck, where my family lives, lies along the Port *Washington,* not Port Jefferson, line), I find myself stumbling down an unknown train platform, until I fall down with my legs dangling over the rails. A bored conductor pulls me out of harm's way and tells me to get some coffee in me. "Michigan," I say to him. "I'm-a college gone."

"Go Blue," the conductor says.

But I will not be going to the university in Ann Arbor. Nor will I be attending Cornell's School of Hotel Administration, to which I am shockingly admitted. Over senior year, I have fallen in love yet again.

• • •

She is a tiny, book-addicted Jewish girl, red hair out of myth, thin lips, and negligible chin like my own. She is from alternative Queens, the part over which the radio station WLIR runs roughshod with its Depeche Mode and its Cure. Her name is Nadine (it's not). She is smart and worldly and not a part of our stoner clique. Somewhere I pick up that one of her parents or grandparents is a Holocaust survivor, knowledge I have no idea what to do with. In any case, Nadine is tough and strong and owns that strange combination of boyishness and femininity I so loved in Natasha, my first crush. When she says "Gary" over the phone in her sexy, cigarette-ruined voice, I think how wonderful that my American name isn't Greg.

Are we going out together? Not really. But we like to hold hands. And we like to sing "I Touch Myself," the surprise hit song of 1991 by an Australian band called the Divinyls. So here we are walking up and down the lengths of Stuyvesant High School, holding hands, singing "I don't want anybody else / When I think *about* you / I touch myself." And this is what I've always wanted: someone to hold hands with while we sing about female masturbation, while others watch. Now I'm a real person, aren't I?

Over at her house we lie next to each other, and I try to kiss her briefly, or I almost accidentally skirt her small breasts through her thick sweatshirt, trying to discern nipple. Or we go see *Terminator 2: Judgment Day,* our hands tensely locked together for 139 minutes (we stay through the credits), and then we walk out into the city heat, still together. Or we go to a bookstore by Penn Station that like so many of them no longer exists, where I shyly pick out something pretentious.

On bad days, Nadine says, "You know you're depressed when you can't even make yourself come."

Nadine is going to an academy for shy people in Ohio named Oberlin, which I recall as once ranking number 3 on the *U.S. News & World Report* list of America's top liberal arts colleges but lately has been plummeting down that list. It also has a good creative writing program, and I can double major in political science for law school. Oberlin's Lowest Average Accepted is about 5 points below my current 88.69, so getting in will be easy, and hopefully there will be enough financial aid not to bankrupt my parents. And if I go to the little school in Ohio, I will have someone to hold hands with when I get there, my sweet nongirlfriend with the sultry voice. I will have a head start.

"I honestly believe that you and Nadine will end up getting married," a Stuy friend of mine, a handsome swarthy Greek whom I have recently introduced to marijuana (pay it forward), writes in my Stuyvesant yearbook. And then his final assessment of my life chances: "Good luck, Gary. You'll need it."

19

HOLD MY HAND

*On the left, one of the first days of the author's Oberlin career.
On the right, one of his last.*

OBERLIN COLLEGE WAS ESTABLISHED in 1833 so that people who couldn't otherwise find love, the emotional invalids and Elephant Men of the world, could do so. The college, to its immense credit, was one of the first in the nation to admit African American students and the first to grant degrees to women. In 1970 it made the cover of *Life* magazine by ushering in the age of the coed dormitory. By 1991, I have concluded that of all the colleges before me, Oberlin would allow me to lose my virginity to an equally hirsute, stoned, and unhappy person in the least humiliating way possible.

And, of course, my main reason for choosing Oberlin. Here, I will have someone to hold hands with from day one, my not-exactly-girlfriend Nadine. Just as I once marched into Stuyvesant with an engineering report on my family's $280,000 Little Neck colonial, at Oberlin my secret weapon will be an emaciated Jewish girl with a sexy burst of red hair and a pack-a-day habit.

My father's Ford Taurus is crammed to the roof with asthma inhalers and Apple IIc paraphernalia. I have already alerted my future roommate to expect a party animal par excellence who will subject him to the Talking Heads album *Little Creatures* without interruption. The roommate, who will prove to be incredibly square and studious, a double major in economics and German from a quiet suburb of the District of Columbia, will get the true Oberlin experience out of me, one hundred thousand dollars' worth in 1995 dollars.

The Taurus is winding its way between battle-scarred Little Neck and our appointment at Oberlin's financial aid office. I talk to my mother or I talk to my father, but they do not talk to each other. There is an unspoken sadness amid the inhalers and the Apple IIc—the sadness of the fact that when they return to New York my parents will definitely get the *razvod*. And so the Talking Heads' "Road to Nowhere," booming out of the Taurus's dying speaker system, feels about right. Ever since we arrived in America twelve years ago, I have been trying to keep my parents together, but today my diplomacy has come to an end.

As we pass from Pennsylvania, which contains the Ivy League university of the same name, as well as well-regarded Haverford and Swarthmore Colleges, and into the flatlands of Ohio, I can't help thinking that had I been a better student this *razvod* would not be happening. If Mama and Papa had been more proud of me, they would stick together if only to say, "Our son goes to Amherst, number two top liberal arts college according to *U.S. News & World Report*."

Nadine and I have chosen to live in the same dorm.

• • •

I have never properly been off the Eastern Seaboard, and the flatness and waterlessness of the passing fields (wheat? corn?) and scrub make me nervous. I cannot comprehend this new terrain, and I cannot locate my place within it. All I can see is a python's embrace of American highways and the top hats of bottom-tier fast-food restaurants, such as the one they call Arby's. And yet, because I am young, I am still hopeful that something good will happen to me, *razvod* or no.

Oberlin College lies southwest of the depressed city of Cleveland, near the even more depressed towns of Lorain, Elyria, and, cruelly enough, Amherst. The also depressed downtown area, a kind of addendum to the college, "boasts" an art deco theater named the Apollo. The town pipes in "Silent Night" all through the greater Christmas season to annoy the Jewish students and faculty. There is a five-and-dime store to go along with the Christmas music and the general feeling that time has left us all far behind. Young peasants and underemployed workers from the local farms like to tear down North Main Street in their pickup trucks shouting, "Queerberlin! You guys are a bunch of fucking Democrats."

The college's architecture is designed for LSD and psychedelic-mushroom experimentation, as it makes sense only when it is melting. Heavy blocks of Ohio sandstone have gone into everything from a turreted Gothic hall to a Mediterranean-style, red-tile-roofed chapel. Amid these iconoclastic structures can be found one of Newark Airport's lost terminals, here reconfigured into a suicidal dorm named South, and the Conservatory of Music by Minoru Yamasaki, the designer of the original World Trade Center, which uncannily resembles a three-story version of that doomed structure. The two seasons are winter and summer. When the leaves turn color for that twenty-minute Ohio autumn, the whole crazy ensemble looks as beautiful as anything else in the world.

The human element wanders between these sandstone and cement giants, pissy looking and vegan, suffering from either Low Self-Esteem or Way Too Much Self-Esteem. A boy in a checkered shirt and multicolored Vans will walk by wearing a propeller on his red papal beanie, and if you try to take a picture of him and his beanie he will sneer at your presumption and make fun of you to his female companion whose jeans are a size skinnier than she is. And if you stop taking a picture of him, he will sneer at you for no longer paying attention to him. Lermontov covered all of this in *A Hero of Our Time*.

The first two pages of the *Oberlin Review* from April 5, 1991, bequeath the following headlines: "Discovery of Marijuana Plants Results in Arrests," "Pro-Marijuana Activists Rally," "Porn, Domestic Partnership Head Assembly Agenda." A fourth article, entitled "CF [College Faculty] Discusses Admission Stats," concerns the fact that the year I am admitted to Oberlin, 67 percent of all applicants have received a nod from the admissions office. I would like to have met the one-third of the applicant pool that failed this rigorous admissions challenge. To quote a faculty member from the article: "That level of selectivity is so embarrassingly nil."

I have come to the right place.

. . .

The Subarus of parents are nestling in herds. I do not yet know the significance of this left-wing East Coast car. I also do not understand that many of the parents are themselves academics, many buoyed by family trust funds that will also see their children into the future. There are so many things that I do not know, except for the fact that my parents are about to get the *razvod*. So I kiss them very quickly (Papa, quoting Lenin in part: "You must study, study, and study, Little One") and send them on their way back to Little Neck by way of the inexpensive Motel 6. There they will lie, in my imagination, at opposite ends of the bed, a strange Jewish-Russian silence between them along with some Oberlin promotional brochures, vistas of colorful hippies necking atop a painted rock. In my dorm room, surrounded by my hardworking, completely sober, thoroughly unbohemian new roommate—for his work ethic, he is immediately nicknamed the Beaver—I unpack the Apple IIc and the dot-matrix printer, feeling alone—and not the good alone I felt when I escaped the Sauerkraut Arms—while longing for Nadine's hand.

Here's another thing I don't understand and won't know for several weeks. On the way back home, my parents "make up." In fact, once I depart the family scene the entire trajectory of their marriage changes. They will know as much love and happiness together as people of their geography are allowed. The question I may ask now is *why?* Why does that which I longed for my entire childhood, peace between Mama and Papa, finally happen only as my parents and I separate? Were their daily and nightly fights an attempt to win my audience and attention? Did they enjoy my shuttle diplomacy? My teary "Papa really loves you, and he promises to be a better husband," or practical "Mama has lost her mother and older sister, so we must be especially kind to her and allow her to send up to five hundred U.S. dollars per month to Leningrad." Or, more likely, did the fact that they now had so few people to turn to in this country—so few American or Russian friends and decent, nonwolfish relations—finally leave them no choice but to turn to each other again? Maybe, without me, they finally remembered what they loved about each other in the first place: my father's intellect, my mother's beauty and will.

Will they be lonely without Little Igor? I certainly hope so. The other alternative: They were always better off without me. I was never a part of the family romance. I was only an impediment to it.

Only the full-size bed of the Motel 6 will know.

• • •

And now it is time to claim my own love. Hand-holding Nadine is here, prettier than ever in her neutral gray sweatshirt and denims, even as I bob around her in ugly khaki pants and a tie-dyed T-shirt that my middle-aged want-to-be lover Paulie and I bought at the Universal Studios theme park in Orlando, Florida. ("Check out this T-shirt, Prince Pineapple, *maricón*.") It features Marilyn Monroe's smiling face from *The Seven Year Itch,* and I hope having this retro sexpot across my chest will prove edgy or interesting (it doesn't). There's a poster sale going on at the Student Union, and I buy a copy of Edvard Munch's *The Scream* and a number called *The Beers of the World.* I happily show them off to Nadine, who does not seem at all impressed. She lights a menthol, blows the green smoke out of the corner of her tight little mouth, and we head back to our dorm, a neo-

Georgian brute called Burton that envelops the northern quad within
its two plantation-like wings. With my usual hunger I grab her hand,
humming the Divinyls' "I Touch Myself."

"You know what?" Nadine says. "Maybe we shouldn't hold hands."

Elastic of underwear suddenly flooded with anxiety: "Why not?"

"Just there are a lot of potential rich husbands around here."

She laughs a little.

I laugh a little, too. "Ha-ha," I say.

Back in the dorm, alone, the Beaver off adding more difficult classes
to his overbooked schedule, I lie down on the hard bed and have a
ferocious, unmitigated Oberlin-grade panic attack. Here I am with a
beaver for a roommate, with divorcing immigrant parents, and with
no one's hand to hold in the northeastern corner of a state whose
unironic tourist slogan is "The Heart of It All."

• • •

Oberlin does not have fraternities or sororities. It is also in a dry
county. These and other factors combine to make it difficult for most
students to abstain from quantities of beer and marijuana that rede-
fine the term "copious" (for those interested, there is also a decent
supply of heroin and cocaine). On my first evening at Oberlin I will
smoke a half-dozen joints and drink the Beers of the World, or at least
a six-pack of Milwaukee's Best, the bladder-busting local swill. Half
comatose I will hold hands with the prettiest girl in the dorm, even as
she makes out filthily with a hot resident adviser, everyone laughing at
me, the sad drunk holding on to the beauty as she kisses her aesthetic
equal, a man with long hair as soft and flowing as her own. Stoned, I
grasp the warmth of that hand, forgetting whose it is—Nadine's? my
divorcing mother's?—until I wake up in a room not my own, wearing
some kind of Peruvian poncho and covered in what must be someone
else's drool. In the next year, I will drink and smoke, smoke and drink,
trip and fall, fall and trip, until my endless alcoholic and narcotic exploits earn me my Oberlin moniker: Scary Gary.

• • •

As night falls on Oberlin, Scary Gary and the Beaver dim their lights. The Beav, exhausted from thinking and learning, snores up a storm from the get-go, but Scary Gary is scared shitless of a certain college peculiarity. The bathrooms in Burton Hall are coed.

To me, every Oberlin woman is already an angel, a deeply odorous creature with the potential of drunkenly holding my hand—and now I am supposed to make waste around her? Also the food served in the dining hall, a disingenuous attempt at beef au jus, a hairy salad of destroyed lettuces, a postapocalyptic taco, have made the Second Directive imperative. If I am to go on living, this crap must rush out of me *now* as if I were a re-creation of Frank Lloyd Wright's Fallingwater, a poster of which I probably should have bought instead of Munch's clichéd *Scream.* I circle the bathroom all night long hoping for an opening, so that I may lay a log. At three in the morning, as someone of the fairer sex is loudly vomiting Milwaukee's Best, I slip into the stall as far away as possible, shyly undo my pants, and prepare to let loose. Just then the hipster boots of the girl whose hand I had drunkenly held as she kissed another slide into the stall between me and the vomiter. I tighten some rectal screw inside me, cancel the Second Directive, and run back to my dorm room. And that terrible shitlessness, essentially, is my first year at Oberlin.

• • •

In the morning, although the toilets are coed, the showers on my floor are for men. There are no partitions in the shower room, and we stand about naked with one another, much like in prison or in the navy.

One man walks in with a toy bucket and shovel like kids have on the beach. He sings happily as he sudses himself down. His penis is enormous; even nonerect it describes full arcs in the dense Ohio steam. I try to will myself to grow a little when he's around, so that I won't seem puny, but nothing can hold a candle to his candle. "A mulatto, an albino," the big-dicked fellow cheerfully sings, as every reference in Oberlin in 1991 is to Nirvana's *Nevermind,* every dorm room boasting at least one copy of the iconic album with the underwater baby swimming toward a dollar on a hook.

Men with smaller dicks enter the shower. The complaining begins.

"There's too much reading for English!"

"Ganzel assigned *an entire book* to read!"

"I had to write *two* papers in one week."

The Stuyvesant graduate in me is amused. During my first semester at Oberlin my longest assignment is watching Ridley Scott's *Blade Runner* and then writing a paper describing my feelings about the same. Students, townspeople, and other assorted losers are allowed to teach courses at Oberlin as part of the Experimental College. *These classes are for actual college credit.* The nice sophomore hippie next door teaches an introductory course on the Beatles, which consists of us listening to *Revolver,* getting the munchies real bad, and then ordering in a Hawaiian pizza with ham and pineapple from Lorenzo's (oh, the famished thirty minutes until the damn thing arrives). Sometimes we'll drop acid and try to puzzle out "And Your Bird Can Sing" while walking up to various buildings and leaning on them.

It takes me but a few weeks to realize the frightening new prospect before me. Whereas in Stuyvesant I was at the bottom of my class, at Oberlin I can maintain a nearly perfect average while being drunk and stoned all day long. I get on the phone as soon as the first report card is issued.

"Mama, Papa, I have a 3.70!"

"What does it mean, 3.70?"

"An A average. I can get into Fordham Law easy. Maybe if I graduate summa cum laude, NYU or the University of Pennsylvania."

"Semyon, did you hear what Little Igor has said?"

"Very good, very good," my father says across the telephone line. "*Tak derzhat'!*" Keep it up!

Intense stoner feelings of love wash over me. *Tak derzhat'!* He hasn't used that kind of language with me in half a decade. I remember being a nine-year-old child in our Deepdale Gardens apartment, crawling up his hairy stomach, rooting around his chest hair, cooing with happiness, while he nonchalantly reads the émigré intelligentsia journal *Kontinent*. I call him *dyadya som* (Uncle Catfish). He is my best buddy as well as my papa. "What did you get on your division test?" he asks me. *"Sto, dyadya som!"* ("A hundred, Uncle Catfish!") Prickly kiss on the cheek. *"Tak derzhat'!"*

Does it really matter that upstairs from me, at this very moment, Nadine is holding hands with a guy who looks to me like a famous actor, the one always in rehab or shooting at the police? Does it really matter that outside the window a bunch of hipsters in propeller beanies are tossing around a Hacky Sack, Oberlin's primary sport, without inviting me, because somehow they can *smell* my desperate background, my internship with George H. W. Bush's election campaign, my years as the head of the Holy Gnuish Empire?

Mother: "And what kind of grades are your colleagues getting?"

"People don't really talk about grades at Oberlin, Mama."

"What? What kind of a school is this? This is socialism!"

Socialism, Mama? If only you knew. There's a student dining co-op that doesn't allow the use of honey because it exploits the labor of bees. But all I say is "It *is* ridiculous, but good for me. Less competition."

"I noticed there were not many Asian students."

"Yes," I say happily. "Yes!"

"Mama and I went to an opera last night. Puccini."

My father has said *Tak derzhat'*, and my parents have gone to see Puccini together. This means there will be no *razvod*. We will remain a family.

As soon as I hang up, I lustfully fire up my silver pot pipe and blow smoke at the Beaver until he stalks off for the library. Then, free of his redheaded, freckled, studious presence, I take care of my final need to the sound of "Baby, You're a Rich Man." For this, too, I will receive college credit.

. . .

I like going to classes because I can learn a lot. About the students, I mean. Here the great arias of self-involvement—far more operatic than Puccini's "O Mio Babbino Caro"—wind their way through the boxy little classrooms as professors eagerly facilitate our growth as social beings and master complainers. I learn how to speak effectively within my new milieu. I master an Oberlin technique called "As a."

"As a woman, I think . . ." "As a woman of color, I would specu-late . . ." "As a woman of no color, I would conjecture . . ." "As a her-maphrodite." "As a bee liberator." "As a beagle in a former life."

Only what will I say? Whom will I speak for? I raise my hand. "As an *immigrant* . . ." Pause. All eyes on me. This isn't Stuyvesant; here immigrants are a rare, succulent breed, even if the ones present usu-ally have parents who own half of Lahore. "As an immigrant from the former Soviet Union . . ." So far, so good! Where can I take this? "As an immigrant from a developing country crushed by American impe-rialism . . ."

As I speak, people, by which I mean girls, are looking at me and nodding. I have shed every last vestige of the Hebrew school nudnik and the Stuyvesant clown. The things I say in class are no longer meant to be funny or satiric or ironic; they're meant to celebrate my own importance, forged in the crucible of our collective importance. There is no room for funny at Oberlin. Everything we do must move the human race forward.

. . .

And here's what's happening to me. I'm learning. The truth of the matter is that I should be nowhere near an institution like this. Ober-lin is something nice you do for your child when you're rich. Or at least comfortable. If I would ever have an American child I would happily send her to Oberlin. Let her enjoy the fruits of my labor. Let her have both clitoral and vaginal orgasms inside a gluten-free co-op.

But me? I'm still a hungry, kielbasa-fueled, fucked-up refugee. I still need to build a home in this country and then to buy an all-wheel-drive car to put next to it.

The problem is I learn too slowly. There's a very popular upper-classman who wears a janitor's shirt with the name BOB stenciled over his breast. I have also worked as a janitor before coming to Oberlin. My father got me a job washing floors in a former nuclear reactor in his laboratory. I was paid $10.50 an hour for buffing many hectares of radioactive floors and had to wear a device at all times that looked like a Geiger counter (the present state of my hairline reflects as much). I worked all summer long so that I could have money for pot and beer and Chinese food to buy for a prospective hand-holder, but my parents certainly supplied me with shirts and pants to wear. "Poor Bob," I say. "He only has one shirt. *As an immigrant,* I know what that feels like."

"Who's Bob?"

"Over there."

"That's John."

"Why does his janitor's shirt say 'Bob'?"

My hipster interlocutor looks at me as if I am a complete idiot. Which I suppose I am.

As an immigrant, my job is to fucking learn. And what Oberlin has to teach me is how to become a part of the cultural industries in a handful of American cities. How to move back to Brooklyn's Williamsburg or San Francisco's Mission District and be slightly known among a select group of my own duplicates. How to use the advance for the Serbian rights to my memoir to throw a killer party featuring the world's second-worst banjo player and absolutely worst snake charmer. There's a knock on the door of a labor seminar with my favorite Marxist professor. A package of cheese has arrived from France. *The People's Cheese* we call it. The People's Volvo. The People's Audi TT Roadster. There are other ways to be fabulous, ways I could hardly imagine among the forty-by-one-hundred-foot lots of eastern Queens. You just constantly have to be sure of yourself. You can't announce your ambitions. You have to join a band where you dress like a chicken. You have to complain about the Soviet Union's recent collapse even as your parents celebrate it. You have to bring a beach bucket and shovel to your morning shower. You have to go out with someone for the duration of junior year and get rid of them when you've had enough, and then you have to *complain* about the fact that a human being actually loved you.

The truth is this: The rich will rule even at a place like Oberlin, where their kind is technically forbidden. They will simply invert the power structure to suit their needs. They will come out on top no matter what. Stuyvesant was hard but hopeful; Oberlin, on the other hand, reminds me yet again how the world works. I guess that's why they call it an education.

My hair is growing and curling into locks and reaching toward my ass; my shirts are becoming flannelly just like Kurt Cobain's. A child of Lenin is learning about Marxism in the Rust Belt from faculty whose office doors are festooned with signs reading CARD-CARRYING MEMBER ACLU and LOBOTOMIES FOR REPUBLICANS: IT'S THE LAW.

I am still majoring in politics, still paying respect to my parents' law school dreams, but I am also doing something that Oberlin can respect as well.

I am writing again.

20.

JENNIFER

*My first southern Christmas. Jennifer is holding the rambunctious
Tally-Dog. I am so full of hush puppies and grits it hurts to
lift my head.*

"UH, YOUR TEETH ARE REALLY HURTING ME, Gary. Could we try something a little different?"

I have a girlfriend.

Her name is Jennifer, known to most by her initials, J.Z.

I am lying next to her. I am twenty years old. Back at Stuyvesant, I have spent several nights next to Nadine in her Queens bedroom, both our eyes closed, an eighteen-year-old-sized distance between us, me dreaming of her bony frame, her dreaming, presumably, of another's bony frame, a digital clock soundlessly keeping time by her bedside, wasted time.

If I could compress the unrequited love of the last twenty years it is possible that I could come up with art. But that is not the kind of artist I want to become. When it comes to the world, I want to know it, touch it, taste it, and indefinitely hold it. Twenty years old, post-Leningrad, post–Hebrew school, postchildhood, post-God, I am a materialist without possessions. I do not believe in a Russian soul. The heart is an important organ, but it is just an organ. You are not what you want. You are what wants you back. Everything begins with her. Everything begins on the night when I lie with her in a building elegantly named Keep Cottage, a rambling timber-and-stucco mansion housing one of Oberlin's renowned dining and residential co-ops, the kind where bees are kept safe from exploitation and a lone terrorist known as the Bacon Bomber, operating under cover of night, dusts the next day's hummus supply with his eponymous foodstuff.

I have a girlfriend. I do not fully know how to kiss her, but I have a girlfriend. Thank you, Oberlin College. Without your extended welcome to the weird, without your acceptance of the not yet fully baked, without the fathomless angst you impose on all those who walk under your Memorial Arch, the angst that leads to the hapless intercourse your students have been waiting for throughout their miserable teen-age existences, without these things it is conceivable that I would not have ravaged a woman with my Pentagon-shaped Soviet tusks until my thirties. It is also conceivable that without you I could have gone to Fordham Law School. But more on that later.

• • •

I am twenty years old. It is spring of sophomore year. I should be nineteen, but because I didn't know English when I came to America, I am always one year behind. Jennifer lies in my arms, the soft and nonangular bulk of her, the fact of her and the fact of me. We are floating through space. That is true of everyone on the planet, but it is most true of people who are holding each other for the first time, with their eyes closed at night, half asleep. Next to us, just as a point of reference, her roommate, another Jennifer, whom we will soon nickname the Aryan (she is from North Dakota and has transparent eyes), is snoring with difficulty and occasionally calling out terrible things in her sleep. Every time I drift off into slumber Jennifer's room-mate's grief awakens me, reminds me of what I've been most of my existence—an unhappy person getting by.

But then how to explain the Jennifer in my arms, the warm tattoo her head is making against my neck. How to explain the presence of another in my life, the thing I can only describe as not-aloneness?

• • •

And one more thing I want to tell you. Morning as I walk out of Keep. I'm winding my way through a large chunk of the Oberlin cam-pus, past the cement constructions of the diarrheal new dining hall, past the thousands of bicycles old and new that Oberlin students tend to see as an extension of themselves, one of the few objects they may fully possess without ideological heartache, and into the green colle-giate expanse of my own North Quad, where my New England–style dormitory with my two roommates and our shared three-foot bong awaits my announcement of love.

Rewind my journey seven-eighths of the way; hold it on the path between Keep Cottage and the dining hall. In slow motion, with the tips of my fingers still to my nose, I turn back and look at the array of Keep's bay windows staring back at me. Is she there looking at me, too? What does it mean if she isn't?

It is spring, real spring, which in Ohio must mean the end of April, not March. Where I am standing is a parking lot with a sprinkling of passed-down Subarus and Volvos. And as I look back at Jennifer's window, the ecstasy of our joining is itself joined to the future mo-ment of our parting—because we *must* part eventually, no? And somewhere amid the midwestern spring happiness, among the rebirth and the Easter around me, I can already suss out the death of us, the death of something to which I know I am not yet entitled. My teeth are really hurting her. Can we try something different? Yes, we can try. But will it help?

• • •

We meet during one of those legendary Scary Gary moments of which I myself have no perfect recall. I am being carried through North Quad by a bunch of fellow drunk and stoned revelers, of which I am the drunkest, the stonedest, and, naturally, the scariest. There are three versions of this incident I have heard. In one, I am being carried *out* of my dormitory, because I have thrown a raucous party, angering my roommate, the Beaver, and the Beaver has thrown me out to party elsewhere. In another version, I am being carried *into* the dormitory, *into* the path of the angry Beaver, whose redheaded studies or red-headed sleep I am about to interrupt with my intruding horde. In the third version, which holds to its own kind of recycled Oberlin logic, I am first carried into the dormitory and then carried out of it.

"Party at my room!" I am shouting. "Everybody come! Burton 203!" I have my first growth of goatee at this point, I have my Peruvian poncho with a hemp pin attached to the heart. As I am being tossed up and down by the many weak Oberlin arms, am I thinking of the book I have just read—Nabokov's *Speak, Memory*—in which Vladimir Vladimirovich's nobleman father is being ceremonially tossed in the air by the peasants of his country estate after he has adjudicated one of their peasant disputes? Yes, that is precisely what should be on my mind. Because literature is slowly seeping into my goatee along with the Milwaukee's Best and the vile coat of fried buttery fat surrounding the Tater Tots served in the cafeteria. Inside the dorm room, the Beaver, who, if I take a step back from my growing snobbism, is actually a kind, smart boy named Greg, is trapped behind his economics textbook, as my silver pot pipe is produced, as thirty lungs are readied, as the cans of beer are popped with so many skinny index fingers, as my sophomore next-door neighbor, my Beatles Studies professor, opens the CD tray—remember how it used to sound, the mechanical *woooosh* of a CD player?—and puts in *Rubber Soul*.

Somewhere amidst all this I see a face, a circle of pale within the darkest hair around, and then a chin descending into a perfect dimple. There are at least a dozen women in the crowded, pot-smoke-filled room, and my love forms halos around each of them, even as I try to edit them down to one. My weekly mission is to develop an unrequited crush and then to smoke and drink my way out of it. Tonight, I keep returning to the circle of pale within the nimbus of dark, and to what's underneath: ethnically dark brown eyes and thick eyebrows. She has a loud, sparse laugh that goes away quickly and a slightly unsettled manner, like she doesn't fully belong here. Not in the way that most people really don't belong at Oberlin but in the same way *I* don't belong at Oberlin. As I will soon learn, neither of us really understands why a band must dress like a chicken. And our hearts are at least partly with the Bacon Bomber and his sabotage of the hummus and peanut butter supplies of the co-ops. And our hearts are at least partly in Russia and Armenia, where her father's family is from, and the American South, from whence her mother hails with great difficulty.

I am being a little bit charming. The new kind of charming I've developed, drunk within three seconds of passing out, drunk enough to sway to *Rubber Soul*'s "Nowhere Man," finding a kind of personal beat there, drunk enough to expel large quantities of comical intellectualized thought at anyone caught in my path. Something, something, Max Weber, something, something, Protestant joke, something, something, Brezhnev reference. Those who have come across my first novel will know exactly the song I am singing.

"That is one aspect of you that I especially envy," she will write to me in a letter shortly, "your ability to get people to listen to you, and hold their attention."

Yes. The years of being shunted, of observing from behind a language barrier, of listening from a bedroom adjoining my parents' and trying to figure out a way to douse the flames, have produced a calculating, attention-seeking mammal of few equals.

And from a much-later letter from her: "I felt a kind of desperation in you, a sadness which I saw in Oberlin before we were going out."

She is with her friend Michael, an upstate Jewish polyglot and easily the smartest person within the Oberlin class of 1995 (from which
he will Marshall Scholar his way directly into Oxford). He will become one of my best friends, too. I sit down next to Michael, the
thickness of his glasses matched by the saucerlike depth of my own
contact lenses, and we begin a back-and-forth in Russian that's the
easiest and most true interaction that I've had at Oberlin to date.
Something about the Russian bard Vladimir Vysotsky perhaps? The
collapse of the Soviet Union just a few months ago? The nostalgia that
Nabokov thinks is vulgar *poshlost'*, but that we as boys of nineteen and
twenty are not yet ready to dismiss out of hand? And as we spit out
the Russian, more revelers pour into the room, the funk of my pot
pipe seeping into the floor below and the floor above. But I care for
none of them tonight beyond a bullshit "Hey, wha's up? Beer in the
fridge."

And sometimes she laughs, and sometimes she looks straight ahead
with uncertainty, and sometimes she cocks her head back and takes a
long, thick dredge of Milwaukee. Soon every detail of her background
will be of interest to me, soon every mannerism will be studied with
the kind of microeconomic detail that would have impressed my
roommate. But right now I am onstage. I am on the stage before my
dead grandma Galya singing to her of *Lenin and His Magical Goose*. I
don't have the arrogance to say to the woman in front of me: *You will
love me*. But I do have the arrogance to say, *Why don't you at least* think
about loving me?

It will take her about a year to think about it, the two of us becoming close friends first. But along with my charm I am also learning the
art of desperate persuasion. To quote Louise Lasser: "You're fake and
manipulative!" And finally I will leave her no choice.

· · ·

Her name is Jennifer, and her last name begins with a *Z* and ends in
the common Armenian patronymic suffix *-ian*. For most of her life
she goes by her initials, *J.Z.* Of the American names I deeply covet,

ecumenical Jennifer is up there with Waspy Jane and Suze, and I've also adored the variations of Jenny and even the terse but lovable Jen. But there is something strong and unusual in a woman, even a woman at Oberlin, going by no more than her initials. After it is over between us and I move back to New York, I can hardly look at the subway map because of the prevalence of the J and Z trains as they swing merrily from Manhattan through Brooklyn and Queens, through all the boroughs I know and love.

J.Z. is from the northern suburbs of Raleigh, North Carolina. She speaks with traces of a southern accent, her parents are not academics, and she does not have easy access to money. All these many facts combine to ensure that she is different from your typical Obie.

Her friend Michael is different, too—multilingual and cosmopolitan in a way that belies an upbringing in Plattsburgh, New York, well versed in the martini shake and the use of bitters and colloquial Yiddish. Let me now expand my warm menagerie of friends circa sophomore year, 1992 to 1993. I have two new roommates. Irv (not really his name, though it kind of ought to be) has beautiful C-cup breasts and a Japanese girlfriend from the Conservatory of Music. He is stoned even more than I am and spends a good part of the day sucking with great delicacy upon his own thumb. He will approach a trio of hippie chicks in our dorm with the suave entrée "So I hear you guys are having a bit of a gang bang tomorrow night." My other roommate is Mike Zap, who introduces me to the music and thought of the then-inflammatory rapper Ice Cube. We will begin many evenings with the rousing cheer: "*Po*-lice eat the dick straight up!" per Cube's album *Death Certificate*. Mike is Pittsburghian by nature, covers sports for the *Oberlin Review* (the most thankless journalistic task in our deeply uncoordinated college), and, with his kindness and relative normalness, provides a useful compass for the rest of us freaks. When visiting his home in Pittsburgh's Jewish Squirrel Hill I feel shades of my Hebrew school friend Jonathan, the smooth running of decent parents and functional household, here bound together by two of the most genial animals I have yet come across, a black dachshund named Rudy and a caramel one named Schultz.

The five of us—me and J.Z. and Michael and my roommates, Irv and Zap—together we are what I've always wanted out of life, a community among whom I do not have to feel second-rate. As in love as I am with J.Z., I am also in love with the fact that she and I share our best friends. Two weeks into sophomore year, the enormous three-foot sky-blue bong in our dorm room attracts hordes of first-year students who have heard of its legendary smoky output. The best thing about Big Blue is that it is so big it requires more than one person to operate, and, sure enough, either breasty Irv or Zap with his scruffy new beard and adorable high laugh will do the honors with the bowl and hold the "carb," as I lean back and fill myself with laughter and lunacy. "*Po*-lice eat the dick straight up!" Disgusting, polluted Ohioan winds knock at the bay windows of Noah Hall, but up here we are all in this together. And then, filled with smoke and friendship, I get to shut my eyes and dream entirely of her.

. . .

I pursue her the only way I know how. Fakely and manipulatively. I insult her. Something about her upper chest being covered with freckles, freckles that I dream only of kissing. A tough southern girl, she writes me a letter short on ceremony: ". . . Enough bullshit! You also have some insecurities that you need to address."

What? Me? Insecure?

She closes with the directive "Write what you feel uncensored" next to a big heart and her initials, *J* and *Z*.

Sensing an opening, I pounce. I write what I feel. I write and I write and I write and I write and I write, a flood of lovelorn missives that will have no equal in my life, because my next relationship, a full eight years later, will already take place in the age of email. Even after we break up post-Oberlin, fourteen-page letters come sailing from New York to North Carolina and fourteen-page letters come sailing

back. Hell, we write to each other while we're *at* Oberlin, both of us
guarded and scared of each other, neither of us used to opening our
mouths and letting the emotions change the timbre of our voices.
Emotions are weaknesses where we come from. And when summer
puts an end to Oberlin and we are mostly apart, we write throughout
our working days, me at an immigrant resettlement agency—$8.25 an
hour—and her, for half that sum, behind the counter at an American
automotive store called Pep Boys.

The most beautiful collection of letters and numbers I have ever
seen, on a simple white envelope, about half a year into our relationship:

RESEARCH TRIANGLE AREA

RALEIGH DURHAM CHAPEL HILL

HAPPY HOLIDAYS!! 12/29/92 PM RAL NC #1

RAL NC #1. Someone from America, the real America, has written to
me. In front of my parents' house, the sparse traffic of Little Neck
behind me, I open the Christmas letter, and I go deaf to the actual
world. Her thin red lips are speaking to me, the noise of my parents—
"Igor! Snotty! It is vacuuming time!"—so much Russian nonsense
behind the drawn-out, southern cadences of her voice. I absorb the
letter, the love and the angst both (for she is, like me, not altogether a
happy person), while locked in the upstairs bathroom, the water running. And then with the vacuuming still undone, with my mother's
pristine floors still covered with minuscule traces of dust that upset
her careful world to no end, I begin to write back.

J.Z.—

*The whole idea of living w/you, working out w/you, writing poetry w/
you, cooking grits and okra w/you, is just too astounding for words.*
I'm making great strides in discovering what I'm all about, I'm

*finally being happy about being Gary, and all this has happened because
I finally have a friend who I can share everything with.*

I've had an uneasy feeling about the Bible all my life.

Doesn't our society suck?

I HATE MY HAIR!

*I look like a hunchbacked Jewish goat with a row of teeth like the
Sarajevan skyline after the war.*

I respect your pessimism.

*Is that [North Carolina] Jason guy still bothering you? I don't take
this kissing-on-the-neck stuff lightly you know.*

Why do so many men (and women) fall in love with you so quickly?

*You are my greatest teacher—you've taught me so much of what I
admire and respect about myself.*

• • •

About myself, sure. I am deeply into learning, admiring, and respect-
ing myself. But what about *her?* Lost in the shocking scenario of finally being a Boyfriend, constantly worried that amorous North
Carolinians named Jason will keep kissing her on the neck in my absence, constantly trying to devise ways in which she can love me more,
can I really see the sad, lovely girl in front of me, all five feet and three
inches of her? She is the child of a shattered family, a fun-house image
of what my own family might look like if the *razvod* had gone through.
The sullen Armenian father, a genius at some branch of computer science, alone in his Research Triangle countryside ramble, goading his
children to do worse. The southern mother in her little modern ranch,
dividing her time between eating, sleeping, drinking down glasses of
white wine, and playing bridge. The cold, angry older half sister, radiating negativity out of Dallas/Fort Worth. The younger brother, who
calls her Nate for some reason, lighting his farts and drag racing down
the sunbaked Carolina tar.

In the mail from North Carolina, a postcard with a photo of Yoko and John Lennon's "Bedpeace," and in her pretty scrawl, "We'll be having some of that soon!"

From other letters:

I look like an Armenian marshmallow.

I am just NOW starting to really trust you with everything, Gary. Parts of me which are constantly on guard are finally relaxing with you.

I am going to send you a copy of the [new] David Byrne tape.

A co-worker said to me, You mixed aren't ya? I mean you're not all white?

I cried on the whole way home from work . . . It turns out my grandfather had a heart attack. I love that old man. He really is a good person.

Gary, we're in our prime—let's enjoy it—Oberlin stress is bad!

I can't believe how much your mom criticizes you. She doesn't ever say good things, at least none that I've ever heard. How does that affect you?*

I wish I could fly over to the Shteyni house and rescue you.

Could you have Nina [my mother] pray for my grandfather?

Can you imagine our wedding? Jews, Armenians and Southerners.

Dude, there is no jokin' around about the Mississippi River!

I love you, Gary.

I feel that I must type that last one over again, because when I first read those words, they were not read only once.

"I love you, Gary."

---

* From a future girlfriend in 2004, a hotel room in Prague or maybe Vienna (increasingly it is hard to tell the two apart), after she has just met my parents for the first time: "Why are they so mean to you?" Me: "Oh, it's just cultural." Her: "Boy, *that* sounds like an excuse." Me: "Let's *not*, okay?"

...

The plane touches down in Raleigh-Durham. Early summer, just a few weeks after Oberlin has closed for summer fumigation and ideological reset, but we cannot wait to see each other a day longer. I'm covered in a plaid thrift-store shirt, *très* Keep Cottage, where we first kissed, which I wear all the time because it makes me feel loose and boyfriend-like. There's a string around my neck with a single marble-like blue bead that I don't dare take off, even in the shower, since it is a gift from her. For the next half decade, whenever I am anxious, I will spin the bead between my thumb and index finger. Even when she is gone. Especially when she is gone.

I've had three Bloody Marys on the plane because that's what LaGuardia-Raleigh jet-setters like me are keen to do. And also because by this point in my life I can't survive a few hours without a drink. Outside I can already sense a different world, her world. Looking out the plane window, I see nothing but North Carolina green. Forest upon forest, blessed by the mellow local sun, cut apart by small rivulets of sprawl that the migrating Yankees are said to be bringing with them as they take over the college towns of Durham and Chapel Hill and beyond.

...

There she is past baggage claim, my pale half-Armenian marshmallow now made slightly red by the aforementioned sun, just as I've been reddened by the aforementioned vodka. (I am now twenty-one, and my bingeing is legal.) She is wearing the vintage green-and-gold, vaguely Asian-styled silk shirt that I bought for her twentieth. I hug her. Boy, do I hug her.

"Easy. Easy there, Shteyni-dawg." Shteyni-dawg is my nickname, used not just by J.Z. but our friend Michael, Breasty Roommate Irv, and Kind Rapping Roommate Zap.

And I think:

Oh, my God, I am not alone.

So many miles from my parents, and there is my girlfriend in my arms, and scattered across the Eastern Seaboard, with a brief jaunt into the Pennsylvania hinterlands for Zap, are my friends.

Easy there, Shteyni-dawg.

She has an Oldsmobile 88, a big red southern monster, and as she drives I lean over and kiss her neck. She is wearing the lavender perfume we bought from a street vendor near Fourth Avenue. I am covered in Drakkar Noir or Safari for Men or a cologne of equally debilitating pungency. Something, after all, has to announce the fact that I am still a Russian immigrant.

Or am I?

When I walked into the Sheep Meadow in Central Park after my first day of Stuyvesant, I thought a part of me broke. A connection to the past. A straight shot from Uncle Aaron's labor camps and the bombs of the Messerschmitts to the wield of my father's hand and the lash of my mother's tongue to the boy who writes "Gary Shteyngart" and "SSSQ" on his Hebrew school assignments. Maybe the connection didn't break. Maybe it just bent. And now in J.Z.'s car it is bending further. The past, which stretches indefinitely behind me, and the future, which stretches for another fifty years at best, are evenly matched. Nothing in the genetic program I've been given has prepared me for someone like her, for the unconditional warmth of her interethnic nose, for "Dude, there is no jokin' around about the Mississippi River!" Nor for the deep existential melancholy that weighs us both down like the hot and wet southern summer around us.

Her mother's home, unlike my mother's, is unkempt, the heavy furniture sunk into carpets, every square inch haunted by a furry beast of a corgi named Tally-Dog, which, when confronted by my Drakkar Noir stink, knows only one mode: bark. To my greatest horror, three minutes into the visit, I pull an albino roach out of the sink by one of its antennae, thinking it is one of my own hairs gone prematurely gray.

But her mother is sweet and interested in me, staring out from her large golden glasses with good cheer and an early evening buzz. She is a big woman prone to the colors purple and lavender, often layered together. And from the moment I cross her threshold, it is clear that I am welcome here, and welcome to her daughter's love.

On the previous summer's visit to Little Neck, J.Z. accidentally breaks my mother's desk lamp, for which we are promptly billed eighty dollars by my no-nonsense mater. (We split the eighty, not a trifling amount for two financial aid students.) That, and the sight of my father walking down the stairs in his tight soccer shorts, his shining testicles spilling out of both sides, provide J.Z. with a quick but potent overview of Shteyngart family life in medias res.

Down here, testicles are kept away from public sight. In fact, there is a southern rule that a man must keep one foot on the floor when inhabiting a room with a woman of tender age. It is the most wonderful rule in Christendom, this tense little caveat, because when the house is cleared of her mother, J.Z. and I run for the bedroom and collapse into each other, disappearing our ugly Oberlin clothes in just a few simple motions, as David Byrne starts singing:

And she was lying in the grass.
And she could hear the highway breathing.
And she could see a nearby factory.
She's making sure she is not dreaming.

I know he's singing about J.Z., about the rosiness of her body, the hard dough of her shoulders, the seriousness of her eyes. He's singing about her and not me; he's letting me leave myself and be with her. *And she was.*

After we shower off a little in the cramped bathroom and rejoin the Carolina humidity, we talk about death. For my twenty-first birthday, upon my request, J.Z.'s mother has given me a book called *We Don't Die: George Anderson's Conversations with the Other Side,* a tender little bit of hucksterism about a medium who communicates with the deceased. Ever since my first breathless encounter with asthma I have sensed that the curtain between our world and nonexistence is as thin as a kopeck. But now that I have found a pair of depthless brown eyes to stare into mine on a frilly bed in North Raleigh, the thought of departing this earth truly breaks my heart. "I don't want to leave you," I say to J.Z., meaning that I don't want to leave her in five days, when I will have to go back north. But what I really mean is that I don't ever want to leave her, or to leave the pleasures we just had, or to leave the strangeness of David Byrne's voice, or to leave the memories that we are putting together every day. After college we will move to New Mexico, we decide. Smoke pot and make love amid the cacti. She wants to become some sort of healer. I already know that I want to write.

Her granddaddy is southern through and through, courtly and folksy—"He's more nervous than a cat in a room full of rockin' chairs"—with a deer hanging in his smokehouse in Fayetteville, with enough authority to command the head of the table at his daughter's house, and with the kindness to let a perfect stranger from New York sit by his side and be treated like an old friend. He says grace over the food, mentioning Jesus Christ, Our Lord, at which J.Z. and I give each other curt Oberlin smiles. Granddaddy, he's *Jew*-ish.

But after dinner Granddaddy comes over to the kitchen and says, "That's a fine division of labor you have here. She's washing the dishes, and you're drying them. You two are good together." Right then and there I want to marry J.Z., marry her whole family, lighted farts and all. And when her grandpa dies of a heart attack a few years later, I will feel her pain, feel it as an extension of my own hurt, because my own grandmother is so very sick.

• • •

We fight. The truth is I don't know how to do anything—drive a car, fry an egg, be a man—and as progressive as we are, she still wants me to be strong for her. Eventually, when we drive from North Carolina to her sister's house in Dallas, Texas, she will order me behind the wheel, and, somewhere in Alabama, I will drive the Oldsmobile 88 directly into the wall of a Shoney's franchise. J.Z.'s favorite phrase, spoken with a well-practiced scowl, those dark Armenian eyes sheltering a yellow flame: "Well, *that's* ridiculous."

But instead of being contrite, I go on the offensive. I'm a New Yorker. Why shouldn't I be able to drive an Oldsmobile from Raleigh to Dallas without hitting some disgusting southern chain restaurant? Even if they did reward my vehicular assault on their dining room with a signature Monte Cristo sandwich ("Y'all must be tired"). Wasn't she there with me and her friend Michael when we watched Woody Allen's *Manhattan* together? Didn't she guzzle down Michael's martinis and whiskey sours as he and I cracked Jewishly about the artist Sol LeWitt? Isn't this the life she signed on for with a New York intellectual in the making?

Apparently not. For here I am trying to climb the sheer cliff face of North Carolina's Grandfather Mountain, using the ladders and cables to try to hang on to the damn thing, as cloud cover swirls *beneath me,* promising a truly sharp and jagged death if I let go of the rope. I am a classic acrophobe, worried that a part of me *wants* to let go of the rope. But I know that if I can't drive a car or ride a bike or play fetch with a disgruntled Welsh corgi, I should at least climb a mountain with this nimble countrywoman, who even now is bounding up the wall of rock with mountain lion dexterity.

Or, as I'll write to her after I get back to Little Neck: "I'm not good at adjusting to a new environment, especially when I feel like I can lose you by doing something wrong."

Or, as I'll write to her after we break up: "When I think of the most important moments of our relationship, I seem to see myself staring at the dashboard of your car."

Yes, in the passenger's seat, staring at the clicking odometer on that enormous chrome dashboard, staring at the passage of trees and hills and the Blue Ridge Mountains, staring at the scenery of the country that's been promised to me on my certificate of naturalization. And there she is, driving for me, one of her hands on the wheel, the other maneuvering the drinking straw to her lips, the perspiring, transparent cup full of southern ice tea, which, for those not in the know, is the best ice tea in the world.

And at night, in the half-deflated tent that I have failed to correctly pitch, in some national park, with the last sparks of our lovemaking extinguished, with our stomachs filled with hush puppies and grits and fried haddock, I lie there reading *We Don't Die: George Anderson's Conversations with the Other Side* by flashlight, hoping against hope that everything Stuyvesant and Oberlin have taught me—the immateriality of our personalities, the quickness of our time on this earth—is not altogether true.

21.

SIGN YOUR NAME (ACROSS MY HEART)

So ready for heartbreak.

IN THE MIDDLE OF ALL THAT JENNIFER, something else happens, which, I suppose, can be called college. When I close my eyes, I see myself walking down the ramp of the Mudd library, a kind of post-modern academic fortress, replete with moat, my backpack burdened down with statistics on Khrushchev-era barley harvests. My senior thesis in the politics department will be called "Back in the USSR: The Evolution of Current Reintegrationist Trends," anything to take me back to the country that has just fallen apart so unceremoniously. When I keep my eyes closed for a few beats more, I see Big Blue, the bong I am athletically smoking as Ice Cube instructs his nonexistent female audience: *Bitch . . . you should have put a sock on the pickle.* When

I keep my eyes closed for another second longer (I promise you, I will open them soon), I am back in the West Village with my roommate, C-cup Irv, the two of us tripping out on 'shrooms at his parents' house, as those fascinating new fractal patterns bloom and die on the screen of his Mac desktop.

"Dude, this guy in the Con[servatory of Music] fucked me," Irv tells me.

Me, nonjudgmental, used to anything by now: "Cool. How did it feel?"

"Pretty good. Like I had a piece of shit up my ass."

All this is leading somewhere.

. . .

Now that I have true friends who tell me about what goes inside their asses, now that I am able to talk honestly about my life with a woman who loves me ("I love you, Gary," to quote yet again from her letter), I can finally begin to think of myself as a serious person. And that seriousness will not lead to Fordham Law School, where I would most certainly clown around for the first two difficult years and then fall into a disastrous cocaine-fueled tailspin by the third. For me, this means the one thing I pursue with competence and with passion. I write.

Let me reiterate: I don't know how to do anything. No fried egg, no coffee, no driving, no paralegaling, no balanced checkbook, no soldering a fatherboard onto a motherboard, no keeping a child warm and safe at night. But I have never experienced that which they call writer's block. My mind is running at insomniac speed. The words are falling in like soldiers at reveille. Put me in front of a keyboard and I will fill up a screen. What do you want? When do you want it? Right now? Well, here it is.

My output is a story a week or a batch of poems. I write as soon as I wake up, the hangover still pulsing in the damaged front of my brain, to the *thwacka-thwacka* sound of roommate Irv's first vigorous masturbation. I write before coffee; I write with Big Blue gurgling in the corner; I write like a child who needs to prove something. The Oberlin creative writing department takes me on, takes me in. There is a professor called Diane Vreuls (such a strong Dutch last name), tall and striking, approaching retirement, who gets what I'm doing. In her tiny cramped office in the basement of the building that resembles the first three floors of the World Trade Center, she points out a passage where one of my characters crawls through the woods. "How does he crawl, Gary?" she asks. And then she gets down on all fours, and, with all six feet of her plus the gray halo of long hair, she crawls every which way. And I get it. And I understand how it's done. How the words convey the world around me and the world trapped inside me.

I am walking on water. Yes, that's what writing can do. I am walking across the Atlantic Ocean at a diagonal, looping up the English Channel, making hash of the Danish archipelago, sliding up the Baltic Sea, down the Gulf of Finland. "Well, we know where we're going," David Byrne is singing on the stereo, "but we don't know where we've been."

I am going to Moscow Square, to Tipanov Street, but what I don't know how to do yet is to go beyond my childhood courtyard with its sooty black pipe and rusty rocketship.

To the Chesme Church. To the helicopter launching pad. Up, up, into the air and between the spires.

• • •

I write with J.Z. cross-legged across the bed from me, buried in statistics and psychology textbooks. Years later, she will become a healer, just as she promised herself.

I'm desperately trying to have a history, a past. I'm flooding myself with memory, melancholy and true. Every memory I repressed at the Solomon Schechter School of Queens, where I pretended to be a good East German, is coming back to me. I write about eating *pelmeni* dumplings with my mother by the mermaid statue in Yalta. I write about the mechanical chicken I used to play with in the Crimea.

About the girl with the one eye in our first apartment in America, the one who played Honeycomb license plates with me. I proudly use words I just picked up, words like "Aubusson," writing next to it, in parentheses, "French rug." I stick the Aubusson into a kind of literary action story called "Sundown at the International," complete with "jet-black Sikorsky helicopters." Fifteen years later, that story will be expanded into the novel *Absurdistan*.

Sometimes my writing sucks, but sometimes it strives for the truth and it works. My parents are fighting across its pages. I am learning English. I am learning to be second-class. I am learning *Adonai Eloheinu, Adonai Echad*. Faced with an American pizza parlor, my "mother instructs me to order a pizza with meat on it so that I'll have a complete meal." My imagination is allowed to roam in all directions, even ones that fail (*especially* ones that fail). I hand in a truly strange character sketch of Nikita Khrushchev celebrating a lonely seventieth birthday on a collective farm. I write about my grandmother's fictional meeting with Pope John Paul II.

And then it all comes to a halt.

Oberlin imports a hot young teacher, a disciple of the guru editor Gordon Lish, famous for his editing of Raymond Carver and his grueling $2,600 workshops back east. Every story I hand in comes back with "Gary, I know what Gordon would say about this story so let me save you $2,600." At first, I don't give a fuck what Gordon would say, and, given Oberlin's impressive tuition, my parents (and the federal government) have paid way more than $2,600 for this class anyway. But the teacher wears skimpy outfits—a tiny floral spaghetti-strap number in the middle of the Ohioan winter—and she breaks our flannelled hearts with each and every workshop. I want to please her badly. So I begin to write in the terse, indecipherable bullshit-mysterious style that Gordon Lish, somewhere in Manhattan, is clearly asking of me. "The *shuka* is in the pot." Whatever that means. Several of my classmates decide to quit writing once the semester is over, which, subconsciously, may be the goal of the entire Gordon

Lish program, to reduce beginners to nothing, to clear the decks of those who would disobey the master. On certain cold days, I unwittingly fall into a Hebrew school prayer on the way to class, rocking back and forth to keep warm, chanting, "*Sh'ma* Oberlin, Gordon Lish *Eloheinu,* Gordon Lish *Echad.*" (Hear, O Oberlin, the Gordon Lish is our God, the Gordon Lish is One.) But it doesn't help. The spaghetti-strap teacher tells me what I am writing is not literature, although she does have more hope for me than the other students because "I have a better understanding of grammar."

The Lish professor is there only for a semester, and then I am returned to Diane. It takes me a while to recover. Diane is tough with me but also patient and kind. More important, she knows how to laugh with every inch of her six-foot-long Dutch-Serb body, ridiculous laughter, Eastern European laughter. People who think literature should be *Serious*—should serve as a blueprint for a rocket that will never take off—are malevolent at best, anti-Semitic at worst. Within Diane's welcome embrace I stop writing "The *shuka* is in the pot." I return to the work at hand. I plow on Napoleon-like toward Moscow Square and then toward Moscow itself.

• • •

There is an exchange program with the Moscow State Institute of International Relations, an elite institution that once educated the Soviet Union's future diplomats. Moscow is not St. Petersburg (hometown patriots might say it is the opposite), but Moscow is *really* Russia, by which I mean Asia. It is my holy truth.

I am all set to go to Moscow for my junior year, to reclaim the Little Igor inside me.

And then the women in my life tell me no.

My mother is scared of Russia in 1993. Yeltsin's tanks firing at the parliament building. Chechnya getting ready for full-scale war. Gunfights in broad daylight. In the decade since we've emigrated, my parents have never said one good word about the country, other than to praise its many bearded writers and creamy Eskimo ice cream. The Internet as we now know it is not yet a fact, but Mother presents me with a Xeroxed wire piece about some hapless student thrown to his death out of the window of a Moscow University dorm.

I write a story called "Three Views from the Avenue of Karl Marx," an earnest homage to my uncle Aaron and the labor camps. My professor tells me to send it off to *The New Yorker,* nearly precipitating a happy heart attack on my part. Am I really that good? My mother reads it, sighs, and tells me, "That's not how it happened." The details are all wrong.

I am heartbroken. Oddly enough, the pain feels similar to being called a Red Gerbil in Hebrew school. There, I was ridiculed for being an inauthentic American, and now I am being charged with being an inauthentic Russian. I do not yet understand that this very paradox is the true subject of so-called immigrant fiction. When the inevitable rejection slip comes from *The New Yorker,* I decide I have to go back to Russia to get the details right.

But then there is the other woman.

J.Z. understands that I need Russia for my stories. But she doesn't want to lose me for a year. We are just getting started. We are so very much in love. And so I have a choice: my writing or, possibly, my girlfriend.

It is not even a choice.

Fuck Russia. I will spend a semester with J.Z. in then-trendy Prague.

Within minutes the brick and mortar appeared on both sides of the road, like a signpost signaling VLADIMIR'S CHILDHOOD, NEXT HUNDRED EXITS: an endless stretch of rickety plaster Soviet-era apartment houses, each edifice peeling and waterlogged so that the inadvertent shapes of animals and constellations could be recognized by an imaginative child. And in the spaces between these behemoths were the tiny grazing spaces where Vladimir sometimes played; spaces adorned with a fistful of sand and some rusty swings. True, this was Prava and not Leningrad, but then these houses formed one long demented line from Tajikistan to Berlin. There was no stopping them.

These sentences appeared in my first novel, *The Russian Debutante's Handbook*. Needless to say, Prava is a kind of Prague, and Vladimir, the hero, is a kind of me. When I saw those Soviet bloc apartment buildings, *paneláks* in Czech (literally "prefabricated panel housing"), out of the window of a bus from Prague's airport, J.Z.'s hand clasped in mine, I knew I wanted to write a novel, and I knew what it would be about. When you're twenty-one there really is only one subject. It appears in the mirror each morning, toothbrush in hand.

The semester in Prague was my reconnaissance mission. In practical terms, I learned nothing, not even Czech, which should have been fairly easy for a Russian speaker. Maybe I learned that a half draft of pilsner spilled over a plate of onions and cheese and then sopped up with thick country bread could make me happy.

Along the way, some things happened that happened also in my novel. In a small village north of Prague, I was nearly beaten to a pulp by Czech skinheads who mistook me for an Arab. I was saved by my New York State driver's license and my American Express card, proof of my non-Arabian nature. (In the novel, my hero, Vladimir, gets the beating from which I escaped, and then some.)

Then there were some things that happened *nearly* as they did in my novel. Jealous after J.Z. had danced with an Australian or an Israeli, I drank myself so stupid that I found myself crawling along the tram lines to our dormitory, my death forestalled only by the ferocious nighttime clang of the number 22 tram and the intervention of an equally drunk Czech policeman.

And then there were some things that didn't happen in the novel at all. On Buda Hill, overlooking the bulbous and overdone Hungarian parliament building, J.Z. stared into my camera lens, her black hair

picked up by the wind, the combination of Armenian and southern
Wasp features finally settling into something undeniably Eastern European, the smile that wasn't, the pale beauty that was.

• • •

A cold, rainy, muddy, miserable day in late May. The Oberlin College
commencement exercises of 1995. Two-thirds of the manuscript of
what will be my first novel is under my arm. I am happy and I am
scared. J.Z. and I are breaking up. It is not anyone's fault. She wants
to return to North Carolina. I want to be in New York, where I mistakenly think another love will quickly swoon into my arms.

But I don't want to end my Oberlin story there. Let me go back a
year. There is a dorm called South, which, as I've mentioned, resembles a lost terminal of Newark Airport. This is where I've just had an
asthma attack, my first in five years and the worst one of my life.

It's been several weeks since I've checked out of Oberlin's pitiful
hospital, several weeks since J.Z. held the phone clamped to her ear,
my mother relaying to her my health insurance information as I
struggled to breathe in my sweaty little dorm bed; the two women in
my life, their Russian and southern accents, my mother's awful exact-
ness, J.Z.'s love and fear.

She has nursed me back to health, has spent every hour by my side.
The circles under my eyes are larger than usual. Because of the asthma
I haven't been able to smoke pot in weeks, and I'm nervous and depleted. One of the many things I never learned how to do is dance.
But tonight J.Z. says she will teach me. She puts on Terence Trent
D'Arby's "Sign Your Name (Across My Heart)," the 1988 slow jam
that has somehow survived the full Kurt Cobaining of Oberlin's ste-
reos. She puts her hands on my hips, and I put mine on hers. I let my
eyes fall shut. Slow, rhythmic breathing. The ugly dorm, the sad college, the unhappy students. I sway in one direction; I sway in another.
What am I doing wrong? I don't want to have another asthma attack.
My hands are resting on my lover's hips, and part of me, perhaps because of the recent asthma, has left my body. What I don't yet know is

that this *will* be my last asthma attack ever. But for now the two of us are still here, swaying to Trent D'Arby's earnest crooning.

"J.Z.," I say, "I don't know how to do this."

She keeps her hands on my hips. Her dark hair with its brown highlights pools across my chest.

And then, suddenly, I do.

22.

THE BENEFACTOR

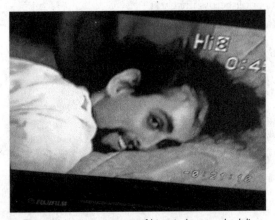

The author is tripping out of his mind on psychedelic mushrooms while being videotaped for a documentary called Only Children *by his new friend John.*

ON THE NINE-HOUR DRIVE HOME from Ohio, my diploma in hand, my parents and I stop in for a McDonald's lunch. Remarkably, the hamburgers haven't changed in price over the years, so I order three, plus a medium Coke and medium fries, and my parents also go in for a hamburger each and share some of my medium fries as well as their own private small Coke. Because of my fine grades and impending job as a paralegal, and then, presumably, ascension to law school, all of us are a happy family and five times sixty-nine cents for the hamburgers plus another three dollars and fifty cents for the hamburger accessories seems well within reach. We've earned this now. Across the aisle I espy one of the prettier Oberlin graduates, a girl who uses lipstick, and we both roll our eyes at one another, as if to say, *Ugh, can you believe we're at a McDonald's?* If only I could tell her how much each bite with my parents really means to me.

The other thing I'm excited about is going back to New York, the place I know will be my home for the rest of my life. With J.Z. no longer my girlfriend, going home means mainly one thing: going back to my new best friend.

Allow me to backtrack to sophomore year.

• • •

My college roommate C-cup Irv and his parents live in Washington Square Village, two pieces of colorful NYU Warsaw Pact architecture set around a pleasant private park. Across the hall from Irv lives a sound editor who is friends with the former head writer of the soap opera *As the World Turns*. I want to say this soap opera writer, John, is *x* years old, but in the two decades I've known him he has never revealed his age. It's not that he lies about it. It's that he does not confess his age to *anyone*. "Too traumatic," he whispers when asked, his face folding into a sort of grieving Jewish turtle expression, the kind my people reserve only for talk of their own extinction. In his apartment, I once found a college graduation photograph, which had John's graduation date written on the back. He lunged across the room to grab the photo from me, demolishing a coffee table in the process, then yelping in pain on the floor while triumphantly holding on to the graduation photo. So how old is John? Since you can never really tell the age of Americans who lumber toward nonbeing on their own schedules, let's just say that when I first meet him in 1993, he is old enough for me to turn him into a parental figure and young enough for me to understand him as a friend.

In 1993 John has left the soap opera world and is writing a script about a college-aged kid who kills his parents. (Vaguely appropriate, given that at the time I am trying to kill my own parents, or at least the first twenty years of my life spent with them.) His friend, the sound editor, suggests a suitable candidate from my generation. Enter Oberlin roommate Irv, the proud sexual omnivore and keeper of Big Blue, our three-foot bong. Enter Maya (name changed), a sweet, damaged round girl who is a dominatrix in the Vault, New York's premier sadomasochist club, whom I will also pluck from life and pin, with a modicum of blood spilled, onto the pages of my burgeoning first novel under the name Challah.

Enter me.

John invites me out. I am so impressed to be meeting a real writer I tell John I will gladly pay for dinner. I take him to a fancy Indian place called Akbar on Park Avenue and Fifty-Ninth, where Paulie, my lecherous high school boss, used to take me. The restaurant has stained-glass ceilings that dazzle my Little Neck eye, and the waiters seem very proud of their powerful tandoor oven, from which emerges my very first pillowy naan bread, the steam rising magically around my fingers as I tear it apart.

I do not realize that this is the last fancy meal I will pay for in the next five years, nor that I am about to turn in one benefactor for another, this one without the urge to bend me over his desk. The writer Chang-rae Lee (about whom later) will remark that my characters are usually sons in search of fathers. It would be hard for me to argue his point.

At dinner, I am looking at a balding, curly-haired man in wire-rimmed glasses, part of his face hidden beneath a bushy mustache, his crisp Frank Stella shirt tucked into his denims. This is how I picture the cool, high-end fathers of Oberlin students who live in off-campus houses with funny names like Banana House or Eek-a-House! where everyone is in a band or very close to someone in a band.

Here is what John sees seated before him at Akbar. A twenty-year-old boy with scraggly, ass-length hair, outrageous, sparse Soviet teeth that would not flatter an Appalachian beaver (until my parents replace them in a year, I speak with a hand constantly held in front of my mouth, like a shy Japanese girl), and the pride of my wardrobe, a silk summer jacket, the kind worn by the actor Don Johnson in the TV serial *Miami Vice,* which I also wear with the sleeves partially rolled up, even during the month of January.

John takes all this uniqueness with good cheer, as my orthodontia and I question him about the writing life—I am particularly impressed that he has written for *Knots Landing,* a spin-off of my beloved *Dallas*. I have sent him some of my work from Oberlin, in particular a short play, which he has marked with encouragement ("funny," "good passage") and precise criticism ("get specific," "awkward phrase"). At dinner, I am full of follow-up questions. *How* may I best fix this awkward phrase? *What* does getting more specific mean?

John is a Manhattanite through and through, as complicated and as rooted in place as anyone I've ever met, versed in restaurants and theaters and a market called Fairway, on Broadway at Seventy-Fourth Street, which stocks foods such as I could have only imagined: lemon anchovies, Roman artichokes, Idiazabal cheese from the Basque country. He also has no children, which is fortuitous for me but perhaps not so much for him.

Within a few months of our Akbar dinner, the Don Johnson jacket will be gone, traded in for one of John's old Armani blazers.

Within a few months, we will be on the phone almost daily, me pressing him on the latest draft of a story or a poem with bratty impatience, as if his entire world revolves around my creative needs. "Have you read it? John? Hello? I cannot wait any *lon*-ger. Talk to me, Haimosaurus!" (John is not tall, but there is something colossal yet haimish about his presence and gait, reminding me of a powerful Hebraic dinosaur.)

Within a few months, I think seriously of transferring to Columbia or, more in tune with academic reality, NYU, to be closer to my new role model. Only my budding relationship with J.Z. will keep me at Oberlin.

Within a few months, John will take me, J.Z., and roommate Irv out to the River Café for my twenty-first birthday, and I will run off with my girlfriend to the parking lot to kiss her in front of the world's most important skyline for at least as long as it takes a medium-rare filet mignon to grow cold.

Within a few months, J.Z. and I will be staying in his empty new apartment, sleeping together on his bare hardwood floors.

Within a few months, he will drop the idea of his script and start making a documentary film about me, Irv, and Maya the Domina-trix, which will eventually be titled *Only Children,* because he and his three subjects share an interesting quirk—a paucity of siblings.

And within a few years, I will drive him completely and conclu-sively around the bend. And he, in turn, will deposit me in front of the New York Psychoanalytic Institute.

• • •

John figures out that I'm a jerk pretty quickly. It happens while he's filming a dinner with me, Irv, and his parents at their Washington Square Village pad. I love Irv's apartment unreservedly, because it is at the center of the island where I want to live and because the laws of parenting, as I have known them, do not apply around here. There are garbage cans perched on shelves for no good reason, and most of the belongings are stuffed into bulging bags from the Duane Reade phar-macy. "You're supposed to be the adult!" Irv's mother yells at John, banging on his bedroom door. The three of us are huddled together, puffing reefer, a towel stuffed under the door Irv's mama is trying to demolish. Irv, hurriedly putting out the joint: "Just a minute, Mom! We're *working.*" And then we all laugh, mother included, at John's lack of adulthood. Back in the living room, John shows us some footage of Maya the Dominatrix, whom he, in his infinite sympathy, is about to install in her own apartment, as she's about to go homeless.

And I let loose. From behind my Russian rabbit teeth, a torrent of hatred so misdirected at a girl whose life is sliding off the rails, who has done me no harm, who is closer to me than I think. *She's fat. Sub-urban. Unsophisticated.* This from a boy who has just scribbled "Au-busson" into his writer's journal and underlined it no fewer than thrice.

"How can you say that?" John asks.

But I say more and more and more about the woman with the jangles of chains atop her cleavage, a woman who has just been pum-meled with a cane at her job in a Manhattan S&M dungeon while sick with anemia and a bleeding ulcer, who has been in and out of homeless shelters and mental institutions since being abandoned by her family at age sixteen.

"So many people move to the East Village and then go to the opposite extreme of their suburban experience," I say, venomously, to the camera. "That is so *old*. To make her character interesting, she has to be engaging and intelligent."

"She's not a character!" John shouts.

Drunk off of Irv's Japanese plum wine (the strange tipple of choice that summer), and constantly fussing with my cheap new contact lenses, I am in high dudgeon, incensed that John would speak up for this fat suburban dominatrix. *You can't adopt her,* I want to say to him. *You have to adopt me!* Because no one can have more pain than I can.

Partly, this is what being of college age is about, being an expert on everything. But also I am saying exactly what my parents would be saying about Maya. Spoiled American. Didn't go through what we went through. Wasting her life. In fact, with my thick new stubbly goatee and my joyous sarcasm, I am a direct stand-in for my father. If only I could have one of those UN placards to place in front of me every time I sit behind a desk. Republic of Fatherlandia.

One night during summer break from Oberlin, after getting John to buy me dinner at Le Bernardin or La Côte Basque or some little East Ninth Street joint with perfect butter-and-garlic-soaked snails, the kind of food I could only have imagined while watching *Dallas* and eating my mother's farmer's cheese with canned peaches, we find ourselves in the subway. I am so happy to be back in Manhattan, so happy to be with my new best friend, so happy to have been so well fed, each hundred dollars spent on me equal to a new kind of love. Even the number 1 train slowly clanging along from downtown to midtown, even its crowded melancholy, pleases me to no end. I have to say something to immortalize this moment.

"I don't understand why people want to root for the underdog," I say.

And John just looks at me. At my gaping teeth. At my Don Johnson sleeves. He doesn't want to say what he's thinking. That to him

I'm an underdog. That he knows who I am. That he's scared of what I might become. That his own mother had told him growing up, over and over, "I'd divorce your father if it wasn't for you." That he was president of his Salem, Oregon, high school class, the boy who crowned the Queen of the Sweetheart Formal but still hid in the library with his sandwich when it came time for lunch. That he failed his parents by never becoming a lawyer, much as I will fail mine in the years to come.

. . .

He is a father figure to me. And I, strangely enough, am a father figure to him. Angry, controlling, steeped in the monstrous narcissism of the underappreciated child, unable to part with money: how familiar I must seem to my new friend. When John's mother was dying, his father, a successful businessman, wouldn't leave the car in a one-dollar hospital parking lot. "How can he spend the dollar," John's psychoanalyst told him, "when he's losing so much."

And so John's unstated mission becomes this: How can he stop me from becoming my father? The first part of his plan, oddly enough, is for me to understand and acknowledge my love for my father, my childhood desire to emulate him.

My first year at Oberlin I wrote a poem called "My Reflection" about a trip Papa and I had taken to visit a distant relative in Florida. At a roadside diner, when my father had gone to the bathroom, the waitress had mistaken him for my brother and told me he looked dashing. When my father came out, I scurried off to the bathroom myself and tried to pose like him in the mirror, pleased that he looked so young, thinking that maybe he would not die during my lifetime. "I counted five gray hairs on top of my head" is the last line of the poem.

As part of his documentary, as part of his effort to show the audience that I am not just a full-time jackass, John has me walking around town reading "My Reflection" in various locations. He takes me to the Meatpacking District, which at the time is as blood soaked as the name implies, and asks me to read the poem while standing against a wall. "John, this wall is unsanitary," I say. "John, it smells like lobster."

"Just read the poem," he says.

"It's too much of a high school poem," I whine. "It's not inventive. I can't imagine myself identifying like that with my father. I was trying to write a cute father-and-son relationship poem. This is Hallmark."

John, always ready for an argument with the son he never had, says, "If you hadn't felt it, you couldn't have written it."

"But I'm good at doing this kind of bullshit."

"This strikes a nerve. It exposes something about you that you don't want exposed. Tenderness, empathy, and a bond with your father."

"It's manufactured. My father and I haven't had a real conversation in years." John and I fight on for about an hour, until I stalk off with the words "I hope someone stuffs that camera up your ass." But between us, this passes for friendly banter, and John, undeterred, follows me up a rotting pier jutting out into the Hudson with his camera, the signage reading AREA UNSAFE: KEEP OFF. In 1994, most of New York is still unsafe, so we ignore it. I sit down on the rotting pier and stare into the sunset over Jersey.

"Read the poem," John says.

"You're such an asshole!"

"Read the poem," he says.

"I'm sick of this shit. This is no way to live."

"Read the poem, Gary."

• • •

Later that day, I'm having a predinner glass of Beaujolais at John's apartment. Whenever John is distracted by a phone call I sneak off to the Dell desktop whose gigantic corpus is practically embedded into the herringbone floors of his study, bring a file up on his monitor, and write whatever comes to mind in the middle of one of his Word documents—e.g., "Another fine night here at Château le Moron," which is what I call John's apartment. Any man who fears mortality as much as John does usually keeps an outlandishly exact record of every aspect of his life, and so I find a file that contains the entire song list of a Tony Bennett concert. Sometimes with John, it feels like I'm reliving my childhood, or at least trying to imagine what childhood on these shores might have been like. I find a space between "Tangerine" and "The Best Is Yet to Come" and type in "Duet with Gary."

I'm too young to even understand the significance of what I've typed. The desperate need for adult friendship and guidance, the relief of having found someone who can match my pitch and volume, can understand my song.

Duet with Gary. Have I ever been so sincere in my life? Will I ever be again?

• • •

Returning from Oberlin with my parents after graduation, I am thinking of John and the dinners at La Côte Basque and the easy sophistication and camaraderie that surely await me. Right about now, several hundred miles to the east, he is recording a voice-over to his documentary, introducing me to the viewer.

"I've never ceased to be amazed by Gary's intolerance, meanspiritedness, and selfishness," the man who will one day be the witness at my wedding is saying into his microphone. "I don't know if it was in spite of those traits or because of them that I would come to feel as close to this hostile Russian—too many years younger than me to mention—as I ever have to any friend."

The hostile Russian is on his way home. He is cocky and still coated with praise from the Oberlin College creative writing department. He has just been treated to a McDonald's lunch by his parents, the last such treat he will know in years. More tragic still, he cannot even begin to fathom the possibility of failure.

23

FROM THE DIARIES OF PUSSY-CAKE

The author at a party on his first date with Pamela Sanders. He is so drunk he can barely stand. Notice the desperate white cravat around his neck. Poor author.

L ET'S GO BACK TO THE BEGINNING. To the Strand Book Annex in Manhattan. To the panic attack. To the book. *I am standing there once again in the Fulton Street Strand, holding* St. Petersburg: Architecture of the Tsars, *the baroque blue hues of the Smolny Convent Cathedral practically jumping off the cover. I am opening the book, for the first time, to page 90. I am turning to that page. I am turning to that page again. The thick page is turning in my hand.* What happened at the Chesme Church more than twenty years ago?

When Jonathan and I used to play our Zork computer game after Hebrew school, there was a simple typed command—I—that stood for "inventory." It would tell you how many swords and flasks and assorted magical loot you, the player, possessed at the moment. Curiously, a "Personality Inventory" or "Self-Report Inventory," with its Anxiety and Repression and Ego Strength Scales, is also used by psychologists to evaluate the mental conditions of a test subject. I am just saying.

If I were to type *I* in 1997, at the Strand Book Annex in Lower Manhattan, what inventory would appear?

1. There would be "Me." Ponytail tied back with a girlish scrunchie. Receding hairline out in front. A heavy rotation of dead ficus trees. Five thousand dollars in debt to Chase Visa. A Little Failure of the first order.

2. There would be my new studio apartment in babylicious Park Slope. Three hundred square feet looking out onto a dank courtyard, the kitchen overrun with roaches of all sizes and colors, a gift from the old woman slowly, eternally, dying in the apartment upstairs. No baby.

3. There is my novel, which I've finished but which I also hate. At one point, I decide to throw out the five hundred pages that comprise the last draft. A good Oberlin graduate, I recycle the whole mess first, but, broke and indebted, I use the cheapest recycling bags. I return from work to find out that my recycling bags have burst, and my entire novel is scattered like a blizzard across Seventh Avenue, the Champs-Élysées of Park Slope, my name crowning every page, my friends chuckling at my random prose. "Who's this *Vladimir*?"

4. My friend, adversary, and role model, John. The key to my future sanity.

The problem with Zork's Inventory function is that it never really tells you what you *don't* have. What you want. What you need still.

I no longer have J.Z. She is in North Carolina. Her boyfriend is a drummer who lives in a van. After almost three years of having a companion, someone to drive me to the hospital for my last asthma attack, someone to split a soggy tuna sub with at the Student Union's snack bar, I am alone.

My grandma Polya. Her death is drawn out and cruel. I follow her to different hospitals, Manhattan's Mount Sinai and a lesser one near her apartment in Queens, but it is hard to sit at her bedside, next to the green-hued monitors that chart her failing grasp on the world. She is dying in parts, as most of us do. Skeins of hard-won adulthood peeling off. The kindness is gone from her face, the kindness she once shared only with me, and what is left is a contorted Soviet grimace. I don't know what to do. I give her strawberries to eat. I watch my father howl in anger and sadness. I kiss her forehead at the funeral parlor, and it feels cold and hard like a brick, inanimate. So much for George Anderson's *We Don't Die*.

I watch her body being driven to a Long Island cemetery in a van, not a real hearse, and wish I had the money to upgrade her final voyage. The body of the one woman who didn't consider me a Little Failure or a Snotty or a weakling is covered with dirt, handfuls of which we have all thrown on top of her with our hands, as is Jewish custom.

And the final thing I don't have. *St. Petersburg: Architecture of the Tsars*. After my panic attack is over, I put the book down and walk right out of the Strand Book Annex. Walk right out toward a fresh lunchtime vodka and tonic at the Blarney Stone. No Chesme Church for me. No helicopter either.

But four dry years after I've kissed J.Z. a final goodbye, there will be someone new in my life.

Someone, as they say, special.

. . .

Her name is Pamela Sanders.* We hook up at a social agency conference about the resettlement of Hmong refugees or something of the sort. She is a serious-minded Program Development Specialist who works at the nonprofit I just got laid off from. I am writing grant

* Not her name. Not her name at all.

proposals for a Lower East Side settlement house, my new employ. My title is Senior Grant Writer, but I am sometimes referred to as Señor Grant Writer, and people tell me I am not a team player.

After four lonely years without J.Z., I am primed to like anybody who will touch me, but there's more to Pamela than that helpful distinction. Let me start with how she looks. She has two bodies. An aristocratic upper half that my Petersburg ancestry would probably have termed "cultured"—diminutive shoulders that fit into the hollows of my palms, a well-proportioned Anglo face (here the straight stalk of a nose, there a minimalist attempt at ears), the whole pleasant affair crowned by twenty inches of rich, flaxen hair. But by candlelight a second body reveals itself, as loamy and real as our country's interior: strong, strong legs that conquer the hills of Brooklyn where she lives (Cobble and Boerum Hills, to be exact) with ease; hips wide enough to give birth to the tribe of Joseph; a backside in which one could lose oneself, a scalloped, ridged, white-pink ode to the uncomplicated side of lust. And when she propels this second half out of a pair of tight jeans, I am torn between the biological and the refined—do I grab the ass or kiss the nubbin of a nose, do I go for the part of her golden crown or plunge between the obvious promise of her thighs? After knowing her a few weeks, after falling thoroughly in love, I am, I think to myself, caught in a love triangle between me and these two Pamelas. And then the love triangle gets *really* complicated. She tells me she has another boyfriend.

He is, let's say, Kevin, a thirty-year-old poet who lives with his parents in New Jersey, drops dubious verses about the Greek gods, and weekly crashes at my sweetheart's house in Brooklyn. They have been together for the better part of a decade, the phone bill is in his name, and the answering machine informs the caller that she has reached "the home of Kevin." In photographs he looks like a Greek god himself, a dark, hipster one, assigned by Zeus to some minor precinct, say, Trendios the god of Williamsburg. If the outgoing phone message is any indication, he speaks with a fake aristocratic accent. He also enjoys working with wood. Despite this inclination, he has not had sex with my baby doll for some time.

That is my job. By this point, I am living in a tenement apartment off Delancey Street on the Lower East Side, measuring maybe ten feet by twenty feet (fewer tiny roaches than in my Brooklyn digs, more giant flying water bugs), next to another studio that is home to a couple so loud one could graph their hourly orgasms in a series of parabolas and bell curves. Pamela gets competitive with the neighbors. She hollers during lovemaking as if my tenement building is on fire (frequently it is), urging me to do the same. "Let's show them where the *real* fun is!" she'll say. When it's over, she calls her other boyfriend, makes sure his parents know that, yes, she is still coming over to New Jersey for a weekend of family fun, her tone quiet, familial, obedient.

Once I call her Brooklyn apartment when Kevin is *in situ,* and he tells Pamela he doesn't want "that man," meaning me, ever calling there, meaning her home, again. This puts a crimp in our communication.

I love Pamela. She is what I've been waiting for all my life. A chance to lower myself into complete abasement, a chance to beg for someone's love over and over again, knowing I will never get it. After our first date, when I find out she has a boyfriend, I sign off gallantly in an email, "I am at your disposal."

Except what I've written is: "I am your disposal."

In return for this admission she gives me a present, Michel Leiris's *Manhood: A Journey from Childhood into the Fierce Order of Virility.*

She's in her late twenties, but already there are crow's-feet radiating from the edges of her pale gray eyes. But it's not just her face. Her personality is old. She is a self-described urban hermit and unreformed shoplifter. When I fall ill, she tells me she loves thinking of me as a feverish little nineteenth-century child, with her playing the role of horny older caregiver. When she notices I use Lever 2000 Pure Rain soap (forty-nine cents at the local bodega) she tells me it's bad for my skin and gets me some fancy soap made from olive oil. She plays computer chess until two in the morning. She schedules a week off from work that she promises me will be "FuckFest '99." "I have this tingle in my middle region," she informs me. She calls me Dope, Mr. Shygart, Coy Little Mother, Poochie (as in "Have fun tonight, Poochie"), Pussy-cake, Big Furry Bitch.

"You shouldn't let me get away with this crap," she tells me, after hurting me some more.

On the other hand, she gets upset when I tell her I love her. She tells me I'm quite "dear" to her but that she can't reciprocate all this "love" because of Kevin. "Oh, the complexities of modern life!" I write to her. "So many goofy, earnest middle-class boys to choose from."

But here's the problem. Pamela and I both want to be writers, we both want to be card-carrying members of the East Coast Intelligentsia, but we also both think we're fakes. I'm a Russian immigrant (before the burst of Russian immigrant lit of the early 2000s), and she's working class. To wit, she's from a destroyed family in Washington State, the father a Boeing worker always worried about his next paycheck and the next union strike. Kevin's family *is* her new family, tender, native-born, educated Jewish suburbanites. When she spends the weekend at their house, Kevin sleeps on the floor next to her, pretending they're still together in every way. Neither of them wants to give up the ruse to her adoptive parents.

And here's what really hurts: I can't give her the same kind of family. Not with the greenhorn Shteyngarts in their Little Neck enclosure. Not with my mother's cold cabbage borscht with the surreally large dollop of sour cream, not with their Republican politics, not with their superannuated Ford Taurus leaking quietly in front of the single-car working-class garage.

And when I see my parents through her eyes I do love them more. Because I know behind those accents, behind the fearful, angry, conservative views, there is culture of the kind Pamela can only imagine, the culture of a superpower that was tossed on history's ash heap, yes, but the culture of Pushkin and Eisenstein and Shostakovich and Eskimo ice cream and diapers that had to be washed and hung out to dry, and black-market Grundig radios desperately trying to catch Voice of America and the BBC. But maybe I'm being overly sentimental.

"Don't let that bastard Tolstoy ruin your life," Pamela tells me.

· · ·

Much like Pammy, I lead a double life. With her, I am a Big Furry Bitch. With my friends, I am confident and full of life, proud that I have a girlfriend (most of my friends don't know about Kevin), proud to have rejoined the world of the reproductive. I retreat into food and cocktails to the point where Pamela complains that all I ever talk about is the overpriced crap I put into my mouth. My nonprofit salary goes entirely toward gin fizzes at Barramundi on Ludlow, hookah pipes at Kush on Orchard, oysters at Pisces on Avenue A, yam and roast duck at Le Tableau on Fifth Street. Postgorging, my friends and I head back to my studio to hear MC Solaar drop French-Senegalese beats on my new TEAC stereo, singing along to "Prose Combat" and "Nouveau Western." A typical email to Pam at the time: "We had tapas at Xunta that were nonpareil, dry sausage, blood sausage, olives stuffed with anchovies, sheep's milk cheese, *patatas bravas,* and the ubiquitous garlic shrimp." Oh, that *nonpareil* dry sausage. Oh, those *ubiquitous* garlic shrimp.

So here I am boasting of my gastronomy to Pam, and my lovemaking with Pam to my friends. And there I am in bed in my Lower East Side studio, my futon gently rolling down the sloped floor until I crash headlong into my bookshelf, crying furry Poochie tears because Pam is with Kevin in New Jersey or, worse yet, in her Boerum Hill apartment, having her famous lamb and oven-roasted potatoes like the married couple they should have been.

"If you won't speak to me, *it is better not to live!*" is what I would shout to my mother when she gave me the silent treatment as a child. Now I am, according to Pam, Mr. Shygart, *a coy little mother* who is approaching thirty, with a half-girlfriend, with a job as Señor Grant Writer that pays $50,000 a year. But despite these modest successes, my mother's silence is where I want to be. The truth is I miss her almost as much as I miss Pam. Alone and crying and plotting angry revenge, this is what it feels like to be home. This is comfortable and familiar. The only thing that is missing is the Lightman from my childhood closet.

Desperate, I write to her: "I would love it if Kevin and I could be friends and we could all spend time together."

Even more desperate: "Perhaps we can even form a kind of unconventional family, Marin County style."

My perception of Marin County, California, appears to be flawed at the time.

• • •

Finally, I take it to the next level. I am not to be anywhere near her apartment when Kevin deigns to visit from New Jersey, but one such night I find myself at the nearby Brooklyn Inn, a dusty but attractive joint on Hoyt Street with huge arched windows and a long dark-wood bar. Kevin and Pammy both love the place because it often attracts a certain groomed literary crowd, the people they one day wish to be. At the bar, I guzzle down a vodka tonic, and another, and another, and another, and another, and another and another. How many does that make? My math not so good.

The walk from the Brooklyn Inn to Pamela's takes about five minutes under sober conditions. The main danger for me now is Atlantic Avenue, which has many lanes to cross, by which I mean more than two for certain. A small Japanese car pulling out into traffic bumps me somewhere around the hip, but I shrug it off, waving at the driver not to worry. Eventually, I turn onto leafy, gorgeous State Street, Pam's street, and crawl on all fours up to her buzzer. At the top step, I collapse and take a little breather, gather my anger together. The last time I hit somebody was back at the dacha in upstate New York, the kid I would torture while citing the torture scene from Orwell's *Nine-*

teen Eighty-Four. What I am about to hit now is not exactly Kevin. It is not even Orwell's poor *Vinston.* It is a door. Pamela's front door.

The problem with chronicling the lowest moment of my life is that I can't recall much of it.

Here's what I do remember.

I am hitting the door. The tough Brooklyn door, probably wrought in the time of Walt Whitman, does not budge. Instead my hand turns red, then purple. I feel nothing. Maybe my hip is starting to ache some from being hit by the car on Atlantic.

Then I am inside, because someone (Pam?) has opened the door, and I am racing upstairs to confront my nemesis. The thing about Kevin is that he truly is very handsome. He has a real jaw, a serious nose, and tight clever eyes underneath a well-stocked brow. Immediately, I can tell that I am outclassed.

What happens in the next few seconds, minutes, or hours seems to be this: I scream and cry, something like "I can't take it anymore, I can't take it anymore! It is better not to live!" and Pammy screams and cries with me. Kevin, as far as I can remember, remains fairly immobile and unmoved. He says a few things here and there, perhaps along the lines of *I'm sorry it has to be like this.* But what's truly amazing about this scene is that Pamela and I are essentially putting on a performance for Kevin. The two outsiders, one drunk out of his mind, the other depressed and eternally abandoned, are dancing and singing and weeping for Kevin, our God. I cannot fully choreograph Pamela's dance, but I can surely remember the lyrics to my own. They are in Hebrew, of course, and I learned them in 1979 in a school in Queens.

Yamin, smol, smol, yamin, left, right, right, left, *troo-loo-loo-loo.*

Pamela guides me downstairs, my hand already throbbing to the point where my eyes are clouded in a different brand of tears. She goes no farther than the door I had hit with twenty-seven years of frustration, a door that she slams shut behind her. Angry, accusatory emails will stream in from her end by morning's light. It would appear that by meeting Kevin I have broken the rules of the game.

And outside it is warm either in the fading way of fall or the raptur-

ous, tenuous way of spring. And I am standing there holding my
hand as a bearded, academic-looking man walks a set of Welsh corgis
down State Street, a mirror of some earlier time and place—summer
break, North Carolina—that should have pleased the early Nabokov so.

. . .

Three years later, Pamela Sanders is in a creative writing M.F.A. program at the University of Florida. One night, she sees her latest ex-
boyfriend—a Ph.D. student in English, who, rumor has it, has done
something terrible to her—sitting on the patio of the Market Street
Pub & Brewery. When he gets up, Pamela follows him through the
bar and into the restroom. She is carrying a carpenter's hammer, its
head wrapped in plastic. In the restroom, as he is taking a leak, Pamela
hits the back of his head repeatedly with the claw end of the hammer.
"I'm going to kill you!" Pamela is screaming, according to the arrest
form. "You ruined my life!" He wrestles the hammer from her in the
bathroom, and she runs out of the Market Street Pub, leaving her
victim to stagger back into the bar. He suffers multiple lacerations and
contusions to the head.

Pamela flees the state of Florida; she is charged with attempted
murder. Eventually, she returns to Florida and turns herself in. The
charges are reduced to aggravated battery with a deadly weapon and
she is sentenced to a year in the county pen.

. . .

The first time I hear of the crime it is 2004, and I am at a writers'
conference in Prague, following the publication of my first novel. My
beer-hoisting interlocutor tells me the tale with a smile, which may
indicate that he knows of our past relationship. I can only imagine
how quickly and gleefully a story like this must have spread through
a college town. How quickly the term "Pamma Hamma Slamma"
would be coined. Even before the attack, she was a mystery to many
of her fellow writers and teachers, but several of the women in the

creative writing program rallied behind her, one apparently going as far as to take her into her home, in Gainesville, after she was released on fourteen years' probation. Some time later, she returned to New York City.

"That guy whose head she bashed in," my drinking companion in Prague tells me, "he kind of looked like you! He had a beard!"

I am later told that Pam's fiction was really coming into its own before the attack, something that does not surprise me, because she was always an exceptionally strong writer, if maybe a little too scared of the truth she was leaving behind on the page. But that kind of work requires a bravery different from the kind needed to bash a human being over the head with the claw end of a carpenter's tool in a stinking subtropical bathroom, again and again and again.

24.

RAZVOD

The author posing for his first novel. What he will gain in readership, he will soon lose in hair.

A BOOK FULL OF DYSFUNCTION and hammer-armed assassins needs an adult in the room. Someone has to enter from stage left, *way* left, and tell our deluded hero, *You can't live like this anymore.* Someone with two ounces of wisdom and at least as many of kindness needs to change our hero's life. How romantic it would be if said person was a willowy American blonde or a sharp-tongued Brooklyn girl. Nothing doing here. We all know who it's going to be.

But, oh, thank God there is *someone.* No, let me be emphatic: Thank God there is him.

When I graduate from Oberlin, John is at the center of my life and the center of my abuse. I hate him so much for being from a prosperous American family, for being older than me, for being generous to Maya, whom he's installed in the first decent apartment of her life and who, thanks to his kind offices, no longer has to whip businessmen inside a Manhattan dungeon. And I hate the little muscle under his left eye, the one that twitches when we watch something sad at Lincoln Plaza Cinemas, the one that allows the sheen of liquid to coat the bottom lid, the one that shows that he is human and aware of the pain of others. That, more than anything else, is unforgivable to me and to my origins. So I respond by sabotaging his documentary, by offering him nothing but clownish songs and stupid accents whenever he flips on the camera. I want to punish John for trying to see beyond my goatee and spiteful tongue. I want to make him pay for his curiosity and his love.

But despite this hatred, I want his life, too. I pass by the Frank Stella shop on Columbus where John gets some of the shirts he wears effortlessly to places like Le Bernadin or a production of Mamet's *Oleana*. To me, Frank Stella, this old-fashioned middle-class shop, looks like nothing less than a well-lit jewel box. Just the simplicity of it, the lack of pretension, the lack of Stuyvesant striving to be the best. If only my eye could twitch and cry. If only the silent coldness inside me could dissipate. If only my apartment had green silk curtains, a 1920s burgundy mohair couch, and a letter from Bette Davis thanking me for sending flowers when we stayed at the same hotel in Biarritz. If only I could drink a few glasses less each day.

When I come home after a day of paralegaling to discover the world's biggest water bug flapping around my studio, I call John and beg him to come over and kill it. He won't, but it's a relief to be able to call him and tell him something no one else must know. That I'm scared.

John is generous enough to go over dozens of drafts of my first novel, for which I reward him with five years of derision. "The Challah character [read: Dominatrix Maya] needs more development," he tells me.

"Well, what do *you* know?" I say, seething like a small samovar on his plush mohair couch. "*You're* just a television writer. *You've* never written a novel." And what I'm really telling him is: *Why do I have to work so hard, why do I have to rewrite this fucking novel over and over again just to get a little bit of your praise? Why don't you just adore me like my grandmother did?*

When I'm with my real parents, I regale them with funny tales of Rich American John—"A woman comes every week to clean his apartment and he pays her handsomely!"—a profligate, silly individual whom we may all safely look down upon. And yet, despite his Americanness, or perhaps because of it, we also respect him. At Thanksgiving family dinners he tries to steer them from their dreams of law or accountancy for me, telling them stories of his own years as a television writer. "And how much money did you make from this writing business?" my father wants to know.

He tells them. "Ooooooh." It is a fine figure. "Gary's very talented," John says to my parents. "He can make it as a writer." And I blush and wave it away. But I am thankful. A soft-spoken American whose apartment my parents and I have estimated to be worth close to a million 1998 dollars is my advocate.

Later, I realize that just as I tried to puff up my family's barely existing wealth when I was in high school, I am attempting to make John richer and more generous in the eyes of my parents, my friends, myself. I am trying to make John the parent who would take me right out of Solomon Schechter. The parent who would say, "We can do better than this." The truth is, John's father did not own half of Salem, Oregon, the glittering state capital from which John hails, as I always claim to others. He owned a hardware store. The Upper West Side apartment, bought in the mid-1990s, cost John two hundred thousand dollars, not one million. The single Armani blazer he owned and bequeathed to me was hardly the Gatsbyesque wardrobe I made it out to be. And even those trips to Le Bernadin or La Côte Basque were rare. More often than not there was sugar-cane shrimp at the Vietnamese joint around the corner from his house. But, honestly, who cares? I was just happy to be with him.

No, I want the safety of John's imaginary riches to rescue me from my mother's $1.40 Kiev-style chicken cutlet. "When you have to pay for everything, you will know that life is hard," my mother says the night she sells me the stack of butter-stuffed poultry and a roll of Saran Wrap for twenty dollars even.

And I realize then the dissonance between my parents and John. We're in America, and, frankly, life is just not *that* hard. She *needs* to make it harder. For her. For me. Because we never really left Russia. The orange Romanian furniture, the wood carving of Leningrad's Peter and Paul Fortress, the explosive Kiev-style cutlets. All of it means one thing: The softness of this country has not softened my parents.

At the dinner table in Little Neck on the Night of the Cutlets, John and my parents are discussing what to inscribe on my grandmother's gravestone. A year has passed since she died.

My father wants to write the English translation of a Russian inscription, which translates roughly as "Always mourning son."

"But you won't always be mourning," says John. "You'll always miss her, but you won't be mourning."

My father looks mildly horrified by John's pronouncement. *He'll always miss her?* What kind of American bullshit is this? His mother has died, so he has to literally be the *always mourning son.*

My mother has another suggestion for the gravestone. "Always struggling son." She explains for the benefit of our American guest: "Gary's father thinks he has to struggle. He has to feel this pain forever. Some people"—meaning our kind—"always want to feel guilty." She comes up with a few more gravestone inscriptions. "Always painful mourning." "Constantly painful mourning."

My father will take John up to his monkish attic space to show my friend the lay of his land. "And here I have my Sony radio. And here is some Chekhov and Tolstoy. And here are Pushkin's letters." How happy I am to see the two most important men in my life talking to each other, being chums across the distance of time and culture. That one term, *Sony radio,* is enough to make me cry cutlet-dense filial tears. John is doing it again; he's softening my family for me.

Finally, outdoors in his overgrown beefsteak tomato and cucumber garden, the sun setting behind him, my father speaks into John's camera: "When Gary was six years old he was running on the street, kissing me, hugging me. Now he doesn't want to hug me, he thinks it's not necessary. But I need this. I feel lost now. Not only because I don't have my mother anymore, but because nobody needs me so much like she needed me."

John and I talk about our parents all the time, me only half listening, or quarter listening, to his stories, him immersed in mine. He points out what I sometimes can't see through both my rage and my love (at a certain point, the two have become indistinguishable): They paid for my college; they bought me my new teeth so that I could smile. If his father, a successful businessman in Salem, Oregon, could worry about payment at a one-dollar parking lot, what can be said of my mother, a woman born in the year after the Siege of Leningrad was broken?

Empathy is the first part of this parental program.

And then, a managed distance.

• • •

The years roll by. 1999. I am dating Pamela Sanders, weeping at the presence of Kevin and his powerful woodworking tools. My novel keeps going through draft after draft. Somebody has to be blamed for all this and since I can't rise up against either my parents or Pamela, it will have to be John.

For years I've been trying to squeeze him dry. To my friends, who never meet him, he is the Benefactor, aka Benny. The thousands of dollars he's been lending me have been flowing into my caviar party fund. Several times a year, my two-hundred-foot studio is crammed with about as many celebrants, who gorge on the finest champagne and silver-gray beluga that I've sourced from a questionable Brighton Beach store. The reason for these parties is always vague. My hairdresser is moving to Japan. My hairdresser is moving *back* from Japan. "Caviar courtesy of my benefactor!" I shout over the MC Solaar and the happy giggling of my Osaka hairdresser. "Somebody out there really loves me!"

And then it ends. And then John has had enough.

• • •

Before the advent of the electronic in-box, I manage to save nearly all the letters and postcards that come my way. A sensible gift of habit, I believe, from my mother, who throws nothing out. Or, perhaps, the inheritance of a totalitarian culture where everything will be used as evidence. In any case, John's letters to me are at the top of the pile. By the time he's had enough of me, they are as long as twenty-four pages and they render the truth of my life in those days better than I can.

You are not a child and I am not your parent.

There is practically nothing writerly about your process. Your acute and omnipresent anxiety causes you to function much more as an accountant or a producer, with his eyes on the bottom line and no understanding of how artists function, rather than as a young writer, trying to develop a first novel, a new career. In short, you are as mean and ungenerous to yourself as your parents are; they taught you well.

You are no longer twenty as you were when we met. You are pushing thirty. The wounded child in a defensive rage has become an adult man hurting himself and inflicting pain on others.

You are still close enough to the beginning of adulthood that you can change.

Do you want to spend your life as a frightened angry person taking your deepest fears and problems out on innocent bystanders, as well as on yourself? In five or ten years, you could be a father bestowing upon his children the same kind of misery that you now enjoy. That's how it works.

Your inability to empathize makes it difficult for you to put yourself in the skin of the characters you write.

You have to decide to take yourself seriously, not in a phony self-pitying way, but in a serious, dignified way.

It's impossible to discuss these issues for long without thinking of the role your drinking plays. Last spring's birthday dinner comes to mind,

when you drank a bottle of wine at Danube and a large pitcher of
sangria at Rio Mar. About half way through the evening you were
incoherent, uncomprehending and slurring your words. A highlight was
a disjointed monologue about how you have no drinking problem.

When do you reach the point that you are no longer so fragile that
you can't see beyond your own pain?

When do you stop being pitiable Gary hiding in the Stuyvesant
bathroom and emerge to become a man who stands up to the inner
demons that are driving him?

When I first read these dispatches, a Pamela Sanders–grade anger
boils within me. Fucking John. What does he know about writing?
Or hiding out in bathrooms? He's just a television writer. And, anyway, I'm too old to have a father figure. I'm "pushing thirty," as he,
the man obsessed with his own mortality, has just reminded me. But
the thought of going it alone, with nothing but the pricey Kiev-style
cutlet awaiting me in Little Neck, turns my anger to despair. I must
find a new way to manipulate John, to keep my caviar fund intact, to
keep the Duet with Gary humming along. As a gesture of kindness, I
take John out to Barney Greengrass for sturgeon and eggs. At first I'm
excited by the idea that I'm repaying a vast debt to John by buying
him some animal protein on a lazy Sunday afternoon, but perhaps it
is the Russian nature of the sturgeon that turns my mood from mag-
nanimous guest of the Upper West Side to pure Leningrad citizen,
circa 1979. When the $47.08 check is slapped on the table, the color of
my face turns from lox to whitefish, and I have a minor panic attack
on the spot. *No! No! No! My American papa has to pay for this, not me. If*
he doesn't pay, then I have nothing but my real parents! I run out of the
restaurant, the edges of my eyes blurring with crazy tears, leaving
John to settle the bill once more.

And then, finally, after all the bilked meals and goods and services
and cash, and in response to yet another one of my requests for cash,
there is this:

We the undersigned agree to all the terms specified herein.

Gary will borrow the sum of $2200 from John.

The term of the loan is two years.

*On the 27th of each month, Gary will pay to John $50.00 of the
principal.*

*In addition, on a quarterly basis, i.e. every three months, on the 27th
of the month, Gary will pay to John one quarter of the year's worth of
interest on the remaining principal. The rate of interest will equal the
interest which is being paid at that time on a two-year United States
Treasury Bill.*

*Gary further acknowledges that part of his stated purpose in borrow-
ing the money is to embark in psychotherapy or psychoanalysis with a
trained certified professional, preferably a psychiatrist or psychoanalyst
M.D. He hereby gives his word that this was not merely a ploy to receive
the loan but that he does indeed intend to proceed with this plan.*

• • •

It gets easier.

It gets easier fast.

It is fashionable now to discredit psychoanalysis. The couch. The
four or five days a week of narcissistic brooding. The reaching over to
pluck Kleenex from the quilted tissue box beneath the African pietà
thing. The penis-y Freudianism underlying it all. I have made fun of
it myself in a novel called *Absurdistan,* my hero, the overweight and
self-indulgent Misha Vainberg, son of a Russian oligarch, constantly
calling his Park Avenue shrink while the real post-Soviet world disin-
tegrates around him and people die.

The truth of it is that it is not for everyone. It is not for most people.
It is difficult, painful, and tedious work. It feels, at first, like a diminu-
tion of power rendered upon a person who already feels powerless. It
is a drain on the bank account and it takes away at least four hours a
week that could be profitably spent looking oneself up on the World
Wide Web. And, quite often, there is a seeming pointlessness to indi-

vidual sessions that makes my days studying Talmud in Hebrew school brim with relative insight. But.

It saves my life. What more can I add to that?

• • •

I hit the couch four times a week. I mean that literally. I jump on that couch; I hear the thwack of my body against it, as if I'm saying to my analyst, who is partly a stand-in for John: *Fuck you. I don't need this. I'm more* real *than this* talking. *I'm more real than your* silence. I hate my shrink so much. The smug, silent authority who charges me fifteen dollars a session. The money, the money, the money. I am always the keeper of accounts. And always will be.

"I think you're charging me too much," I say into his silence.

He's ripping me off, there's no doubt about it. The gray-haired, gray-bearded, native-born presence is taking money from me, fifteen dollars at a time. My mother was right about everything. This country was built on the coins of fools like me. "Hide your quarters," she would warn me before my college friends came over to visit my apartment.

Thwack, the angry retort of my body against his couch.

Well, I'm not going to be different. I'm not going to be one of those people. The animal petters. The smilers. The helpers. The Benefactors. The sandwiches-for-the-homeless makers. Stop pushing me. Stop pushing me with your silence.

"What else comes to mind about that?" my analyst says after I quiet down.

What else comes to mind about that? I want to get up and beat you like you once beat me. I want to have that power over you. I want to be so big that all you can do is hide your head beneath my assault, offer me up your pretty little ears.

You with your innocent silence. You think I don't see your rage? Every man has it. Every man, every boy, has the power to humiliate another with his strength.

"I think you're charging me too much," I say.

• • •

Four times a week, I have a lunch date with reality. I talk, he listens. Later I find out that he is half Anglo and half Armenian, just like J.Z., and I wonder if being in the company of a person who shares in at least some of her nucleic acids soothes me. In the intervening years, she, too, has become a doctor.

Reality. I'm learning to separate the real from the not. As soon as I say something out loud, as soon as I publicize it into the afghan-carpeted Park Avenue air, I realize it is not true. Or: It doesn't have to be true.

I think you're charging me too much.

I am a bad writer.

I should be with a woman like Pamela Sanders.

I do not have a problem with alcohol or narcotics.

I am a bad son.

I am a bad son.

I am a bad son.

• • •

There is usually a lag between understanding and action. But I move quickly.

I break up with Pamela Sanders, taking myself out of the path of her wrath and her hammer. At first, I offer her the choice of ending her relationship with Kevin. She tells me that she feels like Kevin and I are both pointing guns at her head.* Yes, I want to tell her, but only my gun is cocked and loaded.

New Year's Eve 2000 is coming up and she has not been invited to any parties. "What are you doing around New Year's? Parties?" she asks me with a new shyness. I email her, telling her I have plans, typing the words reluctantly, because I know what it's like to be lonely on

---

* The image of Pamela Sanders plus a weapon pointed at a head is what in creative writing classes is called "foreshadowing."

an important date and because I still love her. She buys me a much belated birthday gift, a book.

Its title is *St. Petersburg: Architecture of the Tsars.*

Several months after I begin analysis, I do something I've been scared to do since I canceled my junior year abroad in Moscow. Despite my mother's insistence that I will be killed and eaten right in front of the Hermitage, I buy a ticket back to St. Petersburg, Russia. And so, beneath my sweaty polyester ski hat, I am standing in front of the Chesme Church, its "sugarcoated spires and crenellations," trying not to pass out. I still don't understand the why of it, but at least I am here. At least I am trying.

Half a year into analysis, I apply to creative writing programs. Not to Iowa, because the pain of that rejection still blinds me, but to five others. I am accepted by all of them. The most promising one appears to be Cornell, which in addition to covering tuition and fees also gives a healthy stipend of twelve thousand dollars per year.

I happily call my parents to tell them that I've been accepted to an Ivy League school not focused on hotel administration. But, as a lark, I have also applied to Hunter College's new writing program, directed by one of my favorite contemporary writers, Chang-rae Lee. Reading his novel *Native Speaker* has severely shaken my perception of what fiction about immigrants can get away with. There are scenes in *Native Speaker* that are not teased out with bullshit laughter and hairy ethnic weeping but shouted, with anger and resignation, at the sky, scenes that make me question the relative insignificance of what I am trying to do with a "comic" novel still called *The Pyramids of Prague.*

I get an acceptance call from Chang-rae, and he invites me over to his office in one of the two skyscrapers that form most of Hunter's unapologetically urban campus. The elevator smells like the French fries being French-fried in the second-floor cafeteria, and the whole building seems powered by their delicious grease. The fear of meeting one of my favorite writers is only partly offset by the Cornell acceptance letter, which I've folded talismanically into my front shirt pocket. In the years before analysis, I would have had a spontaneous eruption of stomach flu or jaundice and found a way to avoid seeing my literary hero. Or, had I made it into the Hunter building, I might have passed out in the fry-smelling elevator.

The fearsome literary presence I've expected is actually a skinny Korean American man, maybe four inches my better in terms of height and seven years in terms of age, wearing jeans and an unassuming checkered shirt. Perhaps that bastard Hemingway is to be blamed for the image of the male writer as a grenade that's just been uncapped and rolled across the floor—writers of my generation, for the most part, look very much like the rest of humanity. But all I can do is sweat humbly before my idol.

We sit down and shoot the shit. He tells me he just started this program at Hunter, and he needs good students like me. He's read the first thirty pages of my novel, and he's impressed. I tell him about Cornell and all the gorgeous funding that awaits me in Ithaca. He agrees that it's a deal too good to refuse. I take out a copy of his latest novel, *A Gesture Life,* which he signs to me "With warmth and admiration," a series of four words which floor me with their unexpected solicitude. *He* admires *me*? As I prepare to leave, he asks if he can do one more thing that maybe, just maybe, could entice me to go to Hunter instead of Cornell.

Two weeks later, at a SoHo restaurant called, appropriately enough, the Cub Room, I meet Cindy Spiegel, Chang-rae's editor at Penguin Putnam and one of the rising stars of publishing. I have a speech prepared. I know the novel isn't good enough yet. But I can work hard. I've already worked on it for close to six years, first at Oberlin and then with my friend John. I can work more. It's really no trouble. I have a job, but I can work after work. I can work during work. I can skip breakfast and work. I can skip sleeping and work.

Before I can unbosom myself of the well-rehearsed and patented "Stuyvesant Immigrant Work Song," before the appetizers even arrive, Cindy offers me a book deal.

I want to pause here for a second. I would love to re-create what Cindy said about my novel and how I felt in the first few moments when I realized my life's dream would somehow collide with my reality. But I remember nothing of that afternoon, except walking out of the Cub Room and into one of those ridiculous spring days, one of those days that somehow push aside New York's heat and cold and make life seem much too easy. And I remember breathing in the scent of a blossoming tree and not knowing the name of it, just walking beneath a cloud of its honey and perfume. What had just happened to me? Something happened that was the opposite of failure. Something so big my English cannot even say what it is.

• • •

As a teacher of creative writing, a lifestyle choice nearly as maligned as psychoanalysis, I often look out at the table and see myself at age twenty-eight or thereabouts. Another desperate young man at the end of his options, insecure, anxious to be praised, betting his literary future, his *romantic* future, on his work.

In the year 2000 it is still possible to woo a girl with a book deal. And woo I do. But what's so amazing is how quickly I am wooed back. How soon a number of warm and attractive women are keen to walk down the street with me, hand in hand, to see *Cabaret Balkan* or whatever foreign nonsense is playing at the Film Forum, without a second wood-carving boyfriend waiting for them on their Brooklyn couches. I quickly settle down with an interesting one, an Oberlin graduate with some jet-setting predilections—one of our first dates takes place in Portugal. Lisbon's airport handily features a shop selling engagement rings, and my new *sposami subita,* with the thick pretty eyelashes and the sexy way of wearing a simple hoodie, encourages me to buy her an engagement ring right there (she is of a certain Asian culture that stresses matrimony). I almost do so, but a slight panic attack keeps me from shaving the remaining points off my credit score.

But it's my happiest panic attack to date. I'm not stupid when it comes to these matters. I know how little attraction I pose for most women à la carte. And what I realize is that with Chang-rae's single gesture, I will never have to go home to an empty bed again. From this point forward, I will know love whenever I need to know it.

· · ·

The early joys of my impending publication, and then the joys of actual publication, are without equal in my life. There's something outrageously simple about extending yourself toward a goal the way a plant seeks the sun's rays or a gopher the crunch of easy soil beneath his paws, and then getting *exactly what you want,* sunshine or some prized tuber.

My would-be bride and I are now living in a small but affordable duplex in the far West Village—her real estate acumen is without equal. My psychoanalysis is going well, even though a part of me misses the pain of being with a Pamela Sanders. Each day, out of habit, I bring up my cheek for my new girlfriend to slap, and each day she doesn't slap it. "I just can't seem to spoil you enough," she tells me, as we lie in bed surrounded by an impromptu meal of Popeyes fried chicken, Doritos Cool Ranch–flavored tortilla chips, and non-diet Coke. It's not true, what she said. I learn how to be a spoiled little bastard pretty quickly, but each time she tells me I can't be spoiled, I block out some space in the bathroom to cry happily to myself.

And each day I make the trip to one of those Hudson Street media bodegas that feature a complete selection of the latest Albanian and Eritrean news sources. There, I scoop up the dozens of publications that are running advance and nearly all favorable(!) reviews of my first book. Places I've understood to exist only vaguely, Boulder, CO, and Milwaukee, WI, and Fort Worth, TX, harbor people who have not only read all 450 pages of my meandering manuscript but also approve of what I'm trying to say.

Which is what exactly? *The Russian Debutante's Handbook,* about to sail into Barnes & Noble and destined to enjoy a slight commercial success, is if anything an unfaithful record of twenty-seven years of my life. It is filled with Nat Sherman cigarettes, guayabera shirts and janitor pants, words like "venal" and "aquiline," cats named Kropotkin, dying beloved grandmothers, Eastern European castles brooding over urban hilltops, midwestern collegiate panic attacks, sedulous Jewish roommates from Pittsburgh, large female American backsides, cheerless Soviet cartoon crocodiles, eyebrow waxing, aged balsamic vinegar, and the age-old questions of whether it is better to be an alpha or a beta immigrant, and whether it's okay to bring others into the world when you are not happy with who you are. It is a catalog of the styles and mores of a particular era as recorded by an outsider fast becoming an insider. It is a very long document in which a troubled young man talks to himself. It is a collection of increasingly desperate jokes. To this day, some people tell me it's my best work, implying that it's all been kind of a downhill slog from there. After finishing the book you hold in your hands, I went back and reread the three novels I've written, an exercise that left me shocked by the overlaps between fiction and reality I found on those pages, by how blithely I've used the facts of my own life, as if I've been having a fire sale all along—everything about me must go!

On so many occasions in my novels I have approached a certain truth only to turn away from it, only to point my finger and laugh at it and then scurry back to safety. In this book, I promised myself I would not point the finger. My laughter would be intermittent. There would be no safety.

· · ·

With my first novel about to be born in the late spring of 2002, I feel my life shifting irrevocably; all those tectonic plates that once shuddered against each other are finally aligning to make a permanent surface upon which I can grow plants and herd cattle. It gets easier. But there's something my analyst knows that I don't: This burst of sheer joy will not last long. Already, the mechanisms at my disposal are working to revert myself back to the mean, to the unhappiness, to the drinking. A particularly cruel and personal review finally comes by way of the West Coast and that is the one I savor, the one I draw comfort from, the one I memorize. But this will not be my worst review by far.

The phone rings in my West Village duplex, with its childish trip-
tych of cosmonaut Yuri Gagarin stretching along an entire wall, with
its sense of a happy new couple trying out life together. Another terrific early review has just landed on my laptop, and tonight we are
going to my favorite sushi restaurant, on Hudson Street, to celebrate.
The day before, David Remnick, the editor of *The New Yorker* and my
father's future nemesis, had called me personally to ask if I could write
an article on Russia for the venerable magazine.

I pick up the phone eager for whatever else the world can provide me.

It is my father's voice. "*Mudak*," he says. My mother's howling takes
up the rest of the conversation.

The Russian word *mudak* stems from the ancient term for "testicles," and in a rural sense connotes a castrated piglet. In a modern
sense it is perhaps closest to the American "dickhead." In my father's
arsenal of words I know that it is the nuclear option, and that's what
it feels like when he says it: like being deposited in the middle of
Threads or *The Day After*. Dead trees are whistling around me; a bottle of milk is melting on my doorstep. "*Attack warning red!*" "Is it for
real?" "Attack warning is for bloody real!"

Mudak. Added to Snotty and Weakling and Little Failure, this may
be the final word to grace the tombstone of our relationship. Because
while the hurt is still thrumming in my ear—*why can't you be proud of
me in my finest moment to date?*—I am back on my psychoanalyst's
couch trying on the new words I've just taught myself.

I am not a bad son.

Through the howling coming at me from across the East River, I
discern the source of my parents' anger, the *mudak*-inciting pain. A
Jewish newspaper has sent a reporter to meet my parents in their natural habitat and in her subsequent article has suggested that my parents somewhat resemble the hero's parents in my novel.

"We don't ever want to speak to you again," my mother is shouting
at me.

If you won't speak to me, it is better not to live!

Those are the traditional expected words on my end. But what I say instead is: "*Nu, khorosho. Kak vam luchshe.*" Well, that's fine. Do as you please.

And that stops the howling. And that makes them backtrack, if not apologize. But it is too late. The *razvod* has been signed and notarized, not between my mother and my father but between them and me. I will continue to see them and love them and call them each Sunday night, as mandated by Russian law, but their opinions of me, the fanged hurt of their own childhoods, will not rend my world asunder, will not send me to the nearest bar, will not be unleashed upon the woman I share my bed with.

· · ·

But then there's also this. My mother, a financial administrator at a New York nonprofit, the hardest-working person I have ever known, dutifully going over a letter with me over the phone while I'm at Oberlin, making sure those nefarious articles are in place. "Igor, is it 'We have submitted budget for third quarter, fiscal 1993,' or 'We have submitted *the* budget for third quarter, fiscal 1993'?"

"Submitted *the* budget," I say, literally rolling my eyes, holding the phone away from me as if I am speaking to a younger version of myself. "I have to go, Mama. Irv is here. We're going to [light up a spliff and] see a movie." But how can I, the Red Gerbil of Solomon Schechter School, not recognize what it's like to be ashamed of what comes out of my mouth, or, in my mother's case, what is painstakingly typed beneath the letterhead of her agency? "Mama, your English is so much better than the Americans who work with you," I say to her. "You really don't need my help."

But she does. And now I've published a book that mocks, gently, but sometimes not so gently, a set of parents that are not entirely dissimilar from my own. What does that feel like for them? What does it feel like to pick up a book, or an article in a Jewish newspaper, and not fully understand the subtlety, the irony, the *satire* of the world depicted therein? What does it feel like to be unable to respond in the language with which that mockery is issued?

And as I'm suing for my *razvod*, how can I also not celebrate my parents, my exes? After all, they could not have known that all these years I had been sitting there with the only thing truly at my disposal, the only thing truly mine. My notebook. Taking notes. "When a writer is born into a family, the family is finished"*—Czesław Miłosz.

My father's favorite saying to me: "Maybe after I die, you will come pee on my grave." It is supposed to be sarcastic, but what he's really saying is "Don't let go."

"Don't let go of me." Because sometimes it may seem like I have. Because instead of my fighting back, instead of my indignation, what he hears is silence.

When he tells me that one of my postcollege girlfriends is too fat, that he's personally affronted by her weight, although he does "respect her right to exist," there is silence.

When my mother tells me, before I am to go off on a trip to India, that I shouldn't get any vaccines "because they will give you autism," that canard of the extreme right wing, there is silence.

Silence instead of the yelled rebuttals, the peeing on the grave, which they're used to, which feels familiar and pee warm. "It would have been better if you had told me you were a homosexual," my father said when I told him I had started psychoanalysis. Beyond the post-Soviet distrust of the practice—mental hospitals were used by the Soviet state against its dissidents—there is another fear. You can fight with your gay son, tell him he is a disgrace in your eyes. And he will fight back, will beg for your love. But what do you tell someone who is silent?

And within that silence, time itself has stopped. Within that silence, the words hang in the air, fluttering in Cyrillic, not entirely painless but without the power to bring back the small, unquestioning child at their mercy.

---

* And, I might add, if the family isn't finished, then the writer is.

Don't get any vaccines. They'll give you autism. Don't write like a self-hating Jew. Don't be a mudak. *Soon you will be forgotten.* How can I not hear the pain in that? *His* pain? *Her* pain? How can I not publicize that pain?

And how can I not travel, across eight time zones, to its source?

25.

THE CHURCH AND THE HELICOPTER

THE FINAL REVELATION

Author and Lenin rekindle their bromance on St. Petersburg's Moscow Square.

'M BACK IN RUSSIA. It is June 17, 2011, the temperature is cold and gloomy, but with some outlandish bursts of warmth. In other words the temperature and the way I feel about the country of my birth are one and the same. Since my first return to Russia in 1999, I've been back almost every other year, dutifully taking down everything I see, categorizing each kernel of buckwheat and pale sheet of salami, testing myself by walking into the Chesme Church where the maquettes of gallant eighteenth-century Turkish and Russian fighting ships once faced off in their eternal Anatolian battle. I've shared vodka shots with weeping policemen in Haymarket Square, slipped on in-

numerable patches of ice, nearly been sliced in half by a Georgian ruf-
fian; in other words, done all the things one normally associates with
a trip to the former Soviet Union.

I am on the morning's first speedy train between Moscow and St.
Petersburg. The train is called the Sapsan, named for the mythical
peregrine falcon, the world's fastest animal, and designed by the
equally mythical engineers of Siemens AG. I am hungover to the
point where even the gentle German rocking of the Falcon brings on
serious flashes of nausea. In the past few years I've been careful about
my drinking. But on the night before my current Moscow-Petersburg
journey, spurred on by that most lubricated of creatures, an aging
Russian intellectual, I drank myself to the point where I wedged myself into the cupboard of a Moscow bar. I remember a pleasant young
American television executive working on some suspicious-sounding
international project telling me, "Wow, you really *do* drink like a Russian."

Afterward, blankness, the flash of a hipster hotel on a trendy island
off-shore from the Kremlin, a hundred-dollar last-minute cab to the
train station, and here I am in the *biznes*-class carriage of the Falcon,
a thirty-eight-year-old man about to start writing his first memoir.
Which is what brings me to St. Petersburg in 2011. Even as I am inching my way between Russia's two biggest cities, my parents are chart-
ing their path across the Atlantic. My mother has not been to Russia
in twenty-four years, since her mother died, and my father in thirty-
two years, or from the time he left the Soviet Union in 1979.

We are all coming home.

Together.

• • •

A wind whips the Falcon into the station. It is early summer, but the
St. Petersburg skies are gray, that unremitting gray of upstate New
York in winter. The days are almost at their longest, the light is flat
and cruel; soon, there will be no real sunset. At night, by moonlight,
the sea wind sends the Finnish clouds on secret missions over the city.

I've booked two sleek hotel rooms across from the train station near Uprising Square for me and for my parents, but when I show up, tired and haggard from my insomniac trip to Moscow (its purpose: an article about a Muscovite magazine called *Snob*), I am told my room isn't ready. To my exhaustion is added a strand of fear. What if I don't get any sleep before my parents arrive? They have come at my request, have traveled to a country they don't particularly want to remember. Over the years I'm the one who's returned so many times, have penned so many nightmarish scenarios about the place, and now I'm the one who has to protect them. But from what? From memory? From skinheads? From the treacherous wind? All I know is that I need to be my best for them. My mother is in her mid-sixties and my father in his early seventies. By Russian standards, they are already advanced pensioners. Finally given the room key, I plop down on all that cheap blond wood, large TV flashing images of all the other properties owned by the hotel chain, which, par for the global course, is based in Minneapolis but administered out of Brussels. Two tidy Ativan tablets touch the tip of my tongue, and the usual ragged, unsatisfying, chemical sleep approaches.

· · ·

The terrible marimba of the phone alarm. The fumbling for the toothbrush. The elevator descends with me partly in it. And then they are standing there before me in the busy lobby, two skinny people hemmed in by fat provincial tourists representing several countries. "Hey!" I shout, ready for an embrace.

"Little son!" my mother shouts. And I am smaller.

"Little one," my father says. And I am smaller still.

"Welcome," I say, for some reason, in English. And then in Russian: "Are you tired?" And as soon as the first words of Russian—*Vy ustali?*—get an exit visa out of my mouth I recoil from myself, shocked by hearing my own goofy adolescent bass around my parents. Granted, with my ever-growing American accent, I do not sound entirely native when I *govoryu po-russki* with cabdrivers, hotel clerks, or even my good Petersburg friends. But right now I sound like a child just getting his mouth around his first Russian words. Or is it because I'm trying to speak to my parents with grown-up authority? Trying, against all reason, to be their equal?

How much time have I spent in the last twelve years running up and down this exhausted, melancholy city, retracing their steps, trying to somehow make them my own. And then with the first Russian words out of my mouth, I realize the truth of the matter. It's not possible to make their lives my own. While my mother and father are here, this is their country. And so my responsibilities lighten. And so I realize that what I have to do for the next week is to ignore my own goofy Russian bass and, simply, to listen.

• • •

To the Minnesota tidiness of their room, my mother has added her own tidiness, a system of packing of infinite complexity, so that most of the contents of their three-story house have been condensed and magically transported to the old homeland. Plastic bags beget plastic bags, there are umbrellas, rain jackets, hoods, money pouches, and, from tomorrow's breakfast table, yogurts, heavy bottles of water, a range of fortifying snacks. She will leave the hotel as provisioned as an astronaut testing the first reaches of an inhospitable planet. In her bones, this may still be her country. But she will not touch it with her hands the way I do, trying to lyricize the filth and the decay.

My mother is in her suburban gray sweatpants, bustling around the hotel room, hours of preparation still ahead of her before we head out to dinner. My father sports his STRIPED BASS CONSERVATION PARTICIPANT cap, a new Banana Republic jacket, and swish sunglasses, looking surprisingly Western by way of eastern Queens. Only the combination of black socks and leather sandals betrays him as a true native of this land.

Their strength amazes me. After two flights totaling fifteen hours, after lugging their considerable luggage across half the city via buses and metro—they will not spend the money for a taxi from the airport—they are still alert and vital, ready to down 250 grams of vodka at the Metropol restaurant down Nevsky Prospekt, the city's main axis. This is the superhumanity of the immigrant, but woe be to the all-too-human offspring living in the shadow of such strength. Woe be to the sensitive one who requires one milligram of a benzodiazepine just to fall asleep after a journey of a few hundred kilometers taken aboard a peregrine falcon, versus the many thousands they have traveled aboard British Airways' economy class.

"Igor, you look good," my mother says. "Not like you're tired."

"I wouldn't say so," my father quickly intervenes, the fur sticking out of his shirt in the approaching twilight. For the longest time, he would wear my clothes, my hand-me-ups from Stuyvesant, all those peacock Union Bay and Generra shirts, so small and weak on his muscular body. "There are terrible circles under his eyes," my father says, beholding me fully. "And what do you have on your forehead? Those two lines?"

They are called wrinkles, I want to say, but I do not want to appear mortal in front of him. "I leaned against the seat in front of me on the train," I lie.

Throughout this trip, I will capture little instances of my family reflected in shop windows, my parents looking younger than their ages, younger than many of the people around them, while I look at least two decades beyond my years, the dead graying hair, the sunken eyes, and all the imprints from the years of hard living, those two telltale lines cracked into my forehead. How did it happen that I have aged in tandem with the citizens of St. Petersburg, the city in which my parents had reached their own middle age, while they have seemingly reversed time like true Americans?

My greatest fear: dying before they do. Growing up, it had been the reverse. I couldn't understand how to be on this earth without them. But now every time I board a plane for some ragged destination, I feel their fear ascend through the air alongside me, the "autistic" vaccinations coursing through my blood.

"I will wash quickly under the armpits," my father says, while my mother continues her endless grooming, warning us that "a woman is a long song."

Settling in with his clean armpits, my father, the long journey behind him, begins to talk amiably, almost contentedly, about coming "home": "You know, little son, you could write an entire book about me. I'm not an extraordinary person, but because my life was so varied, all my studies, and jobs in different places, there was much that was interesting.

"You understand, little son, that just like you, I'm a lonely [*odinokii*] person by nature. I don't want to say that I like loneliness. Sometimes I like it, sometimes I don't."

Maybe this is the time for me to say, *I love you*. Or, better still, *I am you*. Maybe this is the flip side of the silence I have mastered. The inability to say what needs to be said until it is too late.

My mother sticks her head out of the bathroom. "Hey, guys!" she says happily. "I was so unattractive. But now I feel refreshed!"

• • •

We are heading up Nevsky Prospekt. The broad Nevsky cuts across the center of St. Petersburg at a northwestern tangent, as if trying to lead the way to Scandinavia. In the times of Gogol and Pushkin most everything happened along this street, from commerce to love to café-scribbled poetry to the choosing of seconds for duels. Today, it is still the place for a long aimless walk from the low-rent Uprising Square to the city's focal point, Palace Square, where the de-tsared Winter Palace sits on its haunches in a green provincial funk. On Nevsky, chicken is fried in the Kentucky manner, and stores like H&M and Zara will, if given the chance, clothe a newly middle-class person from the *shapka* on her head to her galoshes.

St. Petersburg is a sad place. Its sadness lies in a mass grave in its northeastern suburbs along with the 750,000 citizens who died of hunger and German shelling during the 871-day siege, which began in 1941. Petersburg never truly recovered. It is impossible to walk down Nevsky, alone or with my parents, and not feel the oppression of history, the weight on our own family and on every family that has lived within this city's borders since 1941. CITIZENS! a preserved sign at the northern mouth of Nevsky declares, DURING ARTILLERY BOMBARDMENT THIS SIDE OF THE STREET IS THE MOST DANGEROUS. And so it is.

• • •

We are strolling past outdoor patios heaped with sushi and sunlight. Women are already dressed for June's gentle heat, looking as reproductive as their counterparts in New Jersey, only distinguished by the Orthodox crosses on their lovely bare necks. Indians with cameras press around us, preserving every cornice and portico for their prodigious zip files.

"This city always bring on sadness," my mother says. "All of us children were sad growing up. There was a lot of dreaming."

"On Rubenstein Street, I had my first love," my father says. "Right over there."

Much as I mercifully lack writer's block, my mother has never been at a loss for a stray conversational tangent. "Before we left for America," she says to me, "I went to the Eliseev store to buy you chicken cutlets. There was nothing to eat. So I was told to go to the Store of Children's Nutrition. I spent two hours standing in line there, and right under my nose, they ran out of cutlets. I came home and I had nothing to feed you."

I try to think of the time when I went without chicken cutlets. But all I see is my grandmother Galya, the one we left behind to die in Russia, dutifully feeding me cheese as I work away on *Lenin and His Magical Goose,* her meaty beak bent over my efforts.

• • •

"The Coliseum Movie House," my mother announces. "This was the first time I saw Sophia Loren! The line was around the block. I also saw *Divorce, Italian Style*. Stefania Sandrelli was playing in it, so there were only these little fold-out seats left. I fell out of my seat from laughing. Can you believe it? That's how hard I was laughing. Marcello Mastroianni and all that. I was sixteen. Can you imagine that? Almost fifty years ago."

"When we get to Liteiny Street, we'll have a big talk," my father says.

I have never been a fan of "big talks."

We are approaching Liteiny Street.

• • •

"Little son, let's go for a moment just down this block. It's a moment of great sadness."

My father seems quite intent on leading me past a pretty young woman smelling a daisy. We are approaching the portico of the cream-colored two-hundred-year-old Mariinskaya Municipal Hospital, one of the city's largest.

"I spent time here," my father says. "In the *nervnoye otdeleniye*."

I run the Russian through my mind. The sky is pressing down on us with a heavy gray lid. The *Nervous* Department? What exactly is he trying to say? My father was a mental patient? For the first time on this trip, I feel danger. A traveler's danger. Like when I took the wrong taxi in Bogotá a year ago, speeding away from my hotel instead of toward it.

"How old were you?" my mother asks.

"Let's see. My mother was . . ." He has to think of her age first, before he can determine his own. *Children, obey your parents in the Lord, for this is right.* "So I was twenty-three," he concludes.

The information hovers in front of me, still in the form of a question. *My father was a twenty-three-year-old mental patient?* I finger the calming Ativan pill, the lone resident of my jeans pocket. The taxi is still hurtling toward the Colombian jungles, toward the band of rebels who will hold me hostage for decades.

"So young," my mother says.

"I was in the crazy ward," my father says. "And they thought I would remain a *durak* [idiot] forever."

"This street leads to Pestelya Street, where my friend lived," my mother says, apropos of nothing.

"And so, little son," my father interrupts her, "it's a long story. I was in the hospital, they performed terrible experiments on me, and I almost died."

I make an affirming noise. *Uhum*.

"They made me drink buckets of valerian root, bromine, so that I wouldn't have any male desires."

Oho, I say. I cannot even begin to imagine what he's saying.

"*Uzhas,*" my mother says. Horror.

"And there were real crazy people in there. There was one old guy he would shit himself every week and smear the shit on the wall."

"The Tsar's Pierogi!" my mother reads a passing sign with interest.

"And he'd scream, 'Down with Lenin and Stalin!'" My mother laughs. "They'd pacify him and then in a week he'd be back at it. We had quiet crazy people, too. I was the quietest." My mother laughs with her head thrown back. "But I could have been loud. After this they gave me a *spravka* [certificate] attesting to my stay, and they wouldn't take me in the army."

"But what brought this on?" my mother asks.

"I was sitting at home, reading a book, and then my mother found me on the floor, foaming at the mouth, convulsions, like an epileptic. That was the first and last time."

Ativan in my mouth, I ask the next question: "What was the diagnosis?"

"Soldering of the vessels in the brain." As soon as he says it, I think what my psychoanalyst back in Manhattan will soon affirm. The Soviet diagnosis is complete nonsense.

"When your father proposed to me," my mother says, "he said, 'I have a certificate. I have a mental illness.' And I thought: What a typical Jewish trick. He's completely healthy. He just doesn't want to serve in the army. But it turned out it was the truth.

"We're so stupid when we're young. Someone tells you they're mentally ill, why would you marry him? But I thought, He's such a smart, serious person. It can't be. I would notice if he were psychotic. But sometimes, especially as he's aged, you can see that he really *is* mentally ill." My mother laughs. The simple trill of her laugh has not declined over the years; if anything it's been buffeted by her endless sorrows and disappointments.

By his early twenties my father has failed his exams and has been kicked out of Leningrad's Polytechnic Institute. "My mother used to nag me," he says. "'What's wrong with you? What's wrong with you?'"

"Just like I used to do to you," my mother says to me, laughing some more. She switches to English: "Failure! Failure! Failure!"

My father's eyes dart around his fabulous sunglasses, his teeth are relatively straight and white for this part of the world, his beard is white flecked with gray, as mine is already flecking at an accelerated pace. As an old friend of his had just said to me: "You are an exact copy of your father. You have nothing of your mother's." Which is not entirely true. My father has been adjudged more handsome than I. But if the poem I wrote in college, "My Reflection," can be believed, we are almost brothers. Our brain scans would probably attest to that as well. The Ativan is melting under my tongue, entering the bloodstream.

Later my father will tell me about another "treatment" he received at the hospital. They puncture his spine with a needle and blast oxygen into it, trying to "unsolder" the blood vessels of his brain. He comes out a wreck, scared of taking the tram, afraid of leaving his room. The middle half of his twenties are a wasteland of depression and anxiety. It is impossible to know what led him to foam at the mouth and convulse in the first place, but my psychoanalyst believes a neurological episode, a grand mal seizure, for example, may have been the cause. Treatments for neurological disorders generally do not include placement in a clinic where psychopaths smear their feces along the wall, injection of oxygen into the spine, and the administration of bromine to fight a young man's erections.

• • •

I part ways with my parents for the evening. I meet my good friend K in the southern suburb in which he lives. We share a spicy kebab at an Armenian joint. We tell jokes about a certain horse-faced leader in the Kremlin, and I drink as much vodka as I can. He has work tomorrow, but as we embrace and he puts me on a tram back to Uprising Square, I don't want to leave him. Drunkenly, I watch the city assemble itself outside my tram window, the Soviet giving way to the baroque.

My father was a mental patient.

So now I forgive him?

But it was never about forgiveness. It is about understanding. The whole psychoanalytic exercise is about understanding.

What did he say when I told him years ago I was seeing a psychiatrist? "It would have been better if you had told me you were a homosexual."

But he knows, doesn't he?

He knows what it's like not to have control over yourself. To see the world pass right through your hands.

Is he trying to settle up with me?

I wander into the new Galeria mall, a behemoth by Uprising Square, filled with Polo and Gap stores, and all the other purveyors of the Hebrew school clothing I never owned. It's sad to reach out to past hurts and find nothing there. Just the splash of my sneakers against the cold Galeria marble, the echoes of my footsteps, because at this late hour on a weekday I am practically alone.

In my hotel room, with my parents just a floor above me, I put my head to my pillow and think of my wife. I think of the warmth of her. I think of the relative silence of her own immigrant family, the silence that I crave. My wife. Even though I am "the writer," she reads more than I do. She folds the pages of the books she reads when she wants to remember something important. Her favorite books are accordions, testaments to an endless search for meaning.

I think of my mother and father. Of their constant anxiety. But their anxiety means they still want to live. A year shy of forty, I feel my life entering its second half. I feel my life folding up. I sense the start of that great long leave-taking. I think of myself on the subway platform at Union Square. I am invisible, just a short obstacle others have to get around. Sometimes I wonder: Am I already gone? And then I think of my wife and I feel the whoosh of the number 6 train, the presence of others, the life still within me.

Why did he tell me this today?

• • •

The Admiralty building on the banks of the Neva River, headquarters of the Russian navy, has been built in the same loud Empire style as the hospital where my father spent part of his life. The Admiralty, a kind of early-nineteenth-century skyscraper, is topped by a gilded spire itself topped by a small sail warship, which appears regularly on local souvenirs and whose platonic shape delighted me as a child, a golden addendum to the warships in the Chesme Church. To the southwest of the Admiralty building lies the vast central Admiralteiskii Rayon, a district of initial grandeur and increasing shabbiness. This is where my mother hails from.

My mother studied and later taught piano. I believe the reverence of music she shared with my opera-obsessed father allowed these two dissimilar people to fall in love. The story of my mother's introduction to music is slightly different from the story of my first encounter with words at the behest of her mother, Grandmother Galya.

"When I was five," my mother says as we exchange the colonnaded riverbanks and canals for the shawarma-reeking depths of her neighborhood, "my father bought me a balalaika that cost forty rubles. This was the last money we had and it was supposed to be used for food. My mother [Grandmother Galya] took the balalaika and smashed it against the wall of our apartment. I started to cry. My mother comforted me by saying, 'I know you're crying not because I smashed the balalaika but because you can see how upset I am. You're very sensitive.'"

My mother is changing history. She is making her balalaika-smashing mother into a heroine. Does she want me to do the same for her? Is that what good children do for their parents? What about good writers?

I think back to the Kiev-style cutlet she sold me when I had graduated from Oberlin. I see mother's laughing face as she puts the twenty-dollar bill she's inveigled out of me in the pocket of her pink pullover. She is happy. Haggling with her son is fun, especially since he always loses. At money matters he is also a failure. And she is laughing because she can feel that part of this must be a joke. She understands the absurdity of the moment. She will often begin an anecdote with the words "Guys, you want to laugh?" And then she will laugh herself as if to demonstrate what it's all about.

She is laughing. But is she sad? Is part of her sad? What is it like to be her at the moment she takes my money? What does it feel like to sell your broke son a horrible piece of chicken at retail? How many years must pass before I feel sad for her? *Is this the moment? Is this why I brought them back here?*

The balalaika smashes against the wall. The five-year-old girl begins to cry. And then, here in the present, the sound of a violin fills the street. We are approaching the college where the post-smashed-balalaika phase of my mother's musical education took place. My mother poses for the camera mock-solemnly and gives it a four-finger pioneer's salute. In the lobby a plaque commemorates alumni lost in the Second World War. NO ONE IS FORGOTTEN, it says. Next to the plaque are the usual bearded luminaries of the nineteenth century and next to the luminaries stands a new ATM machine. An incredibly Russian-looking boy with several layers of disheveled blond hair and a perfect potato nose is hitting the accordion pretty hard.

I can see the immediate disappointment on my mother's face, the sadness of return, the letdown of memory. "Everything used to *shine* around here," she says. "Now everything looks so unkempt."

"There's a fine stink here," my father says, screwing up his Americanized nose at the produce of so many armpits.

"The first time I came in here, I heard a girl playing the piano," my mother says. "I nearly dropped. I said to my father, 'I want to study here! I *will* study here.' And I was accepted. No one expected that of me. Stalin spent a lot of money on this stuff. He loved music."

• • •

We trudge out of the music school and toward the distant Pryazhka River. "Why are all the windows boarded up?" my mother asks, as we approach the house where she grew up. SALE, a sign says in English. APARTMENTS, 228 METERS. "Look, they've set everything on fire!" Indeed, one of the windows has been blown out, the surrounding frame charred black.

My mother looks around the building's ruined courtyard uncertainly. "Petya Zabaklitski from our class, he lived in that entryway over there, every day he would run ahead and wait for me. And whenever I walked home he would shout, 'Yasnitskaya [my mother's maiden name] *the Jewess* is coming. Yasnitskaya *the Jewess* is coming!' This was the first sorrow of my life."

• • •

My father grew up in the village of Olgino, northwest of the city center in the so-called resort area of Petersburg, which hugs the northern banks of the Gulf of Finland. Several redbrick mafioso-style estates, their boundary walls sprinkled with security cameras, have appeared along its rutted streets, but Olgino still feels like a half-wrecked semirural neighborhood moored in some failing periphery. We could be in Michigan or Sicily or North Africa or Pakistan. Only the weather betrays our latitude.

Today is cold and rainy, but the village is swaddled in the unkempt greenery which my father is clearly delighted to see. We are approaching a ramshackle green house built in some indeterminate Soviet style of rural housing, New England barn meets Russian *izba* meets instant decay.

"Here would pass a herd of cows," he says. "In the morning I would have to push out our cow, Rosa, so that she would go into the forest with the other cows. There was a shepherd with a cattle prod. Oy, my heart is starting to jump!"

There is laughter coming out from under his baseball cap. The snow-white goatee is mirthful. He speaks without pause. "Our house was one of the biggest houses, fifteen-twenty families lived in it. Here there were little garden plots." We walk by a vast rotting woodpile. "Here was our veranda." We walk by boarded-up windows. "Here we planted flowers." A collapsing brick shack sheltering an old Suzuki four-by-four. "Here Aunt Sonya had a little barn, sheep, pigs, cows. We had a good warm barn, you could keep a cow or a piglet there in winter. Here was the outhouse. Always tons of shit there. Frozen shit in the winter. Here lived a girl named Gelya, when boys my age or older would see her we'd always shout 'Gelya, *opa*! Gelya, *opa*!' And she would laugh." He makes a humping motion at the invisible Gelya.

"Be careful, there are stray dogs here," my mother says.

We pass by an old Soviet radio jamming tower. "After I was released from the hospital," my father says, "I was still half-crazy. My heart kept trembling. My mother and I rented a room here in the summer. I lived here from May to November, and I was mostly alone. Every day I'd go to the gulf," the nearby Gulf of Finland, "swimming morning and night, even when there was ice. This saved me. This made me a human being again, as opposed to an invalid."

My father traces his weak nerves back to his life with Ilya, or Ilyusha in the diminutive, his cruel, erratic, alcoholic stepfather, whom my father eventually overpowered. "We lived in a room a hundred sixty square feet," my father says. "Ilya was capable of anything."

"And you fought with him?" I ask.

Proudly: "I beat him! Until he bled! *Until he bled!*"

My mother laughs. "A good little son you were."

"My mother would come home and she would find out. We'd be silent, but there would be traces of blood on the curtains and elsewhere. My mother, of course, loved me more than him."

We are passing a line of birches, so clean and bright in the miserable weather. My father introduces a new subject. "Why am I so strong [*krepkii*], even to this day? Because from seven to five I worked hard. And I also played sports. Skis, skates, running, swimming. If you do farm work, you don't even need to exercise.

"I learned to love the peasant's work. Jews weren't supposed to do that. And in tsarist Russia Jews weren't even given land, because they were supposed to be lazy and good for nothing.

"I still have very good memories of Olgino. Because I am basically a country person. I like reading and music and all that. But I don't like big cities. Not Manhattan, not Leningrad. To go to the opera, the museum, *fine*. But I like to be surrounded by trees, forest, grass, fresh air, fishing, and sunshine."

We walk toward the gulf which restored his sanity.

• • •

We find ourselves back on Nevsky Prospekt, approaching the sienna-colored tower of the old city *duma,* or assembly. This is where first dates in Petersburg often begin, and my parents were no different. They met on the steps beneath the Italianate tower, where today, dozens of teenaged and twenty-something boys and girls are huffing away at cigarettes, tapping away on their phones. "When we first met I couldn't understand what she was," my father says. "It was as if some kind of orange had walked up to me."

"I painted my cheeks with orange powder," my mother explains. "My friend had a boyfriend who knew how to get anything. And so for New Year's he got everyone Polish powder, which was orange. But we were all very proud of it. All of Leningrad was orange. Anything Polish was a big deal. Such pretty packaging."

"So," my father continues, "I was standing there and I saw this orange person. And I thought this is not one of ours! It must be a foreigner. She was more yellow than a Chinese."

"I'm telling you it was the Polish powder!"

"I was wearing a hat that looked like—"

"A pierogi."

"That looked like a pierogi. It was called a *khrushchyovka*. Gray and made of sheep. And I was also wearing a handsome French coat."

"*Very* handsome," my mother says, and I breathe in that sentence deeply. My parents still love each other.

On our way back to the hotel, they mention that there is only eighteen thousand dollars left on the mortgage of their Little Neck home and that they will pay this sum off within months. "Now we will be free!" my father says.

Now they will be free.

. . .

We are crossing Moscow Square.

They've put in gaudy fountains next to the pine trees where my father and I would play hide-and-seek. Beneath my Lenin there's a temporary summer stage from which issues horrible thumping Russian pop, something about sun rays and "Get closer / closer to my heart." There are Nike swooshes where the old *gastronom* used to be. Children who have no knowledge of the Great Leader scamper on and off Lenin's podium, singing "la la la la la." A lone boy in camouflage pants is texting with his mouth open. A man is holding a woman's ass by the fountains, his bare shorts-clad legs wrapped around her. This is my sacred space, Moscow Square, June 2011.

We are approaching the building where we lived; beyond it, the Chesme Church. I am breathing hard. I have to pee. My father is telling me how Franklin D. Roosevelt ruined America.

We walk into the peeling entryway of our apartment house. The building is painted in the unappetizing colors of rose and dun, festooned with great loops of graffiti. Runty-looking kids are sitting by some ad hoc storage containers. The grass is overgrown with weeds and daisies.

"Where was the rocket?" I ask, curious about the rusty spaceship where I used to play Cosmonaut.

"The rocket was over there," my father says, pointing at a standard-issue multicolored playground with swings and slides. A touch of sunlight, but no more, falls upon the courtyard where I used to spend my healthy days. The scraggly trees take what they can get.

"I always had nightmares about a big black steam pipe," I say.

"That pipe, little son, was somewhere near here."

"What were you afraid of?" my mother asks. "What did you imagine? You were afraid of tree roots when you were three."

"Freud could have said a lot about all this," I say, forgetting my audience. "He might have said it was about sexuality. The child growing up, afraid of becoming . . ." My mother grimaces. I stop talking.

Our former lives hang above us. Beige brick, casement windows, the occasional wooden or iron balcony, exposed gray piping, black electrical wires.

"It was big and dark," my father says of the pipe.

"Like a rocket," I say. "I always thought there was going to be an explosion. And we'd all be flung into the cosmos."

"No kidding," my mother says. "How could you even have imagined that?"

We return to the street, the facades of our megablock forming a pinkish wave flanked by a column of oaks.

"And over there, to the left, there was a church," my father says.

. . .

The sidewalks have piled against each other like so many adolescent teeth. An unreformed ancient tram passes with a nineteenth-century European clatter. My mother is limping on the way to the church. My father jokes that she's drunk too much beer at Little Jap (Yaponchik), the Moscow Square sushi joint with the casually racist name where we just ate lunch.

"I didn't drink too much," my mother protests, "I didn't eat too much. I have a corn on my foot."

"Can't bring the old lady with us," my father says. "We should have left her home." I laugh, a braying sound. This is how they talk. This is how I never learned to talk. Not in Russian. Not in English. The supposedly funny banter with a twist of the knife. That's what I have my novels for.

My father squeezes her with love. "*Starukha* [old lady]," he says, "let's take her by the arms and legs and throw her in the garbage dump."

"I'm not drunk. I drank half what you drank."

"You drank all the beer."

All of this is said in good humor and could go on for the rest of the afternoon. But it stops.

We are standing in front of *it*. The sky is the same dour gray as every other day, while *it* is the same pastry pink they serve at my mother's favorite Café North on Nevsky. "What a pretty church," I say. "This used to be the museum of . . . the naval fleet, something like that?"

"Yes, because it was the battle of Chesme," my father says.

"I don't remember *any*thing!" says my mother.

Its three spires are poking into the northern murk, there's a sandy lot in front of it. A drunk is sitting on a bench with his arms around one leg. My mother sits down on another bench to treat her corn. "Just go in the church by yourselves," she says. "If there's a toilet, tell me."

"Do you remember we used to launch your helicopter here?" my father says.

"The helicopter, yes."

"Many, many times we launched the helicopter. You liked it so much. And I did, too. I actually liked it, too."

"Where did we find the helicopter?"

"We bought it! Where did we find it? It flew so high, almost to the windows."

"I remember it got stuck one time."

"No, I don't remember that. I don't think so. Many, many times we would launch it. You were so happy."

We come upon a heavy wooden door. My father takes off his cap. Inside the church, a floodlit study in pink and gold. People are crossing themselves with a quiet vengeance. "They sure knew how to build churches in Russia," my father says, impressed. "The most well known of the post-Byzantine style is the Cathedral of St. Sophia in Novgorod. I was there."

We leave the church. And I think: *That was it?* That was the entire visit? That was the sum of fifteen years' worth of panic attacks?

My mother is still sitting next to a dirty flowerpot outside the church, carefully applying Dr. Scholl's to her feet. "You're a comical old lady," my father says to her. She gets up and begins to waddle, penguin-like, away from the church and back toward Moscow Square and the metro that will take us back to our hotel. We pass by a graffito that addresses the three of us Jews specifically: "The Slavic Realm is for Slavs only!"

"His posture has improved so much," my mother says of me. "He's unrecognizable. His walk. It's like he's not my son!"

"He's been going to the gym," my father says. "Feel his arms. How I fought with him to get him to play sports, but he didn't do dick."

"You didn't want to," my mother says to me. "He tried playing ball with you. He built you a little ladder." As I write this, I hold a photo of myself climbing my father's makeshift wooden ladder in our Leningrad apartment, wearing a sailor's outfit and a shit-eating grin. The photo is dated 11/1978, and my mother's handwriting on the back announces: "The famous athlete training at home."

"He was trying to stop you from being afraid of heights," my mother says. "And it worked, you climbed it."

"Yes, you climbed to the top," my father says. "Gradually. At first you climbed two or three steps, and then you got to the top. It's all about training yourself."

"On the one hand, your father taught you well," my mother says. "On the other hand, he always pushed you."

"Pushed me?"

"He wanted you to overcome your fear of heights but then when you got to the top he tried to push you off. And I read in Freud that you should never do such a thing." *She read in Freud?* "It just creates more fear. But your father didn't understand that. He was young himself. Thirty-three years old, what did he understand? Come to think of it, he was maybe about thirty-six when he pushed you off the ladder.*

"He pushed you from the heights, like this!" my mother says, as she makes a pushing motion. She laughs. "He scared you, and you became even more fearful of heights."

"Let's go! Let's go!" my father says. "I have something to show you!"

We're walking by Lensovet (Leningrad Soviet) Street. There are cheap lace curtains in the windows of the apartment blocks. The hotel Mir, which I've once unfairly described as "the worst hotel in the world," sits on one side of the street. We step over crooked tram lines and unkempt vegetation. A soot-covered truck passes by. My father begins to speak rapidly, as if he has been building up the courage to do so.

"As I was telling you, little son, one day when we were walking down this street after launching our helicopter by the church, we were going back to our house and you started to behave rascally [*ty nachal shalit*]. You were still trying to launch the helicopter on the street and there were so many people around. I told you once, twice, you didn't listen, then I swung my fist and you got it in the nose. And the blood began to flow."

My mother laughs. "Oy, how could you do that? I gave my son into your hands, and you would do that!"

"When I came back to Russia as an adult and walked by here I began to feel very scared," I say. "And I had dreams about helicopters."

"Really?" my father says. A sad-looking child peeks out from behind his lace curtains as we walk by a first-floor apartment. We pass a sign for a cell phone company: SIGN UP AND COMMUNICATE FOR FREE.

"And then I bought a book about Petersburg. I was looking at it in the store, and I saw the Chesme Church, and I had a panic attack."

"Oh, Igor, you are so sensitive," my mother says. "And that is why you are a writer."

* He was forty.

"In Russia you could do things like that," I say, meaning punch a five-year-old child in the nose until he bled. "But in America . . ."

"You couldn't do that in America?" my mother asks.

"I didn't want to beat you," my father says. He looks thoughtful. "It was by accident. I waved my hand and hit you in the nose."

"I only really beat you up once," my mother says, "and I was so sad afterward.

"I guess even from the start I was an American mama," she says.

• • •

It is time for me to be silent. It is time for me to listen, not to talk. But it is also time for me to go underground.

It is 2010, a year before this current trip with my parents. I have returned to St. Petersburg to do a reading tour on behalf of the U.S. State Department. With some free time on my hands, I am taking the metro to the southern suburb to see my friend K. The Petersburg metro, built under Stalin, is the most reliable mode of transport in the city, but on that day, just as we are approaching Moscow Square, the train stalls.

I look up at a poster showing a pretty girl of about five holding a paintbrush with white paint smudged on her cheeks and forehead, smiling mischievously. The caption reads:

WHAT WOULD A RESPONSIBLE PARENT DO?

a) Put her in the corner
b) Enroll her in art school
c) Suggest that you paint together
                    —Russia Without Cruelty to Children!

The panic attack begins immediately. My breath is gone. I look up at the grimy ceiling of the metro car, trying to see right through it to my freedom, but all I can see through the deep tunnel and the Soviet wiring is Moscow Square and Lenin and the Chesme Church and something I cannot articulate.

An organization called Russia Without Cruelty to Children! is suggesting that the worst Russian parents are capable of is placing their
playful, paint-splattered children in the corner. What I wouldn't have
given for that corner, that mythical, bloodless corner.

But right now, there is no place to sit on the crowded train. No *corner*
for me to hide in. The train is not moving. Maybe it will never move!
Maybe I will be stuck here with this paint-splattered, smiling girl forever. I turn to my fellow standing passengers, each of them rendered
faceless by my panic attack, and begin to formulate what to say in Russian. "*Gospozha*," I would start, to the most matronly and kindest of the
faceless bunch. "*Missis*. I need to get off this train immediately. Please
summon the conductor."

But I know I can't say it. I know this is no longer my city and these
are not my people. But is it still my language? I close my eyes and
begin to remember the words of my father's letters.

Good day, dear little son.

A trickle of breath.

*How are you doing? What are you doing? Are you going to climb the
"Bear" Mountain and how many gloves have you found in the sea?
Have you learned to swim yet and if so are you planning to swim away
to Turkey?*

More breathing, shallow, but familiar. I whisper the words to myself, the way I used to whisper to myself in Russian in the first grade
of Hebrew school, the American children thinking me a lunatic.

One day in Gurzuf, a submarine named Arzum *sailed in from Turkey.
Two commandos wearing Aqua-Lungs departed the boat and swam for
the shore. Unbeknownst to our border guards they headed for the mountain, for the forest. In the morning the Soviet border guards saw fresh trails
on the beach of the "Pushkin" sanatorium and called on the border guard,*

who summoned their search dog. She quickly found the two hidden Aqua-
Lungs under the rocks. It was clear—an enemy. "Search!" the border
guards commanded the dog, and she immediately ran in the direction of
the International Pioneers Camp. Story to be continued—at home.

The loud but happy turn of the wheels beneath us. We are moving again! We are coming into the station, we are coming into Moscow Square. I unclench my worried fists, open my eyes, and stare into the angelic face of the five-year-old girl with the paint smeared on her cheeks and forehead.

Little son, there are only a few days left until we meet again, do not be
lonely, behave yourself, listen to your mother and your aunt Tanya.
Kisses, Papa.

The doors swoosh open as if they've been pulled apart by giants. *"Moskovskaya,"* a recorded voice announces the station.

Am I home?

• • •

"To Citizen Shteyngart P., NOTIFICATION, Your husband Sergeant Shteyngart Isaac Semyonovich, fighting for the Socialist Motherland, true to his military oath, evincing heroism and courage, was killed 18 February 1943."

We are outside the tiny village of Feklistovo, where, in 1943, the German line extended southwest of Leningrad. The Red Army attempted to break through the German encirclement and end the siege of the city on several occasions. Here, in one such attempt, my grandfather Isaac, my father's father, an artillerist, was killed in battle.

Twenty-six million died on the Russian side in World War II, nearly 15 percent of the population. It is not an exaggeration to say the ground trod by my sneakers was once steeped in blood. It is not an exaggeration to say that those of us who are Russian, or Russian American, or Russian anything, are the offspring of these battles.

Outside the unremarkable soldiers' mass grave, squared away be-tween some fields and huts, there's a local gentleman in a straw hat selling flowers. "He's going to rip him off," my mother says of the straw-hatted man, as my father ventures out of the car with about four dollars' worth of Russian currency. When my father returns with a modest bunch of red roses, she tells him: "Later, he'll come and resell the flowers you put on the grave."

We are facing a monument of the Soviet socialist realism school, a soldier with a rifle slung over his chest, a silver helmet lying by his feet, surrounded by overgrown weeds. TO THE SOVIET WARRIORS WHO DIED IN BATTLES FOR THEIR MOTHERLAND 1941–44.

It is a sunny day, the first beautiful day of our trip. There's the smell of frying sausages from the nearby country houses. Two grandmoth-ers are sitting on a bench by the mass grave. "I come from Lenin-grad," one of the grandmothers says. She's in full babushka regalia, black raincoat and green kerchief wrapped around her head. "I have a dacha here."

"I live here," says Babushka Two.

"In 1943, my father died here," my father says.

The grannies are silent for a moment.

"*Da*," they finally say.

"In February 1943," my mother says. The fact that she has memo-rized the exact month of her husband's father's death is touching. I will memorize it, too.

"Maybe we'll even find his name, son," my father says as we begin to scour the overwhelming lists of the dead inscribed on the pink and white marble plates flanking the silver soldier statue on all sides. Somewhere amidst these green pastures, the hillocks covered with violets and daisies, my grandfather's bones are buried.

"At least it's a quiet place for a grave," my father says.

"A good, quiet place," my mother says, as if slotting herself into a Carver story. "The air is good."

My father speaks: "Goodbye, goodbye, Father. I probably won't come back again until my death. Forgive me. For everything."

I laugh nervously. "You're not guilty," I say.

"I have a sense of guilt," my father says. "That he didn't live enough. In '43 he was twenty-nine, maybe thirty. He didn't see anything. What was it for? He left a little son, a wife." He shakes his head.

"Oh, son," he says to me, "why didn't me and my mother come here earlier? I don't know why she didn't care about these things. We could have been here a hundred times. Of course, she was upset."

What I notice is that he has stopped calling me "little son." Now I am *just* his son. Now I stand at exactly the same height as him and our relationship is clear.

"Son, please read the prayer for me." From his Velcro money pouch, my father pulls out a pamphlet with Jewish prayers to be said at a grave site. "Where's the main prayer?" he asks. *"Baruch . . . ?"*

As I write this, I'm looking at a photograph of my father in his early seventies holding an umbrella in the forecourt of Versailles, his right foot raised off the ground as if he is Gene Kelly, one of my Stuyvesant sweaters billowing out above his khaki pants. He is smiling at my mother and her camera, smiling fully, with teeth, in the American manner. "Singer in the rain," my mother has written on a Post-it note in her careful English script. She has stuck the note above my father's dancing figure.

The day after we visit my grandfather's grave, we will go to the Great Choral Synagogue of St. Petersburg. I will ask my father if he ever visited the temple during his Soviet days. "Yes, five or six times," he will say. "The first time I came, my aunt who later killed herself, Aunt Sima, she had her wedding here. I was about seventeen years old. And while that ceremony was taking place a girl entered. I remembered her my whole life. She wasn't a beauty. She was dark, dark. A good Jewish face. And some kind of strange, almost glowing dark eyes. My whole life I have felt those eyes looking at me."

"Lord, who should sojourn in thy tabernacle?" I read from Psalms 15:1 in English. "Who shall dwell upon thy holy mountain? He that walketh uprightly and walketh righteously and speaks with truth in his heart . . . He that does those things shall never be moved."

I begin the mourner's Kaddish. "*Yitgaddal veyitqaddash shmeh rabba*," I say in Aramaic. My father bows slightly to God's will with each cadence.

"בְּעָלְמָא דִּי בְרָא כִרְעוּתֵהּ," I say.

"וְיַמְלִיךְ מַלְכוּתֵהּ," I chant.

I can read the prayer, but I cannot understand it. The words coming out of my mouth are gibberish to me. And they can only be gibberish to my father's ear as well.

I chant the words and he says "Amen" after each stanza.

I chant the gibberish backwards and forwards, tripping over the words, mangling them, making them sound more Russian, more American, more holy. We haven't found my grandfather's name, Isaac, amidst the acres of marble covered with Ivans and Nikolais and Alexanders. But the sun shines generously. Cows are mooing and grass is being mowed. A small airplane, surely our heraldic symbol, is landing nearby. This part I know well.

וְאִמְרוּ אָמֵן.

Ve'imru, Amen.

Let us say, Amen.

И СКАЖЕМ: АМЕН!

ACKNOWLEDGMENTS

• • •

AND I THOUGHT writing novels was hard.

The task of sailing into the past was made that much easier by David Ebershoff, my editor, who knew exactly when to furl and unfurl the sails, if that's the right metaphor. (Is it? Or is it trim the sails? I wish I were Waspier.) I also want to thank everyone at Random House for their continued belief that I'm an okay guy and writer, including Gina Centrello, Susan Kamil, Barbara Fillon, Maria Braeckel, Sally Marvin, Denise Cronin, Joelle Dieu, Rachel Kind, and Toby Ernst. My agent, Denise Shannon, continues to keep me solvent and is a terrific reader to boot. My thanks to Dmitry Dolinsky for his expert help with what they call a "flash drive." Patricia Kim took many photos of me wearing a toga.

So many people volunteered their time to remind me of what had happened during the 1980s and early 1990s, a time period many of us are trying to forget. They include Jonathan, J.Z., Ben, Brian, Leo, Maris, and Jessica.

Finally, my parents provided enough stories to fill several volumes and were kind and patient enough not only to answer all my nagging questions but to accompany me to Russia for a week of fish pie and remembrance. I would also like to thank all my "first responders," people who took the time out to read early drafts of this book and offer advice: Doug Choi, Andrew Lewis Conn, Rebecca Godfrey, Lisa Hahn, Cathy Park Hong, Gabe Hudson, Binnie Kirshenbaum, Paul La Farge, Christine Suewon Lee, Kelly Malloy, Jynne Dilling Martin, Caitlin McKenna, Suketu Mehta, John Saffron, and John "Rosencranz" Wray.

PERMISSIONS ACKNOWLEDGMENTS

. . .

Portions of this work appeared in the following publications in different form:

Chapter 1: *Travel + Leisure, The New York Times, The New Yorker*
Chapter 2: *New York*
Chapter 4: *Travel + Leisure; Made in Russia: Unsung Icons of Soviet Design,* edited by Michael Idov (Rizzoli); *The Threepenny Review*
Chapter 6: *The New Yorker*
Chapter 7: an essay first published privately and then in *New York* magazine's *My First New York* (Ecco); *The Threepenny Review*
Chapter 8: *The Threepenny Review, The New Yorker*
Chapter 9: *The Threepenny Review*
Chapter 10: *The Threepenny Review, Granta*
Chapter 11: *Gourmet, The New York Times Magazine, The Threepenny Review*
Chapter 12: *The New Yorker, The Threepenny Review*
Chapter 13: *The New Yorker*
Chapter 14: *The Threepenny Review*
Chapter 15: *The New York Times Magazine, The New Yorker*
Chapter 16: *The New York Times Magazine, The New Yorker*
Chapter 17: *The New York Times Magazine*
Chapter 18: *The New York Times Magazine*
Chapter 21: *GQ*
Chapter 23: *GQ, Granta, The New Yorker*
Chapter 24: *GQ, The New Yorker, Travel + Leisure*

ABOUT THE AUTHOR

• • •

GARY SHTEYNGART was born in Leningrad in 1972 and came to the United States seven years later. He is the author of the novels *Super Sad True Love Story* (2010), *Absurdistan* (2006), and *The Russian Debutante's Handbook* (2002), and the memoir *Little Failure* (2014). *Super Sad True Love Story* won the Bollinger Everyman Wodehouse Prize and was selected as one of the best books of the year by more than forty news journals and magazines around the world. *Absurdistan* was chosen as one of the ten best books of the year by *The New York Times Book Review* and *Time* magazine. *The Russian Debutante's Handbook* won the Stephen Crane Award for First Fiction and the National Jewish Book Award for Fiction. His fiction and essays have appeared in *The New Yorker, Granta, Esquire, GQ, Travel + Leisure, The New York Times Magazine,* and many other publications. His work has been translated into twenty-eight languages.

www.GaryShteyngart.com
Facebook.com/GaryShteyngart
@Shteyngart

Gary Shteyngart is available for select readings and lectures. To inquire about a possible appearance, please contact the Penguin Random House Speakers Bureau at 212-572-2013 or speakers@penguinrandomhouse.com.